ABOUT THIS PUBLICATION

FOR SERVICE ASSISTANCE

Customer Service
1.704.898.0770

North Carolina General Statues is published by The Muliti-Media Group of Greater Charlotte in Charlotte, North Carolina. Copyright 2015 by the Multi-Media Group of Greater Charlotte. This book or parts thereof may not be reproduced in any form, stored in a retrieval system, or transmitted in any form by any means—electronic, mechanical, photocopy, recording or otherwise—without prior written permission of the publisher, except as provided by United States of America copyright law.

The records required by U.S. Code 2257(a) through (c) and the pertinent regulations 28 C.F.R. Cli. 1, Part 75 with respect to this publication and all materials associated with such records are maintained by The Multi-Media Group of Greater Charlotte, Publisher and available for review by Attorney General.

www.visionbooks.org

TID: 5072127
ISBN (10) digit: 1502990482
ISBN (13) digit: 978-1502990488

123-4-56789-01239-Paperback
123-4-56789-01239-Hardback

First Edition

090520140547

Printed in the United States of America

2015 EDITION

North Carolina Criminal Law And Procedure-Pamphlet # 67

Printed In conjunction with the Administration of the Courts

3

North Carolina Criminal Law and Procedure
Pamphlet Reference Guide

9

11

13

§ 120-32.6. Certain employment authority.

G.S. 114-2.3 and G.S. 147-17 (a) through (c) shall not apply to the General Assembly. (2006-201, s. 3; 2011-145, s. 22.5.)

§ 120-33. Duties of enrolling clerk.

(a)   All bills passed by the General Assembly shall be enrolled for ratification under the supervision of the enrolling clerk.

(b)   Prior to enrolling any bill, the enrolling clerk shall substitute the corresponding Arabic numeral(s) for any date or section number of the General Statutes or of any act of the General Assembly which is written in words. The enrolled bill shall have the word "RATIFIED" following the bill number.

(c)   All bills shall be typewritten and carefully proofread before enrollment.

(d)   Upon ratification of an act or joint resolution, the enrolling clerk shall present one true ratified copy:

(1)   To the Governor of any act except acts not required to be presented to the Governor under Article II, Section 22 of the Constitution of North Carolina; and

(2)   To the Secretary of State of:

a.   Acts not required to be presented to the Governor under Article II, Section 22 of the Constitution of North Carolina; and

b.   Joint resolutions.

In the case of any bill presented to the Governor, the enrolling clerk shall write upon the bill the time and date presented to the Governor.

(d1)   The enrolling clerk shall present to the Secretary of State one true ratified copy of:

(1)   Any bill which has become law with the approval of the Governor as provided by G.S. 120-29.1(a);

15

(2)   Any bill which has become law without the approval of the Governor as provided by G.S. 120-29.1(b); and

(3)   Any bill which has become law notwithstanding the objections of the Governor, as provided by G.S. 120-29.1(c).

(d2)   No bill required to be presented to the Governor under Article II, Section 22 of the Constitution of North Carolina shall be so presented until the next business day after the bill was ratified, unless expressly ordered by that house where such bill was ordered enrolled. For the purpose of this section, a business day is a weekday other than one on which there is both a State employee holiday and neither house is in session. No bill required to be presented to the Governor under Article II, Section 22 of the North Carolina Constitution shall be recalled from the Enrolling Clerk or Governor after it has been ratified but before it has been acted upon by the Governor except by joint resolution.

(e)   Repealed by Session Laws 1995, c. 20, s. 1.

(f)   The enrolling clerk upon completion of duties after each session shall deposit the original bills and resolutions enrolled for ratification with the Secretary of State. (1969, c. 1184, s. 3; 1995, c. 20, s. 1; 1997-1, s. 1.)

§ 120-34. Printing of session laws; numbering of session laws.

(a)   The Legislative Services Commission shall publish all laws and joint resolutions passed at each session of the General Assembly and the executive orders of the Governor issued since the adjournment of the prior session of the General Assembly. The laws and joint resolutions shall be kept separate and indexed separately. Each volume shall contain a certificate from the Secretary of State stating that the volume was printed under the direction of the Legislative Services Commission from ratified acts and resolutions and executive orders of the Governor on file in the Office of the Secretary of State. The Commission may publish the Session Laws and House and Senate Journals of extra and special sessions of the General Assembly in the same volume or volumes as those of regular sessions of the General Assembly. In printing the ratified acts and resolutions, the signatures of the presiding officers and the Governor shall be omitted.

The enrolling clerk or the Legislative Services Office shall assign to each bill that becomes law a number in the order the bill became law, and the laws shall be printed in the Session Laws in that order. The number shall be preceded by the phrase "Session Law" or the letters "S.L." followed by the calendar year it was ordered enrolled, followed by a hyphen and the sequential law number. Laws of Extra Sessions shall so indicate. In the case of any bill required to be presented to the Governor, and which became law, the Session Laws shall carry, below the date of ratification, editorial notes as to what time and what date the bill became law. In any case where the Governor has returned a bill to the General Assembly with objections, those objections shall be printed verbatim in the Session Laws, regardless of whether or not the bill became law notwithstanding the objections.

(b)   All index references with respect to the session laws shall refer to the Chapter numbers of such laws in lieu of page numbers, and all index references to resolutions shall refer to the resolution numbers of the resolutions in lieu of page numbers, to the end that the indexes shall thereby be made consistent with the index to the General Statutes which refers to the section numbers and not to page numbers.

(c)   There shall be printed not more than 2,500 volumes of the session laws and 600 volumes of the journals of each house of each session of the General Assembly, all of which shall be bound, and delivered to the Secretary of State for distribution by him under the provisions of G.S. 147-45, G.S. 147-46.1, G.S. 147-48 and other applicable statutes. (1969, c. 1184, s. 4; 1971, c. 685, s. 1; 1983 (Reg. Sess., 1984), c. 1034, s. 179; 1995, c. 20, s. 12; 1997-456, s. 45; 2001-513, s. 16(d).)

§ 120-35. Payment for expenses.

Actual expenses for the joint operation of the General Assembly shall be paid by the State Treasurer upon authorization of the President pro tempore of the Senate and the Speaker of the House of Representatives. Expenses for the operation of the Senate shall be paid upon authorization of the President pro tempore of the Senate. Expenses for the operation of the House shall be paid upon authorization of the Speaker of the House. (1969, c. 1184, s. 5; 1971, c. 1200, s. 6.)

§ 120-36. Legislative Services Officer of the General Assembly.

(a)   The Legislative Services Officer of the General Assembly shall be appointed by and serve at the pleasure of the Legislative Services Commission, and his compensation shall be fixed by the Legislative Services Commission.

(b)   The Legislative Services Officer of the General Assembly shall perform such duties as are assigned to him by the Legislative Services Commission and shall be available to the Legislative Research Commission to provide such clerical, printing, drafting, and research duties as are necessary to the proper functions of the Legislative Research Commission. (1969, c. 1184, s. 6.)

Article 7A.

Fiscal Research Division.

§ 120-36.1. Fiscal Research Division of Legislative Services Commission established.

There is hereby established the Fiscal Research Division of the Legislative Services Commission, which shall be solely a staff agency of the General Assembly, shall be responsible to the General Assembly through the Commission, and shall be independent of all other officers, agencies, boards, commissions, divisions, and other instrumentalities of State government. The Division shall not be subject to the Executive Budget Act or the North Carolina Human Resources Act. (1971, c. 659, s. 1; 2013-382, s. 9.1(c).)

§ 120-36.2. Organization.

(a)   The Legislative Services Commission shall appoint a Director of Fiscal Research, who shall serve at the pleasure of the Commission. The Director of Fiscal Research shall be responsible to the Legislative Services Officer in the performance of his duties.

(b)   The Director of Fiscal Research shall assign the duties and supervise and direct the activities of the employees of the Division.

(c)   The Director and employees of the Division shall receive salaries that shall be fixed by the Commission, shall receive the travel and subsistence allowances fixed by G.S. 138-6 and 138-7, and shall be entitled to the other benefits available to State employees. (1971, c. 659, s. 1; 2006-259, s. 22.)

§ 120-36.3. Functions.

In addition to the functions prescribed in Article 7 of Chapter 120, the Legislative Services Commission, acting through the Fiscal Research Division, shall have the following powers and duties:

(1)   To make periodic and special analyses of past receipts and expenditures and of current requests and recommendations for appropriations of State departments, agencies, and institutions, giving special consideration to the requests and recommendations for appropriations to continue current programs and services;

(2)   To review and evaluate compliance by State departments, agencies, and institutions with such legislative directions as may be contained in the State budget;

(3)   To examine the structure and organization of State departments, agencies, and institutions and recommend such changes as considerations of increased efficiency might indicate;

(4)   To make such other studies, analyses, and inquiries into the affairs of State government as may be directed by the Legislative Services Commission, by the Committee on Appropriations of either house, or by either house of the General Assembly.

(5)   To make periodic reports on the activities of the Division and special reports on the above-mentioned studies, reviews, analyses, evaluations, examinations, and inquiries to the Committee on Appropriations of either house of the General Assembly, or to either house of the General Assembly, as may be appropriate. The reports of the Division shall, where feasible, include

estimates of the financial savings achieved by or anticipated to result from its recommendations. (1971, c. 659, s. 1.)

§ 120-36.4: Repealed by Session Laws 1983 (Regular Session 1984), c. 1034, s. 176.

§ 120-36.5. Office space and equipment.

The Fiscal Research Division shall be provided with suitable office space and equipment. (1971, c. 659, s. 1; 1981; c. 772, s. 7; c. 859, s. 13.3.)

§ 120-36.6. Legislative Fiscal Research staff participation.

The Legislative Services Officer shall designate a member of the Fiscal Research staff, and a member of the General Research or Bill Drafting staff who may attend all meetings of the Council of State, unless the Council has voted to exclude them from the specific meeting, provided that no final action may be taken while they are so excluded. The Legislative Services Officer and the Director of Fiscal Research shall be notified of all such meetings, hearings and trips in the same manner and at the same time as notice is given to members of the Council. The Legislative Services Officer and the Director of Fiscal Research shall be provided with a copy of all reports, memoranda, and other informational material which are distributed to the members of the Council; these reports, memoranda and materials shall be delivered to the Legislative Services Officer and the Director of Fiscal Research at the same time that they are distributed to the members of the Council. (1971, c. 659, s. 2; 1983 (Reg. Sess., 1984), c. 1034, s. 177.1; 1996, 2nd Ex. Sess., c. 18, s. 8(d); 2006-203, s. 60; 2013-234, s. 7.)

§ 120-36.7. Long-term fiscal notes.

(a)   Budget Outlook; Proposed Legislation. - Every fiscal analysis of the State budget outlook shall encompass the upcoming five-year period. Every fiscal analysis of the impact of proposed legislation on the State budget shall estimate the impact for the first five fiscal years the legislation would be in effect.

(b)   Proposed State Buildings. - Upon the request of a member of the General Assembly, the Fiscal Research Division shall prepare a fiscal analysis of proposed legislation to appropriate funds for a State building. The analysis shall estimate the projected maintenance and operating costs of the building for the first 20 fiscal years after it is completed.

(c)   Proposed New Programs. - Upon the request of a member of the General Assembly, the Fiscal Research Division shall prepare a fiscal analysis of proposed legislation to create a new State program. The analysis shall identify and estimate all personnel costs of the proposed new program for the first five fiscal years it will operate. The analysis shall also include a five-year estimate of space requirements, an indication of whether those requirements can be satisfied using existing State-owned facilities, and estimated costs of occupying leased space where State-owned space is not available.

(d)   Proposed Increases in Incarceration. - Every bill and resolution introduced in the General Assembly proposing any change in the law that could cause a net increase in the length of time for which persons are incarcerated or the number of persons incarcerated, whether by increasing penalties for violating existing laws, by criminalizing behavior, or by any other means, shall have attached to it at the time of its consideration by the General Assembly a fiscal note prepared by the Fiscal Research Division. The fiscal note shall be prepared in consultation with the Sentencing Policy and Advisory Commission and shall identify and estimate, for the first five fiscal years the proposed change would be in effect, all costs of the proposed net increase in incarceration, including capital outlay costs if the legislation would require increased cell space. If, after careful investigation, the Fiscal Research Division determines that no dollar estimate is possible, the note shall contain a statement to that effect, setting forth the reasons why no dollar estimate can be given. No comment or opinion shall be included in the fiscal note with regard to the merits of the measure for which the note is prepared. However, technical and mechanical defects may be noted.

The sponsor of each bill or resolution to which this subsection applies shall present a copy of the bill or resolution with the request for a fiscal note to the Fiscal Research Division. Upon receipt of the request and the copy of the bill or resolution, the Fiscal Research Division shall prepare the fiscal note as promptly as possible. The Fiscal Research Division shall prepare the fiscal note and transmit it to the sponsor within two weeks after the request is made, unless the sponsor agrees to an extension of time.

This fiscal note shall be attached to the original of each proposed bill or resolution that is reported favorably by any committee of the General Assembly, but shall be separate from the bill or resolution and shall be clearly designated as a fiscal note. A fiscal note attached to a bill or resolution pursuant to this subsection is not a part of the bill or resolution and is not an expression of legislative intent proposed by the bill or resolution.

If a committee of the General Assembly reports favorably a proposed bill or resolution with an amendment that proposes a change in the law that could cause a net increase in the length of time for which persons are incarcerated or the number of persons incarcerated, whether by increasing penalties for violating existing laws, by criminalizing behavior, or by any other means, the chair of the committee shall obtain from the Fiscal Research Division and attach to the amended bill or resolution a fiscal note as provided in this section. (1991, c. 689, s. 340; 1993, c. 561, s. 21.)

Article 7B.

Research Division.

§ 120-36.8. Certification of legislation required by federal law.

(a)   Every bill and resolution introduced in the General Assembly proposing any change in the law which purports to implement federal law or to be required or necessary for compliance with federal law, or on which is conditioned the receipt of federal funds shall have attached to it at the time of its consideration by the General Assembly a certification prepared by the Research Division, in consultation with the Bill Drafting and Fiscal Research Divisions, identifying the federal law requiring passage of the bill or resolution. The certification shall contain a statement setting forth the reasons why the bill or resolution is required by federal law. If the bill or resolution is not required by federal law or exceeds the requirements of federal law, then the certification shall state the reasons for that opinion. No comment or opinion shall be included in the certification with regard to the merits of the measure for which the certification is prepared. However, technical and mechanical defects may be noted.

(b)   The sponsor of each bill or resolution to which this section applies shall present a copy of the bill or resolution with the request for certification to the Research Division. Upon receipt of the request and the copy of the bill or resolution, the Research Division shall consult with the Bill Drafting and Fiscal Research Divisions, and may consult with the Office of State Budget and Management or any State agency on preparation of the certification as promptly as possible. The Research Division shall prepare the certification and transmit it to the sponsor within two weeks after the request is made, unless the sponsor agrees to an extension of time.

(c)   This certification shall be attached to the original of each proposed bill or resolution that is reported favorably by any committee of the General Assembly, but shall be separate from the bill or resolution and shall be clearly designated as a certification. A certification attached to a bill or resolution pursuant to this section is not a part of the bill or resolution and is not an expression of legislative intent proposed by the bill or resolution.

(d)   If a committee of the General Assembly reports favorably a proposed bill or resolution with an amendment proposing any change in the law which purports to implement federal law or to be required or necessary for compliance with federal law, the chair of the committee shall obtain from the Research Division and attach to the amended bill or resolution a certification as provided in this section. (1995, c. 415, s. 8; 2000-140, s. 93.1(a); 2001-424, s. 12.2(b); 2001-487, s. 79.)

§ 120-36.9: Reserved for future codification purposes.

§ 120-36.10: Reserved for future codification purposes.

Article 7C.

Program Evaluation.

§ 120-36.11. Program Evaluation Division established.

(a)   Division. - The Program Evaluation Division of the General Assembly is established. The purpose of the Division is to assist the General Assembly in fulfilling its responsibility to oversee government functions by providing an independent, objective source of information to be used in evaluating whether public services are delivered in an effective and efficient manner and in accordance with law.

(b)   Director. - The Director of the Program Evaluation Division is appointed by the Legislative Services Commission and serves at the pleasure of the Commission. The Director is responsible for hiring and dismissing employees of the Division and directing the activities of the Division. The Director may not hire or dismiss an employee without the approval of the Legislative Services Officer. (2007-78, s. 3.)

§ 120-36.12. Duties of Program Evaluation Division.

The Program Evaluation Division of the Legislative Services Commission has the following powers and duties:

(1)   To examine a program or an activity of a State agency and evaluate the merits of the program or activity and the agency's effectiveness in conducting the program or activity.

(2)   To develop quantitative indicators for measuring the activities performed and services provided by a State agency and the extent to which the activities and services are achieving desired results.

(3)   To develop unit cost measures to determine the cost of activities performed and services provided by a State agency.

(4)   To determine if a program or an activity of a State agency complies with the agency's mission, as established by law.

(5)   To make unannounced visits to a State agency when needed to evaluate a program or an activity of the agency.

(6)   To make recommendations to improve the efficiency and effectiveness of a State agency.

(7)   To determine the extent to which a State agency has implemented any of the Division's recommendations concerning the agency.

(8)   To require a State agency to submit a written response to a proposed or final recommendation of the Division and to submit a written explanation of the extent to which the agency has implemented the Division's recommendations.

(9)   To make periodic reports of the activities and recommendations of the Division and of any savings achieved by the implementation of its recommendations.

(10)   To receive reports alleging improper activities or matters of public concern listed in G.S. 126-84. The individual making the report may, at the individual's discretion, remain anonymous. Any report received under this subdivision, in whatever form, shall not be a "public record" as defined by G.S. 132-1 and becomes available to the public only as provided in G.S. 120-131. (2007-78, s. 3; 2008-196, s. 2(a).)

§ 120-36.13. Work plan and requests for program evaluation.

(a)   Plan. - The Joint Legislative Program Evaluation Oversight Committee, in consultation with the Director of the Program Evaluation Division, must establish an annual work plan for the Division. The Division must adhere to this annual plan, unless the Joint Legislative Program Evaluation Oversight Committee changes the annual plan to add a new evaluation or remove a planned evaluation. Any enacted legislation that directs the Program Evaluation Division to conduct a study or an evaluation is included in the annual work plan by operation of law; however, notwithstanding any other provision of law, if the enacted legislation did not have an impact statement, as provided in G.S. 120-36.17, completed prior to its consideration by the General Assembly, then the study or evaluation shall be included in the next annual work plan adopted by the Committee and one year shall be added to any required reporting dates included in the legislation, except that the impact statement is not required and the evaluation may be included in the current work plan if the impact statement was not provided pursuant to the time requirements in G.S. 120-36.17(b).

The annual work plan constitutes an information request and a drafting request made by the Committee cochairs to legislative employees under Article 17 of Chapter 120 of the General Statutes. Any document prepared by a legislative employee pursuant to the annual work plan becomes available to the public only as provided in G.S. 120-131. Any document prepared by an agency employee pursuant to a request under G.S. 120-131.1(a1) becomes available to the public only as provided in G.S. 120-131.

(b)   Request. - A request to the Program Evaluation Division for an evaluation of a program or an activity of a State agency must be submitted by a member of the General Assembly. The Director of the Division must review each request in accordance with the following criteria and make a recommendation to the Joint Legislative Program Evaluation Oversight Committee on whether to amend the Division's work plan to include the requested evaluation:

(1)   The work required to conduct the requested evaluation.

(2)   The effect that conducting the requested evaluation will have on the Division's ability to complete its work plan.

(3)   The significance of the requested evaluation compared to the evaluations to be conducted under the work plan.

(4)   Any overlap between the requested evaluation and other evaluations previously conducted by the Division or another agency. (2007-78, s. 3; 2008-196, s. 1(a); 2012-80, s. 2.)

§ 120-36.14. Content of report of Program Evaluation Division.

A report of an evaluation of a program or an activity of a State agency by the Program Evaluation Division of the General Assembly must include the following:

(1)   The findings of the Division concerning the program or activity.

(2)   Specific recommendations for making the program or activity more efficient or effective.

(3)   Any legislation needed to implement the Division's findings and recommendations concerning the program or activity.

(4)   An estimate of the costs or savings expected from implementing the Division's findings and recommendations concerning the program or activity. (2007-78, s. 3.)

§ 120-36.15. Joint Legislative Program Evaluation Oversight Committee established.

(a)   Membership. - The Joint Legislative Program Evaluation Oversight Committee is established. The Committee consists of 18 members as follows:

(1)   Nine members of the Senate appointed by the President Pro Tempore of the Senate. At least two of the members must be a Cochair of the Senate Appropriations Committee or a subcommittee of the Senate Appropriations Committee. At least three of the members must be members of the minority party.

(2)   Nine members of the House of Representatives appointed by the Speaker of the House of Representatives. At least two of the members must be a Cochair of the House Appropriations Committee or a subcommittee of the House Appropriations Committee. At least three of the members must be members of the minority party.

(b)   Terms. - Terms on the Committee are for two years and begin on January 15 of each odd-numbered year. Legislative members may complete a term of service on the Committee even if they do not seek reelection or are not reelected to the General Assembly. Resignation or removal from service in the General Assembly constitutes resignation or removal from service on the Committee. A member continues to serve until a successor is appointed.

(c)   Chairs and Quorum. - The President Pro Tempore of the Senate and the Speaker of the House of Representatives must each designate a cochair of the Committee. The Committee meets upon the call of the cochairs. A quorum of the Committee is nine members. The Committee may not act except by a majority vote at a meeting at which a quorum is present.

27

(d)   Standard Procedure. - In performing its duties, the Committee has the powers of a committee under G.S. 120-19 and G.S. 120-19.1 through G.S. 120-19.4. Funding for the Committee is provided by the Legislative Services Commission from appropriations made to the General Assembly. Members of the Committee receive subsistence and travel expenses as provided in G.S. 120-3.1. The Committee may contract for consultants or hire employees in accordance with G.S. 120-32.02. Upon approval of the Legislative Services Commission, the Legislative Services Officer must assign professional and clerical staff to assist the Committee in its work. (2007-78, s. 3.)

§ 120-36.16. Duties of Joint Legislative Program Evaluation Oversight Committee.

The Joint Legislative Program Evaluation Oversight Committee has the following powers and duties:

(1)   To receive and review requests for evaluations to be performed by the Program Evaluation Division of the General Assembly.

(2)   To establish an annual work plan for the Program Evaluation Division that describes the evaluations to be performed by the Division. The Committee must consult with the Director of the Program Evaluation Division in performing this duty.

(3)   To receive reports prepared by the Program Evaluation Division.

(4)   To consult with an oversight committee or another committee established in this Chapter about a report concerning a program or an activity that is within that committee's scope of study.

(5)   To recommend to the General Assembly any changes needed to implement a recommendation that is included in a report of the Program Evaluation Division and is endorsed by the Committee. (2007-78, s. 3; 2007-484, s. 31.)

§ 120-36.17. Program Evaluation Division impact statement.

(a)   Every bill and resolution introduced in the General Assembly proposing a study or evaluation by the Program Evaluation Division shall have attached to it at the time of its consideration by the General Assembly an impact statement prepared by the Division. The impact statement shall identify and estimate, to complete all studies and reports required by the bill or resolution, all of the following: (i) the number of personnel required; (ii) the total number of hours required; and (iii) the estimated costs.

(1)   If, after review, the Division determines that no estimates are possible, the impact statement shall contain a statement to that effect, setting forth the reasons why no estimate can be given.

(2)   The Division shall indicate whether the Division, based upon its current annual work plan, has adequate and sufficient resources to undertake the study or evaluation as part of the current annual work plan, and shall explain the basis for its determination.

(3)   If the Division determines that it would not be able to undertake the study or evaluation as part of its current annual work plan, it shall indicate a time frame in which it believes the study or evaluation could be accomplished.

(b)   The sponsor of each bill or resolution to which this section applies shall present a copy of the bill or resolution with the request for an impact statement to the Program Evaluation Division. Upon receipt of the request and the copy of the bill or resolution, the Program Evaluation Division shall prepare the impact statement as promptly as possible, but shall transmit it to the sponsor within two weeks after the request is made, unless the sponsor agrees to an extension of time. If the impact statement is not transmitted within two weeks, or by the end of any extension of time as provided under this subsection, then there shall be no impact statement required under this section.

(c)   This impact statement shall be attached to the original of each proposed bill or resolution that is reported favorably by any committee of the General Assembly, but shall be separate from the bill or resolution and shall be clearly designated as an impact statement. An impact statement attached to a bill or resolution pursuant to this subsection is not a part of the bill or resolution and is not an expression of legislative intent proposed by the bill or resolution.

(d)   If a committee of the General Assembly reports favorably a proposed bill or resolution that directs the Program Evaluation Division to conduct a study or evaluation, the chair of the committee shall obtain from the Program Evaluation

29

Division, and attach to the bill or resolution, an impact statement as provided in this section. (2012-80, s. 1.)

Article 7D.

Codification of Statutes.

§ 120-36.21. Codification of Statutes.

The Legislative Services Officer shall assign to staff of the General Assembly the following duties:

(1)   To supervise the recodification of all the statute law of North Carolina and supervise the keeping of such recodifications current by including therein all laws hereafter enacted by supplements thereto issued periodically, all of which recodifications and supplements shall be appropriately annotated.

(2)   In order that the laws of North Carolina, as set out in the General Statutes of North Carolina, may be made and kept as simple, as clear, as concise and as complete as possible, and in order that the amount of construction and interpretation of the statutes required of the courts may be reduced to a minimum, to establish and maintain a system of continuous statute research and correction. To that end the staff shall:

a.   Make a systematic study of the general statutes of the State, as set out in the General Statutes and as hereafter enacted by the General Assembly, for the purpose of ascertaining what ambiguities, conflicts, duplications and other imperfections of form and expression exist therein and how these defects may be corrected.

b.   Consider such suggestions as may be submitted with respect to the existence of such defects and the proper correction thereof.

c.   Prepare for submission to the General Assembly from time to time bills to correct such defects in the statutes as its research discloses. (1939, c. 315, s. 5; 1941, c. 35; 1943, c. 382; 2011-97, s. 1.)

§ 120-36.22. Revisor of Statutes.

The member of the staff of the General Assembly who is assigned to perform the duties prescribed by G.S. 120-36.21(2) shall be known as the Revisor of Statutes. (1947, c. 114, s. 1; 1957, c. 541, s. 10; 1967, c. 260, s. 2; 2011-97, s. 1.)

Article 8.

Elected Officers.

§ 120-37. Elected officers; salaries; staff.

(a)   At the convening of the first session of the General Assembly following each biennial election of members of the General Assembly, each house shall elect a principal clerk for a term of two years, subject to the condition that each officer shall serve at the pleasure of the house that elected him or her and until his or her successor is elected. The reading clerk and sergeant-at-arms of the Senate shall serve for terms of two years, subject to the condition that each serves at the pleasure of the Senate and until the officer's successor is elected. The reading clerk and sergeant-at-arms of the House of Representatives shall serve as provided in the rules of the House.

(b)   The sergeant-at-arms and the reading clerk in each house shall be paid a salary of three hundred eighty-five dollars ($385.00) per week plus subsistence at the same daily rate provided for members of the General Assembly, plus mileage at the rate provided for members of the General Assembly for one round trip only from their homes to Raleigh and return. The sergeants-at-arms shall serve during sessions of the General Assembly and at such time prior to the convening of, and subsequent to adjournment or recess of, sessions as may be authorized by the Legislative Services Commission. The reading clerks shall serve during sessions only.

(c)   The principal clerks shall be full-time officers. Each principal clerk shall be entitled to other benefits available to permanent legislative employees and shall be paid an annual salary of one hundred five thousand three hundred thirty-three dollars ($105,333), payable monthly. Each principal clerk shall also receive such additional compensation as approved by the Speaker of the House of Representatives or the President Pro Tempore of the Senate, respectively, for additional employment duties beyond those provided by the rules of their

31

House. The Legislative Services Commission shall review the salary of the principal clerks prior to submission of the proposed operating budget of the General Assembly to the Governor and shall make appropriate recommendations for changes in those salaries. Any changes enacted by the General Assembly shall be by amendment to this paragraph.

(d)   The Legislative Services Commission may authorize additional full-time staff employees of the office of each principal clerk. The Speaker may assign to the Principal Clerk of the House additional duties for the periods between sessions and during recesses of the General Assembly. The President pro tempore of the Senate may assign to the Principal Clerk of the Senate additional duties for the periods between sessions and during recesses of the General Assembly.

(e)   The principal clerks and the sergeants-at-arms may, upon authorization of the Legislative Services Commission, employ temporary assistants to prepare for each legislative session, serve during the session, and perform necessary duties following adjournment.

(f)   Following adjournment sine die of each session of the General Assembly, each principal clerk shall retain in his office for a period of two years every bill and resolution considered by but not enacted or adopted by his house, together with the calendar books and other records deemed worthy of retention. At the end of two years, these materials shall be turned over to the Office of Archives and History of the Department of Cultural Resources for ultimate retention or disposition. (1969, c. 1184, s. 7; 1977, 2nd Sess., c. 1278; 1979, c. 838, s. 82; 1979, 2nd Sess., c. 1137, s. 8; 1981, c. 1127, s. 9; 1983, c. 761, s. 197; 1983 (Reg. Sess., 1984), c. 1034, s. 208; c. 1116, s. 110; 1985, c. 479, ss. 205, 207; c. 757, s. 189; 1985 (Reg. Sess., 1986), c. 1014, ss. 30, 31; 1987, c. 738, ss. 16, 17; 1987 (Reg. Sess., 1988), c. 1086, ss. 10, 11; c. 1100, s. 16(c); 1989, c. 752, ss. 27, 28; 1991, c. 756, s. 34; 1991 (Reg. Sess., 1992), c. 900, ss. 36, 37; 1993, c. 321, ss. 53, 54; 1993 (Reg. Sess., 1994), c. 769, ss. 7.6, 7.7; 1995, c. 507, ss. 7.9, 7.10; 1996, 2nd Ex. Sess., c. 18, ss. 28.7, 28.8; 1997-443, ss. 33.13, 33.14; 1998-153, ss. 10, 11; 1998-212, s. 28.7(a); 1999-237, ss. 28.7, 28.8; 2000-67, ss. 26.7, 26.8; 2001-424, ss. 32.8, 32.9; 2002-159, s. 35(f); 2004-124, ss. 31.8(b), 31.9(b); 2005-276, ss. 29.8, 29.9, 19B.1; 2005-345, s. 40; 2006-66, ss. 22.8, 22.9; 2006-203, s. 61; 2007-323, ss. 28.8, 28.9; 2008-107, ss. 26.8, 26.9; 2012-142, s. 25.1B(b), (c).)

§§ 120-38 through 120-39: Repealed by Session Laws 1969, c. 1184, s. 7.

Article 9.

Lobbying.

§§ 120-40 through 120-47: Recodified as G.S. 120-47.1 through 120-47.10.

Article 9A.

Legislative Branch Lobbying [Repealed].

§§ 120-47.1 through 120-47.12: Repealed by Session Laws 2006-201, s. 17, effective January 1, 2007.

Article 10.

Influencing Public Opinion or Legislation.

§§ 120-48 through 120-55: Repealed by Session Laws 1991, c. 740, s. 1.2.

Article 11.

Legislative Intern Program.

§ 120-56: Repealed by Session Laws 2011-266, s. 1.10, effective July 1, 2011.

§ 120-57. Legislative Intern Program Council to promulgate a plan for the use of legislative interns.

(a)   For purposes of this section the term "institutions of higher education" means four year colleges and universities and community colleges that offer college transfer programs.

(b)   The Legislative Intern Program Council is hereby empowered and is directed to promulgate for each session of the General Assembly a plan providing for the selection, tenure, duties and compensation of legislative interns. Interns shall be selected from institutions of higher education within North Carolina, including but not limited to all units of the university system and community college system. The selection shall be based upon guidelines set forth by the Legislative Intern Program Council; these guidelines shall permit the proper consideration of each applicant. (1969, c. 32; 1979, c. 1067, s. 1; 2007-201, s. 1.)

Article 12.

Commission on Children with Special Needs.

§§ 120-58 through 120-70. Repealed by Session Laws 1999-395, s. 21B.1, effective July 1, 1999.

Article 12K.

Joint Legislative Administrative Procedure Oversight Committee.

§ 120-70.100. Creation and membership of Joint Legislative Administrative Procedure Oversight Committee.

(a)   The Joint Legislative Administrative Procedure Oversight Committee is established. The Committee consists of 16 members as follows:

(1)   Eight members of the Senate appointed by the President Pro Tempore of the Senate, at least three of whom are members of the minority party.

(2)   Eight members of the House of Representatives appointed by the Speaker of the House of Representatives, at least three of whom are members of the minority party.

(b)   Members of the Committee shall serve a term of two years beginning on January 15 of each odd-numbered year. Members may complete a term of service on the Committee even if they do not seek reelection or are not reelected to the General Assembly, but resignation or removal from service in the General Assembly constitutes resignation or removal from service on the Committee. A member continues to serve until the member's successor is appointed. A vacancy shall be filled within 30 days by the officer who made the original appointment. (1995, c. 507, s. 27.8(a); 2011-291, s. 1.3(b); 2012-187, s. 1.)

§ 120-70.101. Purpose and powers of Committee.

The Joint Legislative Administrative Procedure Oversight Committee has the following powers and duties:

(1)   To review rules to which the Rules Review Commission has objected to determine if statutory changes are needed to enable the agency to fulfill the intent of the General Assembly.

(2)   To receive reports prepared by the Rules Review Commission containing the text and a summary of each rule approved by the Commission.

(3)   Repealed by Session Laws 2009-125, s. 1, effective October 1, 2009.

(3a)   To review the activities of State occupational licensing boards to determine if the boards are operating in accordance with statutory requirements and if the boards are still necessary to achieve the purposes for which they were created. This review shall not include decisions concerning board personnel matters or determinations on individual licensing applications or individual disciplinary actions.

(4)   To review State regulatory programs to determine if the programs overlap, have conflicting goals, or could be simplified and still achieve the purpose of the regulation.

(5)   To review existing rules to determine if the rules are necessary or if the rules can be streamlined.

(6)   To review the rule-making process to determine if the procedures for adopting rules give the public adequate notice of and information about proposed rules.

(7)   To review any other concerns about administrative law to determine if statutory changes are needed.

(8)   To report to the General Assembly from time to time concerning the Committee's activities and any recommendations for statutory changes. (1995, c. 507, s. 27.8(a); 1996, 2nd Ex. Sess., c. 18, s. 7.10(h); 2009-125, s. 1; 2011-291, s. 1.3(b); 2012-187, s. 1.)

§ 120-70.102. Organization of Committee.

(a)   The President Pro Tempore of the Senate and the Speaker of the House of Representatives shall each designate a cochair of the Joint Legislative Administrative Procedure Oversight Committee. The Committee shall meet at least once a quarter and may meet at other times upon the joint call of the cochairs.

(b)   A quorum of the Committee is nine members. No action may be taken except by a majority vote at a meeting at which a quorum is present. While in the discharge of its official duties, the Committee has the powers of a joint committee under G.S. 120-19 and G.S. 120-19.1 through G.S. 120-19.4.

(c)   Members of the Committee receive subsistence and travel expenses as provided in G.S. 120-3.1. The Committee may contract for consultants or hire employees in accordance with G.S. 120-32.02. The Committee may meet in the Legislative Building or the Legislative Office Building upon the approval of the Legislative Services Commission. The Legislative Services Commission, through the Legislative Services Officer, shall assign professional staff to assist the Committee in its work. Upon the direction of the Legislative Services Commission, the Supervisors of Clerks of the Senate and of the House of Representatives shall assign clerical staff to the Committee. The expenses for clerical employees shall be paid by the Committee. (1995, c. 507, s. 27.8(a); 1996, 2nd Ex. Sess., c. 18, s. 8(l); 2011-291, s. 1.3(b); 2012-187, s. 1.)

§ 120-70.103: Repealed by Session Laws 2009-125, s. 5, effective October 1, 2009.

§ 120-70.104. Reserved for future codification purposes.

Article 12A.

Joint Legislative Utility Review Committee.

§ 120-70.1: Repealed by Session Laws 2011-291, s. 1.2(b), effective June 24, 2011.

§ 120-70.2: Repealed by Session Laws 2011-291, s. 1.2(b), effective June 24, 2011.

§ 120-70.3: Repealed by Session Laws 2011-291, s. 1.2(b), effective June 24, 2011.

§ 120-70.4: Repealed by Session Laws 2011-291, s. 1.2(b), effective June 24, 2011.

§ 120-70.5: Repealed by Session Laws 2011-291, s. 1.2(b), effective June 24, 2011.

§ 120-70.6: Repealed by Session Laws 2011-291, s. 1.2(b), effective June 24, 2011.

Article 12B.

Commission on Children and Youth.

§§ 120-70.7 through 120-70.30: Repealed by Session Laws 1989, c. 802, s. 10.3.

Article 12C.

Joint Select Committee on Low-Level Radioactive Waste.

§ 120-70.31: Repealed by Session Laws 2011-266, s. 1.31(a), effective July 1, 2011 and Session Laws 2011-291, s. 1.2(a) effective June 24, 2011.

§ 120-70.32: Repealed by Session Laws 2011-266, s. 1.31(a), effective July 1, 2011 and Session Laws 2011-291, s. 1.2(a) effective June 24, 2011.

§ 120-70.33: Repealed by Session Laws 2011-266, s. 1.31(a), effective July 1, 2011 and Session Laws 2011-291, s. 1.2(a) effective June 24, 2011.

§ 120-70.34: Repealed by Session Laws 2011-266, s. 1.31(a), effective July 1, 2011 and Session Laws 2011-291, s. 1.2(a) effective June 24, 2011.

§ 120-70.35: Repealed by Session Laws 2011-266, s. 1.31(a), effective July 1, 2011 and Session Laws 2011-291, s. 1.2(a) effective June 24, 2011.

§ 120-70.36: Repealed by Session Laws 2011-266, s. 1.31(a), effective July 1, 2011 and Session Laws 2011-291, s. 1.2(a) effective June 24, 2011.

§ 120-70.37: Repealed by Session Laws 2011-266, s. 1.31(a), effective July 1, 2011 and Session Laws 2011-291, s. 1.2(a) effective June 24, 2011.

Article 12D.

Environmental Review Commission.

§ 120-70.41. Commission established.

The Environmental Review Commission is hereby established. (1987 (Reg. Sess., 1988), c. 1100, s. 4.1.)

§ 120-70.42. Membership; cochairs; vacancies; quorum.

(a)   The Environmental Review Commission shall consist of six Senators appointed by the President Pro Tempore of the Senate, six Representatives appointed by the Speaker of the House of Representatives, who shall serve at the pleasure of their appointing officer, the Chair or a Cochair of the Senate Committee on Agriculture, Environment, and Natural Resources or the equivalent committee, the Chair or a Cochair of the House of Representatives

Committee on Environment and Natural Resources or the equivalent committee, the Chair or a Cochair of the Senate Committee on Appropriations - Natural and Economic Resources or the equivalent committee, and the Chair or a Cochair of the House of Representatives Committee on Appropriations - Natural and Economic Resources or the equivalent committee.

(b)   The President Pro Tempore of the Senate shall designate one or more Senators and the Speaker of the House of Representatives shall designate one or more Representatives to serve as cochairs.

(c)   Except as otherwise provided in this subsection, a member of the Commission shall continue to serve for so long as the member remains a member of the General Assembly and no successor has been appointed. A member of the Commission who does not seek reelection or is not reelected to the General Assembly may complete a term of service on the Commission until the day on which a new General Assembly convenes. A member of the Commission who resigns or is removed from service in the General Assembly shall be deemed to have resigned or been removed from service on the Commission. Any vacancy that occurs on the Environmental Review Commission shall be filled in the same manner as the original appointment.

(d)   A quorum of the Environmental Review Commission shall consist of seven members. (1987 (Reg. Sess., 1988), c. 1100, s. 4.1; 1989, c. 727, s. 139; 1991, c. 739, s. 5; 1997-31, s. 1; 2002-176, s. 4; 2003-340, s. 4; 2010-180, s. 2; 2011-291, s. 1.13.)

§ 120-70.43. Powers and duties.

(a)   The Environmental Review Commission shall have the following powers and duties:

(1)   To evaluate actions of all boards, commissions, departments, and other agencies of the State and local governments as such actions relate to the environment or protection of the environment, including but not limited to an evaluation of:

a.   Benefits of each program relative to costs;

b.   Achievement of program goals;

c.   Use of measures by which the success or failure of a program can be measured; and

d.   Conformity with legislative intent;

(2)   To study on a continuing basis the organization of State government as it relates to the environment or to the protection of public health and the environment, including but not limited to:

a.   Improvements in administrative structure, practices, and procedures;

b.   Increased integration and coordination of programs and functions;

c.   Increased efficiency in budgeting and use of resources;

d.   Efficient administration of licensing, permitting, and grant programs;

e.   Prompt, effective response to environmental emergencies;

f.   Opportunities for effective citizen participation; and

g.   Broadening of career opportunities for professional staff;

(3)   To make any recommendations it deems appropriate regarding the reorganization and consolidation of environmental regulatory agencies and the recodification of statutes relating to the environment, including but not limited to:

a.   Ways in which agencies may operate more efficiently and economically;

b.   Ways in which agencies can provide better services to the State and to the people; and

c.   Instances in which functions of agencies are duplicative, overlapping, incomplete in scope or coverage, fail to accomplish legislative objectives, or for any other reason should be redefined or redistributed;

(4)   To review and evaluate changes in federal law and regulations, relevant court decisions, and changes in technology affecting the environment or protection of the environment;

(5)   To review existing and proposed State law and rules affecting the environment or protection of the environment and to determine whether any modification of law or rules is in the public interest;

(6)   To make reports and recommendations, including draft legislation, to the General Assembly from time to time as to any matter relating to the powers and duties set out in this section; and

(7)   To undertake such additional studies as it deems appropriate or as may from time to time be requested by the President Pro Tempore of the Senate, the Speaker of the House of Representatives, either house of the General Assembly, the Legislative Research Commission, or the Joint Legislative Commission on Governmental Operations and to make such reports and recommendations to the General Assembly regarding such studies as it deems appropriate; provided that the Environmental Review Commission shall not undertake any study which the General Assembly has assigned to another legislative commission or committee.

(b)   The Environmental Review Commission may continue the study of environmental agency consolidation and reorganization. The study of environmental agency consolidation shall include, but is not limited to:

(1)   Monitoring the implementation of Session Laws 1989, c. 727;

(2)   Evaluation of the organization, programs, and operation of the Department of Environment and Natural Resources;

(3)   Evaluation of the organization, functions, powers, and duties of the components of the Department of Environment and Natural Resources, including boards, commissions, councils, and regional offices; and

(4)   Recodification of the General Statutes relating to the environment and environmental agencies.

(c)   In addition to its general powers and duties, the Environmental Review Commission shall have the following powers and duties with respect to hazardous waste management:

(1)   To study the current and projected need for hazardous waste treatment, storage, and disposal capacity in the State in light of anticipated generation of hazardous waste and alternatives for hazardous waste treatment and disposal;

(2)   To evaluate the potential for the development of additional hazardous waste treatment, storage, and disposal capacity by the private sector;

(3)   To study the necessity for and scope of hazardous waste treatment, storage, and disposal facilities which are sited, owned, or operated by the State;

(4)   To review progress in securing a volunteer county to host a hazardous waste treatment facility;

(5)   To study incentives and compensation for the community which hosts, either voluntarily or involuntarily, a hazardous waste treatment facility, including any additional incentives and compensation which may be needed, whether there should be differential compensation for a volunteer county, options for use of funds by local governments, distribution of compensation among local governments, and methods of providing flexibility in the development of an incentives and compensation package for a particular local community;

(6)   To review progress in developing interstate agreements for the treatment, storage, and disposal of hazardous waste;

(7)   To assist in the development of cooperative, comprehensive regional approach to hazardous waste treatment and disposal;

(8),   (9) Repealed by Session Laws 2001-474, s. 12, effective November 29, 2001.

(10)   To study the capacity assurance requirement under the Comprehensive Environmental Response, Compensation and Liability Act of 1980, Pub. L. No. 96-510, 94 Stat. 2767, 42 U.S.C. 9601 et seq., as amended, and the Superfund Amendments and Reauthorization Act of 1986, Pub. L. No. 99-499, 100 Stat. 1613, as amended as it relates to the continued eligibility of North Carolina for remedial actions under Superfund;

(11)   To study alternatives available to the State for dealing with hazardous waste and the ramifications of those alternatives; and

(12)   To receive and evaluate reports of every State agency, board, and commission which has any power or duty with respect to hazardous waste management. (1987 (Reg. Sess., 1988), c. 1100, s. 4.1; 1989, c. 168, s. 46(b); c. 727, s. 225(a); 1991, c. 739, s. 6; 1991 (Reg. Sess., 1992), c. 990, s. 4; 1997-443, s. 11A.119(a); 2001-474, s. 12; 2011-266, s. 1.31(b); 2011-291, s. 2.31.)

§ 120-70.44. Additional powers.

(a)   The Environmental Review Commission, while in the discharge of official duties, may exercise all the powers provided for under the provisions of G.S. 120-19, and G.S. 120-19.1 through G.S. 120-19.4. The Environmental Review Commission may meet at any time upon the call of either cochairman, whether or not the General Assembly is in session. The Environmental Review Commission may meet in the Legislative Building or the Legislative Office Building upon the approval of the Legislative Services Commission.

(b)   Notwithstanding any rule or resolution to the contrary, proposed legislation to implement any recommendation of the Environmental Review Commission regarding any study the Environmental Review Commission is authorized to undertake or any report authorized or required to be made by or to the Environmental Review Commission may be introduced and considered during any session of the General Assembly.

(c)   The Commission may contract for consultants or hire employees in accordance with G.S. 120-32.02. (1987 (Reg. Sess., 1988), c. 1100, s. 4.1; 1989, c. 784, s. 5; 2006-255, s. 3.1.)

§ 120-70.45. Compensation and expenses of members.

Members of the Environmental Review Commission shall receive subsistence and travel expenses at the rates set forth in G.S. 120-3.1. (1987 (Reg. Sess., 1988), c. 1100, s. 4.1.)

§ 120-70.46. Staffing.

The Legislative Services Officer shall assign as staff to the Environmental Review Commission professional employees of the General Assembly, as approved by the Legislative Services Commission. Clerical staff shall be assigned to the Environmental Review Commission through the offices of the Directors of the Legislative Assistants of the Senate and House of Representatives. The expenses of employment of clerical staff shall be borne by the Environmental Review Commission. (1987 (Reg. Sess., 1988), c. 1100, s. 4.1; 1996, 2nd Ex. Sess., c. 18, s. 8(f); 2007-495, s. 12.)

§ 120-70.47. Funding.

From funds available to the General Assembly, the Legislative Services Commission shall allocate monies to fund the work of the Environmental Review Commission. (1987 (Reg. Sess., 1988), c. 1100, s. 4.1.)

§ 120-70.48. Reserved for future codification purposes.

§ 120-70.49. Reserved for future codification purposes.

Article 12E.

Joint Legislative Transportation Oversight Committee.

§ 120-70.50. Creation and membership of Joint Legislative Transportation Oversight Committee.

The Joint Legislative Transportation Oversight Committee is established. The Committee consists of 22 members as follows:

(1)   Eleven members of the Senate appointed by the President Pro Tempore of the Senate, at least three of whom are members of the minority party; and

(2)   Eleven members of the House of Representatives appointed by the Speaker of the House of Representatives, at least three of whom are members of the minority party.

Terms on the Committee are for two years and begin on January 15 of each odd-numbered year, except the terms of the initial members, which begin on appointment. Members may complete a term of service on the Committee even if they do not seek reelection or are not reelected to the General Assembly, but resignation or removal from service in the General Assembly constitutes resignation or removal from service on the Committee.

A member continues to serve until his successor is appointed. A vacancy shall be filled within 30 days by the officer who made the original appointment. (1989, c. 692, s. 1.2; 1993, c. 321, s. 169.2(a); 2001-486, s. 2.4; 2011-291, s. 1.7(c).)

§ 120-70.51. Purpose and powers of Committee.

(a)   The Joint Legislative Transportation Oversight Committee may:

(1)   Review reports prepared by the Department of Transportation or any other agency of State government related, in any manner, to transportation, when those reports are required by any law.

(2)   Monitor the funds deposited in and expenditures from the North Carolina Highway Trust Fund, the Highway Fund, the General Fund, or any other fund when those expenditures are related, in any manner, to transportation.

(3)   Determine whether funds related, in any manner, to transportation are being spent in accordance with law.

(4)   Determine whether any revisions are needed in the funding for a program for which funds in the Trust Fund, the Highway Fund, the General Fund, or any other fund when those expenditures are related, in any manner, to transportation may be used, including revisions needed to meet any statutory timetable or program.

(4a)   Examine the importance of railroads and railroad infrastructure improvements to economic development in North Carolina, including improvements to short-line railroads.

(4b)   Study issues important to the future of passenger and freight rail service in North Carolina.

(4c)   Determine methods to expedite property disputes between railroads and private landowners.

(4d)   Study all aspects of the operation, structure, management, and long-range plans of the North Carolina Railroad.

(5)   Report to the General Assembly at the beginning of each regular session concerning its determinations of needed changes in the funding or operation of programs related, in any manner, to transportation.

(b)   The Committee may make interim reports to the General Assembly on matters for which it may report to a regular session of the General Assembly. A report to the General Assembly may contain any legislation needed to

45

implement a recommendation of the Committee. (1989, c. 692, s. 1.2; 1993, c. 321, s. 169.2(b); 2011-291, s. 1.7(d).)

§ 120-70.52. Organization of Committee.

(a)   The President Pro Tempore of the Senate and the Speaker of the House of Representatives shall each designate a cochair of the Joint Legislative Transportation Oversight Committee. The Committee shall meet at least once a quarter and may meet at other times upon the joint call of the cochairs.

(b)   A quorum of the Committee is nine members. No action may be taken except by a majority vote at a meeting at which a quorum is present. While in the discharge of its official duties, the Committee has the powers of a joint committee under G.S. 120-19 and G.S. 120-19.1 through 120-19.4.

(c)   The Committee shall be funded by appropriations made from the Highway Trust Fund to the Department of Transportation. Members of the Committee receive subsistence and travel expenses as provided in G.S. 120-3.1. The Committee may contract for consultants or hire employees in accordance with G.S. 120-32.02. The Legislative Services Commission, through the Legislative Services Officer, shall assign professional staff to assist the Committee in its work. Upon the direction of the Legislative Services Commission, the Supervisors of Clerks of the Senate and of the House of Representatives shall assign clerical staff to the Committee. The expenses for clerical employees shall be borne by the Committee. (1989, c. 692, s. 1.2; 1993, c. 321, s. 169.2(c); 1996, 2nd Ex. Sess., c. 18, s. 8(g); 2013-410, s. 38(f).)

§§ 120-70.53 through 120-70.59. Reserved for future codification purposes.

Article 12F.

Joint Legislative Commission on Seafood and Aquaculture.

§ 120-70.60: Repealed by Session Laws 2011-291, s. 1.2(b), effective June 24, 2011.

§ 120-70.61: Repealed by Session Laws 2011-291, s. 1.2(b), effective June 24, 2011.

§ 120-70.62: Repealed by Session Laws 2011-291, s. 1.2(b), effective June 24, 2011.

§ 120-70.63: Repealed by Session Laws 2011-291, s. 1.2(b), effective June 24, 2011.

§ 120-70.64: Repealed by Session Laws 2011-291, s. 1.2(b), effective June 24, 2011.

§ 120-70.65: Repealed by Session Laws 2011-291, s. 1.2(b), effective June 24, 2011.

§ 120-70.66: Repealed by Session Laws 2011-291, s. 1.2(b), effective June 24, 2011.

Article 12G.

Commission on the Family.

§§ 120-70.70 through 120-70.75: Repealed by Session Laws 1997-443, s. 12.15.

§§ 120-70.76 through 120-70.79. Reserved for future codification purposes.

Article 12H.

Joint Legislative Education Oversight Committee.

§ 120-70.80. Creation and membership of Joint Legislative Education Oversight Committee.

The Joint Legislative Education Oversight Committee is established. The Committee consists of 22 members as follows:

(1)   Eleven members of the Senate appointed by the President Pro Tempore of the Senate, at least three of whom are members of the minority party; and

(2)   Eleven members of the House of Representatives appointed by the Speaker of the House of Representatives, at least three of whom are members of the minority party.

Terms on the Committee are for two years and begin on the convening of the General Assembly in each odd-numbered year. Members may complete a term of service on the Committee even if they do not seek reelection or are not reelected to the General Assembly, but resignation or removal from service in the General Assembly constitutes resignation or removal from service on the Committee.

A member continues to serve until his successor is appointed. A vacancy shall be filled within 30 days by the officer who made the original appointment. (1989 (Reg. Sess., 1990), c. 1066, s. 115; 1997-456, s. 46(a); 1997-495, s. 91(a); 1999-431, s. 3.7(a); 2001-486, s. 2.5; 2011-291, s. 1.5(c).)

§ 120-70.81. Purpose and powers of Committee.

(a)   The Joint Legislative Education Oversight Committee shall examine, on a continuing basis, the several educational institutions in North Carolina, in order to make ongoing recommendations to the General Assembly on ways to improve public education from kindergarten through higher education. In this examination, the Committee may:

(1)   Study the budgets, programs, and policies of the Department of Public Instruction, the State Board of Education, the Community Colleges System Office, the Board of Governors of The University of North Carolina, and the constituent institutions of The University of North Carolina to determine ways in which the General Assembly may encourage the improvement of all education provided to North Carolinians and may aid in the development of more integrated methods of institutional accountability;

(2)   Examine, in particular, the Basic Education Plan and the School Improvement and Accountability Act of 1989, to determine whether changes need to be built into the plans, whether implementation schedules need to be restructured, and how to manage the ongoing development of the policies underlying these legislative plans, including a determination of whether there is a need for the legislature to develop ongoing funding patterns for these plans;

(3)   Study other states' educational initiatives in public schools, community colleges, and public universities, in order to provide an ongoing commentary to the General Assembly on these initiatives and to make recommendations for implementing similar initiatives in North Carolina; and

(4)   Study any other educational matters that the Committee considers necessary to fulfill its mandate.

(5)   Study the needs of children and youth. This study may include, but is not limited to:

a.   Developing strategies for addressing the issues of school dropout, teen suicide, and adolescent pregnancy.

b.   Identifying and evaluating the impact on children and youth of other economic and environmental issues.

(b)   The Committee may make interim reports to the General Assembly on matters for which it may report to a regular session of the General Assembly. A report to the General Assembly may contain any legislation needed to implement a recommendation of the Committee. (1989 (Reg. Sess., 1990), c. 1066, s. 115; 1999-84, s. 20; 2011-291, s. 1.5(d).)

§ 120-70.82. Organization of Committee.

(a)   The President Pro Tempore of the Senate and the Speaker of the House of Representatives shall each designate a cochair of the Joint Legislative Education Oversight Committee. The Committee shall meet at least once a quarter and may meet at other times upon the joint call of the cochairs.

(b)   A quorum of the Committee is 10 members. No action may be taken except by a majority vote at a meeting at which a quorum is present. While in

49

the discharge of its official duties, the Committee has the powers of a joint committee under G.S. 120-19 and G.S. 120-19.1 through G.S. 120-19.4.

(c)   Members of the Committee receive subsistence and travel expenses as provided in G.S. 120-3.1. The Committee may contract for consultants or hire employees in accordance with G.S. 120-32.02. The Legislative Services Commission, through the Legislative Services Officer, shall assign professional staff to assist the Committee in its work. Upon the direction of the Legislative Services Commission, the Supervisors of Clerks of the Senate and of the House of Representatives shall assign clerical staff to the Committee. The expenses for clerical employees shall be borne by the Committee. (1989 (Reg. Sess., 1990), c. 1066, s. 115; 1996, 2nd Ex. Sess., c. 18, s. 8(i); 1997-456, s. 46(b); 1997-495, s. 91(b).)

§ 120-70.83. Additional powers.

The Joint Legislative Education Oversight Committee, while in discharge of official duties, shall have access to any paper or document, and may compel the attendance of any State official or employee before the Committee or secure any evidence under G.S. 120.19. In addition, G.S. 120-19.1 through G.S. 120-19.4 shall apply to the proceedings of the Committee as if it were a joint committee of the General Assembly. (1997-18, s. 15(b).)

§ 120-70.84. Reports to the Committee.

By March 1, 2014, and by January 1, 2015, and annually thereafter, TFA [Teach for America, Inc.] shall report to the Joint Legislative Education Oversight Committee on the operation of its programs under subsection (a) of Section 8.21 of S.L. 2013-360, including at least all of the following information:

(1)   The total number of applications received nationally from candidates seeking participation in the program.

(2)   The total number of applications received from candidates who are residents of North Carolina and information on the source of these candidates, including the number of (i) recent college graduates and the higher institution

the candidates attended, (ii) mid-career level and lateral entry industry professionals, and (iii) veterans of the United States Armed Forces.

(3)   The total number of North Carolina candidates accepted by TFA.

(4)   The total number of accepted candidates placed in North Carolina, including the number of accepted candidates who are residents of North Carolina.

(5)   The regions in which accepted candidates have been placed, the number of candidates in each region, and the number of students impacted by placement in those regions.

(6)   Success of recruitment efforts, including the Teach Back Home program and targeting of candidates who are (i) working in areas related to STEM education, (ii) mid-career level and lateral entry industry professionals, and (iii) veterans of the United States Armed Forces.

(7)   Success of retention efforts, including the Teach Beyond Two and Make it Home programs, and the percentage of accepted candidates working in their placement communities beyond the initial TFA two-year commitment period and the number of years those candidates teach beyond the initial commitment.

(8)   A financial accounting of how the State funds appropriated to TFA were expended in the previous year, including at least the following information:

a.   Funds expended by region of the State.

b.   Details on program costs, including at least the following:

1.   Recruitment, candidate selection, and placement.

2.   Preservice training and preparation costs.

3.   Operational and administrative costs, including development and fundraising, alumni support, management costs, and marketing and outreach.

c.   Funds received through private fundraising, specifically by sources in each region of the State. (2013-360, s. 8.21(b).)

§ 120-70.85. Reserved for future codification purposes.

§ 120-70.86. Reserved for future codification purposes.

§ 120-70.87. Reserved for future codification purposes.

§ 120-70.88. Reserved for future codification purposes.

Article 12I.

Joint Legislative Oversight Committee on Early Childhood Education and Development Initiatives.

§§ 120-70.90 through 120-70.92: Repealed by Session Laws 1996, Second Extra Session, c. 18, s. 24.29(g).

Article 12J.

Joint Legislative Oversight Committee on Justice and Public Safety.

§ 120-70.93. Creation and membership of Joint Legislative Oversight Committee on Justice and Public Safety.

The Joint Legislative Oversight Committee on Justice and Public Safety is established. The Committee consists of 22 members as follows:

(1)   Eleven members of the Senate appointed by the President Pro Tempore of the Senate, at least three of whom are members of the minority party; and

(2)   Eleven members of the House of Representatives appointed by the Speaker of the House of Representatives, at least three of whom are members of the minority party.

Terms on the Committee are for two years and begin on the convening of the General Assembly in each odd-numbered year, except the terms of the initial members, which begin on appointment and end on the day of the convening of the 1995 General Assembly. Members may complete a term of service on the Committee even if they do not seek reelection or are not reelected to the

General Assembly, but resignation or removal from service in the General Assembly constitutes resignation or removal from service on the Committee.

A member continues to serve until his successor is appointed. A vacancy shall be filled within 30 days by the officer who made the original appointment. (1994, Ex. Sess., c. 24, s. 49(a); 1997-443, s. 21.4(a); 2001-138, s. 2; 2011-291, s. 1.4(c).)

§ 120-70.94. Purpose and powers of Committee.

(a)   The Joint Legislative Oversight Committee on Justice and Public Safety shall examine, on a continuing basis, the correctional, law enforcement, and juvenile justice systems in North Carolina, in order to make ongoing recommendations to the General Assembly on ways to improve those systems and to assist those systems in realizing their objectives of protecting the public and of punishing and rehabilitating offenders. In this examination, the Committee shall:

(1)   Study the budget, programs, and policies of the Department of Public Safety to determine ways in which the General Assembly may improve the effectiveness of the Department.

(2)   Examine the effectiveness of the Division of Adult Correction of the Department of Public Safety in implementing the public policy stated in G.S. 148-26 of providing work assignments and employment for inmates as a means of reducing the cost of maintaining the inmate population while enabling inmates to acquire or retain skills and work habits needed to secure honest employment after their release.

(2a)   Examine the effectiveness of the Department of Public Safety in implementing the duties and responsibilities charged to the Department in G.S. 143B-601(1) through (9) and the overall effectiveness and efficiency of law enforcement in the State.

(2b)   Examine the effectiveness of the Division of Juvenile Justice of the Department of Public Safety in implementing the duties and responsibilities charged to the Division in Part 3 of Article 13 of Chapter 143B of the General Statutes and the overall effectiveness and efficiency of the juvenile justice system in the State.

(3)   Recodified as subdivision (a)(13) by Session Laws 2011-291, s. 1.4(c), effective June 24, 2011.

(3a)   Study and evaluate the funding sources and needs of domestic violence programs providing services to domestic violence victims and programs providing treatment to domestic violence abusers.

(4)   Study legal services funding for domestic violence victims and explore additional sources of funding.

(5)   Explore sources of additional funding for all domestic violence programs, including visitation centers.

(6)   Examine current programs and explore new programs to provide effective services to domestic violence victims and treatment to domestic violence abusers.

(7)   Examine law enforcement and judicial responses to domestic violence.

(8)   Review data collected on domestic violence cases pursuant to G.S. 15A-1382.1.

(9)   Study the effectiveness of the Crime Victims Rights Act as it relates to domestic violence.

(10)   Study the needs of juveniles. This study may include, but is not limited to:

a.   Determining the adequacy and appropriateness of services:

1.   To children and youth receiving child welfare services;

2.   To children and youth in the juvenile court system;

3.   Provided by the Division of Social Services of the Department of Health and Human Services and the Division of Juvenile Justice of the Department of Public Safety;

4.   To children and youth served by the Mental Health, Developmental Disabilities, and Substance Abuse Services system.

b.   Developing methods for identifying and providing services to children and youth not receiving but in need of child welfare services, children and youth at risk of entering the juvenile court system, and children and youth exposed to domestic violence situations.

c.   Identifying obstacles to ensuring that children who are in secure or nonsecure custody are placed in safe and permanent homes within a reasonable period of time and recommending strategies for overcoming those obstacles. The Commission shall consider what, if anything, can be done to expedite the adjudication and appeal of abuse and neglect charges against parents so that decisions may be made about the safe and permanent placement of their children as quickly as possible.

(11)   Evaluate problems associated with juveniles who are beyond the disciplinary control of their parents, including juveniles who are runaways, and develop solutions for addressing the problems of those juveniles.

(12)   Identify strategies for the development and funding of a comprehensive statewide database relating to children and youth to facilitate State agency planning for delivery of services to children and youth.

(13)   Study any other matter that the Committee considers necessary.

(b)   The Committee may make interim reports to the General Assembly on matters for which it may report to a regular session of the General Assembly. A report to the General Assembly may contain any legislation needed to implement a recommendation of the Committee. (1994, Ex. Sess., c. 24, s. 49(a); 1997-443, s. 21.4(a); 2001-138, s. 1; 2011-145, s. 19.1(g), (h), (l), (ii); 2011-291, s. 1.4(c); 2012-194, s. 23.)

§ 120-70.95. Organization of Committee.

(a)   The President Pro Tempore of the Senate and the Speaker of the House of Representatives shall each designate a cochair of the Joint Legislative Oversight Committee on Justice and Public Safety. The Committee shall meet at least once a quarter and may meet at other times upon the joint call of the cochairs.

(b)   A quorum of the Committee is nine members. No action may be taken except by a majority vote at a meeting at which a quorum is present. While in the discharge of its official duties, the Committee has the powers of a joint committee under G.S. 120-19 and G.S. 120-19.1 through G.S. 120-19.4.

(c)   Members of the Committee receive subsistence and travel expenses as provided in G.S. 120-3.1. The Committee may contract for consultants or hire employees in accordance with G.S. 120-32.02. The Legislative Services Commission, through the Legislative Services Officer, shall assign professional staff to assist the Committee in its work. Upon the direction of the Legislative Services Commission, the Supervisors of Clerks of the Senate and of the House of Representatives shall assign clerical staff to the Committee. The expenses for clerical employees shall be borne by the Committee. (1994, Ex. Sess., c. 24, s. 49(a); 1996, 2nd Ex. Sess., c. 18, s. 8(k); 1997-443, s. 21.4(a); 2001-138, s. 2; 2011-291, s. 1.4(c).)

§§ 120-70.96 through 120-70.99. Reserved for future codification purposes.

Article 12.

Commission on Children with Special Needs.

§§ 120-58 through 120-70. Repealed by Session Laws 1999-395, s. 21B.1, effective July 1, 1999.

Article 12K.

Joint Legislative Administrative Procedure Oversight Committee.

§ 120-70.100. Creation and membership of Joint Legislative Administrative Procedure Oversight Committee.

(a)   The Joint Legislative Administrative Procedure Oversight Committee is established. The Committee consists of 16 members as follows:

(1)   Eight members of the Senate appointed by the President Pro Tempore of the Senate, at least three of whom are members of the minority party.

(2)   Eight members of the House of Representatives appointed by the Speaker of the House of Representatives, at least three of whom are members of the minority party.

(b)   Members of the Committee shall serve a term of two years beginning on January 15 of each odd-numbered year. Members may complete a term of service on the Committee even if they do not seek reelection or are not reelected to the General Assembly, but resignation or removal from service in the General Assembly constitutes resignation or removal from service on the Committee. A member continues to serve until the member's successor is appointed. A vacancy shall be filled within 30 days by the officer who made the original appointment. (1995, c. 507, s. 27.8(a); 2011-291, s. 1.3(b); 2012-187, s. 1.)

§ 120-70.101. Purpose and powers of Committee.

The Joint Legislative Administrative Procedure Oversight Committee has the following powers and duties:

(1)   To review rules to which the Rules Review Commission has objected to determine if statutory changes are needed to enable the agency to fulfill the intent of the General Assembly.

(2)   To receive reports prepared by the Rules Review Commission containing the text and a summary of each rule approved by the Commission.

(3)   Repealed by Session Laws 2009-125, s. 1, effective October 1, 2009.

(3a)   To review the activities of State occupational licensing boards to determine if the boards are operating in accordance with statutory requirements and if the boards are still necessary to achieve the purposes for which they were created. This review shall not include decisions concerning board personnel matters or determinations on individual licensing applications or individual disciplinary actions.

(4)   To review State regulatory programs to determine if the programs overlap, have conflicting goals, or could be simplified and still achieve the purpose of the regulation.

(5)   To review existing rules to determine if the rules are necessary or if the rules can be streamlined.

(6)   To review the rule-making process to determine if the procedures for adopting rules give the public adequate notice of and information about proposed rules.

(7)   To review any other concerns about administrative law to determine if statutory changes are needed.

(8)   To report to the General Assembly from time to time concerning the Committee's activities and any recommendations for statutory changes. (1995, c. 507, s. 27.8(a); 1996, 2nd Ex. Sess., c. 18, s. 7.10(h); 2009-125, s. 1; 2011-291, s. 1.3(b); 2012-187, s. 1.)

§ 120-70.102. Organization of Committee.

(a)   The President Pro Tempore of the Senate and the Speaker of the House of Representatives shall each designate a cochair of the Joint Legislative Administrative Procedure Oversight Committee. The Committee shall meet at least once a quarter and may meet at other times upon the joint call of the cochairs.

(b)   A quorum of the Committee is nine members. No action may be taken except by a majority vote at a meeting at which a quorum is present. While in the discharge of its official duties, the Committee has the powers of a joint committee under G.S. 120-19 and G.S. 120-19.1 through G.S. 120-19.4.

(c)   Members of the Committee receive subsistence and travel expenses as provided in G.S. 120-3.1. The Committee may contract for consultants or hire employees in accordance with G.S. 120-32.02. The Committee may meet in the Legislative Building or the Legislative Office Building upon the approval of the

Legislative Services Commission. The Legislative Services Commission, through the Legislative Services Officer, shall assign professional staff to assist the Committee in its work. Upon the direction of the Legislative Services Commission, the Supervisors of Clerks of the Senate and of the House of Representatives shall assign clerical staff to the Committee. The expenses for clerical employees shall be paid by the Committee. (1995, c. 507, s. 27.8(a); 1996, 2nd Ex. Sess., c. 18, s. 8(l); 2011-291, s. 1.3(b); 2012-187, s. 1.)

§ 120-70.103: Repealed by Session Laws 2009-125, s. 5, effective October 1, 2009.

§ 120-70.104. Reserved for future codification purposes.

Article 12L.

Revenue Laws Study Committee.

§ 120-70.105. Creation and membership of the Revenue Laws Study Committee.

(a)   Membership. - The Revenue Laws Study Committee is established. The Committee consists of 20 members as follows:

(1)   Ten members appointed by the President Pro Tempore of the Senate; the persons appointed may be members of the Senate or public members.

(2)   Ten members appointed by the Speaker of the House of Representatives; the persons appointed may be members of the House of Representatives or public members.

(b)   Terms. - Terms on the Committee are for two years and begin on January 15 of each odd-numbered year, except the terms of the initial members, which begin on appointment. Legislative members may complete a term of service on the Committee even if they do not seek reelection or are not reelected to the General Assembly, but resignation or removal from service in the General Assembly constitutes resignation or removal from service on the Committee.

A member continues to serve until a successor is appointed. A vacancy shall be filled within 30 days by the officer who made the original appointment. (1997-483, s. 14.1; 1998-98, s. 39; 2009-574, s. 51.1.)

§ 120-70.106. Purpose and powers of Committee.

(a)   The Revenue Laws Study Committee may:

(1)   Study the revenue laws of North Carolina and the administration of those laws.

(2)   Review the State's revenue laws to determine which laws need clarification, technical amendment, repeal, or other change to make the laws concise, intelligible, easy to administer, and equitable.

(3)   Call upon the Department of Revenue to cooperate with it in the study of the revenue laws.

(4)   Report to the General Assembly at the beginning of each regular session concerning its determinations of needed changes in the State's revenue laws.

These powers, which are enumerated by way of illustration, shall be liberally construed to provide for the maximum review by the Committee of all revenue law matters in this State.

(b)   The Committee may make interim reports to the General Assembly on matters for which it may report to a regular session of the General Assembly. A report to the General Assembly may contain any legislation needed to implement a recommendation of the Committee. When a recommendation of the Committee, if enacted, would result in an increase or decrease in State revenues, the report of the Committee must include an estimate of the amount of the increase or decrease.

(c)   The Revenue Laws Study Committee must review the effect Article 42 of Chapter 66 of the General Statutes, as enacted by S.L. 2006-151, has on the issues listed in this section to determine if any changes to the law are needed:

(1)   Competition in video programming services.

(2)   The number of cable service subscribers, the price of cable service by service tier, and the technology used to deliver the service.

(3)   The deployment of broadband in the State.

The Committee must review the impact of this Article on these issues every two years and report its findings to the North Carolina General Assembly. The Committee must make its first report to the 2008 Session of the North Carolina General Assembly. (1997-483, s. 14.1; 2006-151, s. 21.)

§ 120-70.107. Organization of Committee.

(a)   The President Pro Tempore of the Senate and the Speaker of the House of Representatives shall each designate a cochair of the Revenue Laws Study Committee. The Committee shall meet upon the joint call of the cochairs.

(b)   A quorum of the Committee is nine members. No action may be taken except by a majority vote at a meeting at which a quorum is present. While in the discharge of its official duties, the Committee has the powers of a joint committee under G.S. 120-19 and G.S. 120-19.1 through G.S. 120-19.4.

(c)   The Committee shall be funded by the Legislative Services Commission from appropriations made to the General Assembly for that purpose. Members of the Committee receive subsistence and travel expenses as provided in G.S. 120-3.1 and G.S. 138-5. The Committee may contract for consultants or hire employees in accordance with G.S. 120-32.02. Upon approval of the Legislative Services Commission, the Legislative Services Officer shall assign professional staff to assist the Committee in its work. Upon the direction of the Legislative Services Commission, the Supervisors of Clerks of the Senate and of the House of Representatives shall assign clerical staff to the Committee. The expenses for clerical employees shall be borne by the Committee. (1997-483, s. 14.1.)

§ 120-70.108: Repealed by Session Laws 2011-266, s. 1.15, effective July 1, 2011.

§ 120-70.109. Reserved for future codification purposes.

Article 12M.

Joint Legislative Health Care Oversight Committee.

§ 120-70.110: Repealed by Session Laws 2011-291, s. 1.6(b), effective June 24, 2011.

§ 120-70.111: Repealed by Session Laws 2011-291, s. 1.6(b), effective June 24, 2011.

§ 120-70.112: Repealed by Session Laws 2011-291, s. 1.6(b), effective June 24, 2011.

§§ 120-70.113 through 120-70.119. Reserved for future codification purposes.

Article 12N.

Joint Legislative Growth Strategies Oversight Committee.

§ 120-70.120: Expired.

§ 120-70.121: Expired.

§ 120-70.122: Expired.

§§ 120-70.123 through 120-70.129: Expired.

Article 12O.

Joint Legislative Economic Development and Global Engagement Oversight Committee.

§ 120-70.130. Creation and membership of Joint Legislative Economic Development and Global Engagement Oversight Committee.

The Joint Legislative Economic Development and Global Engagement Oversight Committee is established. The Committee consists of 22 members as follows:

(1)   Eleven members of the Senate appointed by the President Pro Tempore of the Senate, at least three of whom are members of the minority party; and

(2)   Eleven members of the House of Representatives appointed by the Speaker of the House of Representatives, at least three of whom are members of the minority party.

Terms on the Committee are for two years and begin on the convening of the General Assembly in each odd-numbered year, except the terms of the initial members, which begin on appointment and end on the day of the convening of the 2007 General Assembly. Members may complete a term of service on the Committee even if they do not seek reelection or are not reelected to the General Assembly, but resignation or removal from service in the General Assembly constitutes resignation or removal from service on the Committee.

A member continues to serve until a successor is appointed. A vacancy shall be filled by the officer who made the original appointment. (2005-241, s. 7; 2011-291, s. 1.10(a); 2011-292, s. 1.)

§ 120-70.131. Purpose and powers of Committee.

(a)   The Joint Legislative Economic Development and Global Engagement Oversight Committee shall examine, on a continuing basis, economic development and global engagement issues and strategies in North Carolina in order to make ongoing recommendations to the General Assembly on ways to promote cost-effective economic development initiatives, economic growth, and stimulating job creation in the global economy. In this examination, the Committee may:

(1)   Study the budgets, programs, and policies of the Department of Commerce, the North Carolina Partnership for Economic Development, and other State, regional, and local entities involved in economic development.

(2)   Analyze legislation from other states regarding economic development.

63

(3)   Analyze proposals produced by the Economic Development Board.

(3a)   Request the Department of Commerce to provide an annual report by January 15 of each year on the effectiveness of the following economic development programs:

a.   Job Development Investment Grant Program (JDIG).

b.   One North Carolina.

c.   Article 3J Credits.

d.   Job Maintenance and Capital Development Fund (JMAC).

(4)   Analyze North Carolina's current international activity in the business, State government, and education sectors.

(5)   Analyze barriers to international trade that may be addressed by legislation.

(6)   Explore ways to increase coordination, synchronization, and intercommunication between State and local governmental entities.

(7)   Collect and analyze data on global business trends.

(8)   Study foreign representation opportunities for North Carolina that could solicit, target, educate, and recruit international businesses to North Carolina.

(9)   Analyze incentives designed to encourage small businesses to export goods and service solutions.

(10)   Study methods for positioning North Carolina as a portal to North America for international trade.

(11)   Explore opportunities to increase foreign direct investment in North Carolina.

(12)   Study any other matters that the Committee considers necessary to fulfill its mandate.

(b)   The Committee may make interim reports to the General Assembly on matters for which it may report to a regular session of the General Assembly. A report to the General Assembly may contain any legislation needed to implement a recommendation of the Committee. (2005-241, s. 7; 2011-291, s. 1.10(b); 2011-292, s. 1.)

§ 120-70.132. Organization of Committee.

(a)   The President Pro Tempore of the Senate and the Speaker of the House of Representatives shall each designate a cochair of the Joint Legislative Economic Development and Global Engagement Oversight Committee. The Committee shall meet upon the joint call of the cochairs.

(b)   A quorum of the Committee is seven members. Only recommendations, including proposed legislation, receiving at least six affirmative votes may be included in a Committee report to the General Assembly. While in the discharge of its official duties, the Committee has the powers of a joint committee under G.S. 120-19 and G.S. 120-19.1 through G.S. 120-19.4.

(c)   The cochairs of the Committee may call upon other knowledgeable persons or experts to assist the Committee in its work.

(d)   Members of the Committee shall receive subsistence and travel expenses as provided in G.S. 120-3.1, 138-5, or 138-6, as appropriate. The Committee may contract for consultants or hire employees in accordance with G.S. 120-32.02. The Legislative Services Commission, through the Legislative Services Officer, shall assign professional staff to assist the Committee in its work. Upon the direction of the Legislative Services Commission, the Supervisors of Clerks of the Senate and of the House of Representatives shall assign clerical staff to the Committee. The expenses for clerical employees shall be borne by the Committee. (2005-241, s. 7; 2011-292, s. 1.)

Article 12P.

Joint Legislative Elections Oversight Committee.

§ 120-70.140. Creation and membership of Joint Legislative Elections Oversight Committee.

The Joint Legislative Elections Oversight Committee is established. The Committee consists of 18 members as follows:

(1)   Nine members of the Senate appointed by the President Pro Tempore of the Senate. The President Pro Tempore shall appoint members proportionally according to the partisan composition of the Senate.

(2)   Nine members of the House of Representatives appointed by the Speaker of the House of Representatives. The Speaker shall appoint members proportionally according to the partisan composition of the House.

Terms on the Committee are for two years and begin on January 15 of each odd-numbered year, except the terms of the initial members, which begin on appointment and end on January 15 of the next odd-numbered year. Members may complete a term of service on the Committee even if they do not seek reelection or are not reelected to the General Assembly, but resignation or removal from service in the General Assembly constitutes resignation or removal from service on the Committee.

A member continues to serve until his or her successor is appointed. A vacancy shall be filled within 30 days by the officer who made the original appointment. (2008-150, s. 1(a).)

§ 120-70.141. Purpose and powers of Committee.

(a)   The Joint Legislative Elections Oversight Committee shall examine, on a continuing basis, election administration and campaign finance regulation in North Carolina, in order to make ongoing recommendations to the General Assembly on ways to improve elections administration and campaign finance regulation. In this examination, the Committee shall do the following:

(1)   Study the budgets, programs, and policies of the State Board of Elections and the county boards of elections to determine ways in which the General Assembly may improve election administration and campaign finance regulation.

66

(2)   Examine election statutes and court decisions to determine any legislative changes that are needed to improve election administration and campaign finance regulation.

(3)   Study other states' initiatives in election administration and campaign finance regulation to provide an ongoing commentary to the General Assembly on these initiatives and to make recommendations for implementing similar initiatives in North Carolina; and

(4)   Study any other election matters that the Committee considers necessary to fulfill its mandate.

(b)   The Committee may make interim reports to the General Assembly on matters for which it may report to a regular session of the General Assembly. A report to the General Assembly may contain any legislation needed to implement a recommendation of the Committee. (2008-150, s. 1(a).)

§ 120-70.142. Organization of Committee.

(a)   The President Pro Tempore of the Senate and the Speaker of the House of Representatives shall each designate a cochair of the Joint Legislative Elections Oversight Committee. The Committee shall meet at least once a quarter and may meet at other times upon the joint call of the cochairs.

(b)   A quorum of the Committee is 10 members. No action may be taken except by a majority vote at a meeting at which a quorum is present. While in the discharge of its official duties, the Committee has the powers of a joint committee under G.S. 120-19 and G.S. 120-19.1 through G.S. 120-19.4.

(c)   Members of the Committee receive subsistence and travel expenses as provided in G.S. 120-3.1. The Committee may contract for consultants or hire employees in accordance with G.S. 120-32.02. The Legislative Services Commission, through the Legislative Services Officer, shall assign professional staff to assist the Committee in its work. Upon the direction of the Legislative Services Commission, the Supervisors of Clerks of the Senate and of the House of Representatives shall assign clerical staff to the Committee. The expenses for clerical employees shall be borne by the Committee. (2008-150, s. 1(a).)

§ 120-70.143. Additional powers.

The Joint Legislative Elections Oversight Committee, while in discharge of official duties, shall have access to any paper or document and may compel the attendance of any State official or employee before the Committee or secure any evidence under G.S. 120-19. In addition, G.S. 120-19.1 through G.S. 120-19.4 shall apply to the proceedings of the Committee as if it were a joint committee of the General Assembly. (2008-150, s. 1(a).)

Article 12Q.

Joint Legislative Emergency Management Oversight Committee.

§ 120-70.150. Creation and membership of Joint Legislative Emergency Management Oversight Committee.

The Joint Legislative Emergency Management Oversight Committee is established. The Committee consists of 12 members as follows:

(1)   Six members of the Senate appointed by the President Pro Tempore of the Senate; and

(2)   Six members of the House of Representatives appointed by the Speaker of the House of Representatives.

Terms on the Committee are for two years and begin on the convening of the General Assembly in each odd-numbered year, except the terms of the initial members, which begin on appointment and end on the day of the convening of the 2013 General Assembly. Members may complete a term of service on the Committee even if they do not seek reelection or are not reelected to the General Assembly, but resignation or removal from service in the General Assembly constitutes resignation or removal from service on the Committee.

A member continues to serve until a successor is appointed. A vacancy shall be filled by the officer who made the original appointment. (2012-90, s. 6.)

§ 120-70.151. Purpose and powers of Committee.

(a)   The Joint Legislative Emergency Management Oversight Committee shall examine, on a continuing basis, issues related to emergency management in North Carolina in order to make ongoing recommendations to the General Assembly on ways to promote effective emergency preparedness, management, response, and recovery. The Committee may examine:

(1)   Whether the State building code sufficiently addresses issues related to commercial and residential construction in hurricane and flood prone areas.

(2)   The public health infrastructure in place to respond to natural and nonnatural disasters.

(3)   Hurricane preparedness, evacuation, and response.

(4)   Energy security issues.

(5)   Terrorism preparedness and response, including bioterrorism.

(6)   Flood and natural disaster preparation and response.

(7)   Any other topic the Committee believes is related to its purpose.

(b)   The Committee may make interim reports to the General Assembly on matters for which it may report to a regular session of the General Assembly. A report to the General Assembly may contain any legislation needed to implement a recommendation of the Committee. (2012-90, s. 6.)

§ 120-70.152. Organization of Committee.

(a)   The President Pro Tempore of the Senate and the Speaker of the House of Representatives shall each designate a cochair of the Joint Legislative Emergency Management Oversight Committee. The Committee shall meet upon the joint call of the cochairs.

(b)   A quorum of the Committee is seven members. Only recommendations, including proposed legislation, receiving at least six affirmative votes may be included in a Committee report to the General Assembly. While in the discharge of its official duties, the Committee has the powers of a joint committee under G.S. 120-19 and G.S. 120-19.1 through G.S. 120-19.4.

(c)   The cochairs of the Committee may call upon other knowledgeable persons or experts to assist the Committee in its work.

(d)   Members of the Committee shall receive subsistence and travel expenses as provided in G.S. 120-3.1, 138-5, or 138-6, as appropriate. The Committee may contract for consultants or hire employees in accordance with G.S. 120-32.02. The Legislative Services Commission, through the Legislative Services Officer, shall assign professional staff to assist the Committee in its work. Upon the direction of the Legislative Services Commission, the Supervisors of Clerks of the Senate and of the House of Representatives shall assign clerical staff to the Committee. The expenses for clerical employees shall be borne by the Committee.

(e)   In appointing members to the Committee, the President Pro Tempore of the Senate and the Speaker of the House of Representatives shall take into consideration the goal of having members appointed to the Committee who have knowledge and experience relating to areas that are most impacted by disasters and emergencies. (2012-90, s. 6.)

§ 120-70.153: Reserved for future codification purposes.

§ 120-70.154: Reserved for future codification purposes.

Article 12R.

Joint Legislative Oversight Committee on Unemployment Insurance.

§ 120-70.155. (Expires July 1, 2023) Creation and membership.

(a)   The Joint Legislative Oversight Committee on Unemployment Insurance is established. The Committee consists of eight members appointed as follows:

(1)   Four members of the House of Representatives appointed by the Speaker of the House of Representatives.

(2)   Four members of the Senate appointed by the President Pro Tempore of the Senate.

(b)   The members serve for a term of two years. Members may complete a term of service on the Committee even if they do not seek reelection or are not reelected to the General Assembly, but resignation or removal from service in the General Assembly constitutes resignation or removal from service on the Committee. A member continues to serve until a successor is appointed. A vacancy shall be filled by the officer who made the original appointment. (2013-2, s. 10; 2013-224, s. 19.)

§ 120-70.156. (Expires July 1, 2023) Purpose and powers of Committee.

(a)   Purpose. - The Joint Legislative Oversight Committee on Unemployment Insurance is directed to study and review all unemployment insurance matters, workforce development programs, and reemployment assistance efforts of the State. The following duties and powers, which are enumerated by way of illustration, shall be liberally construed to provide maximum review by the Committee of these matters:

(1)   Study the unemployment insurance laws of North Carolina and the administration of those laws.

(2)   Review the State's unemployment insurance laws to determine which laws need clarification, technical amendment, repeal, or other change to make the laws concise, intelligible, and easy to administer.

(3)   Monitor the payment of the debt owed by the Unemployment Trust Fund to the federal government.

(4)   Review and determine the adequacy of the balances in the Unemployment Trust Fund and the Unemployment Insurance Reserve Fund.

(5)   Study the workforce development programs and reemployment assistance efforts of the Division of Workforce Solutions of the Department of Commerce.

(6)   Call upon the Department of Commerce to cooperate with it in the study of the unemployment insurance laws and the workforce development efforts of the State.

(b)   The Committee may report its findings and recommendations to any regular session of the General Assembly. A report to the General Assembly may contain any legislation needed to implement a recommendation of the Committee. (2013-2, s. 10; 2013-224, s. 19.)

§ 120-70.157. (Expires July 1, 2023) Organization of Committee.

The Speaker of the House of Representatives shall designate one representative as cochair, and the President Pro Tempore of the Senate shall designate one senator as cochair. The Joint Legislative Oversight Committee on Unemployment Insurance may meet upon the joint call of the cochairs. A quorum of the Committee is five members.

The Committee may meet in the Legislative Building or the Legislative Office Building. While in the discharge of its official duties, the Committee has the powers of a joint committee under G.S. 120-19 and G.S. 120-19.1 through G.S. 120-19.4. The Legislative Services Commission, through the Legislative Services Officer, shall assign professional staff to assist the Committee in its work. The House of Representatives and the Senate's Directors of Legislative Assistants shall assign clerical staff to the Committee, and the expenses relating to the clerical employees shall be borne by the Committee. The Committee may contract for professional, clerical, or consultant services as provided by G.S. 120-32.02. Members of the Committee shall receive subsistence and travel expenses at the rates set forth in G.S. 120-3.1, 138-5, or 138-6, as appropriate. (2013-2, s. 10; 2013-224, s. 19.)

§ 120-70.158. (Expires July 1, 2023) Sunset.

This Article expires July 1, 2023. (2013-2, s. 10; 2013-224, s. 19.)

Article 13.

Joint Legislative Commission on Governmental Operations.

§ 120-71. Purpose.

The rapid increase in the functions and costs of State government and the complexity of agency operations deeply concern the General Assembly. Members of the General Assembly have the ultimate responsibility for making public policy decisions and deciding on appropriations of public moneys. Knowledge of the public service needs being met, having evidence as to whether previous policy and appropriations have resulted in expected program benefits, and data on how State government reorganization has affected agency operations are most important.

Legislative examination and review of public policies, expenditures and reorganization implementation as an integral part of legislative duties and responsibilities should be strengthened. For the purpose of performing such continuing examination and evaluation of State agencies, [and] their actual effectiveness in programming and in carrying out procedures under reorganization, the General Assembly herein provides for the continuing review of operations of State government. (1975, c. 490.)

§ 120-72. Definition.

For the purposes of this Article, "program evaluation" is defined as: an examination of the organization, programs, and administration of State government to ascertain whether such functions (i) are effective, (ii) continue to serve their intended purposes, (iii) are efficient, and (iv) require modification or elimination. (1975, c. 490.)

§ 120-73. Commission established.

There is hereby established the Joint Legislative Commission on Governmental Operations, hereinafter called the Commission, which shall conduct evaluative studies of the programs, policies, practices and procedures of the various departments, agencies, and institutions of State government. (1975, c. 490.)

§ 120-74. Appointment of members; terms of office.

The Commission shall consist of 42 members. The President pro tempore of the Senate, the Speaker pro tempore of the House, the Deputy President pro tempore of the Senate, the Majority Leader of the House of Representatives, and the Majority Leader of the Senate and the Speaker of the House shall serve as ex officio members of the Commission. The Speaker of the House of Representatives shall appoint 21 members from the House, at least five of whom are members of the minority party. The President pro tempore of the Senate shall appoint 21 members from the Senate, at least five of whom are members of the minority party. Vacancies created by resignation or otherwise shall be filled by the original appointing authority. Members shall serve two-year terms beginning and ending on January 15 of the odd-numbered years. Members shall not be disqualified from completing a term of service on the Commission because they fail to run or are defeated for reelection. Resignation or removal from the General Assembly shall constitute resignation or removal from membership on the Commission. (1975, c. 490; 1977, c. 988, s. 1; 1979, c. 932, s. 9; 1981, c. 859, s. 85; 1985, c. 757, s. 142(a)-(c); 1991, c. 72, s. 1; 1995, c. 542, s. 24.1(a); 1997-495, s. 92; 1999-405, s. 1; 1999-431, s. 3.5(a); 2001-486, s. 2.6; 2011-291, s. 1.2(c).)

§ 120-75. Organization of the Commission.

The President pro tempore of the Senate and the Speaker of the House of Representatives shall serve as cochairmen of the Commission. Either of the cochairmen may call a meeting of the Commission. (1975, c. 490; 1977, c. 988, s. 2; 1981, c. 859, s. 86; 1991, c. 72, s. 2.)

§ 120-76. Powers and duties of the Commission.

The Commission shall have the following powers:

(1)   To conduct program evaluation studies of the various components of State agency activity as they relate to:

a.   Service benefits of each program relative to expenditures;

b.   Achievement of program goals;

c. Use of indicators by which the success or failure of a program may be gauged; and

d. Conformity with legislative intent.

(2) To study legislation which would result in new programs with statewide implications for feasibility and need. These studies may be jointly conducted with the Fiscal Research Division of the Legislative Services Commission.

(3) To study on a continuing basis the implementation of State government reorganization with respect to:

a. Improvements in administrative structure, practices and procedures;

b. The relative effectiveness of centralization and decentralization of management decisions for agency operation;

c. Opportunities for effective citizen participation; and

d. Broadening of career opportunities for professional staff.

(4) To make such studies and reports of the operations and functions of State government as it deems appropriate or upon petition by resolution of either the Senate or the House of Representatives.

(5) To produce routine written reports of findings for general legislative and public distribution. Special attention shall be given to the presentation of findings to the appropriate committees of the Senate and the House of Representatives. If findings arrived at during a study have a potential impact on either the finance or appropriations deliberations, such findings shall immediately be presented to the committees. Such reports shall contain recommendations for appropriate executive action and when legislation is considered necessary to effect change, draft legislation for that purpose may be included. Such reports as are submitted shall include but not be limited to the following matters:

a. Ways in which the agencies may operate more economically and efficiently;

b. Ways in which agencies can provide better services to the State and to the people; and

c.   Areas in which functions of State agencies are duplicative, overlapping, or failing to accomplish legislative objectives, or for any other reason should be redefined or redistributed.

(6)   To devise a system, in cooperation with the Fiscal Research Division of the Legislative Services Commission, whereby all new programs authorized by the General Assembly incorporate an evaluation component. The results of such evaluations may be made to the Appropriations Committees at the beginning of each regular session.

(7)   To evaluate and approve or deny requests from the Department of Transportation regarding the funding of federally eligible construction projects as provided in the fourth paragraph of G.S. 136-44.2.

(8)   The Joint Legislative Commission on Governmental Operations shall be consulted by the Governor before the Governor does any of the following:

a.   Repealed by Session Laws 2007-117, s. 2, effective July 1, 2007.

b.   Authorizes expenditures in excess of the total requirements of a purpose or program as enacted by the General Assembly and as provided by G.S. 143C-6-4.

c.   Proceeds to reduce programs subsequent to a reduction of ten percent (10%) or more in the federal fund level certified to a department and any subsequent changes in distribution formulas.

d.   Takes extraordinary measures under Article III, Section 5(3) of the Constitution to effect necessary economies in State expenditures required for balancing the budget due to a revenue shortfall, including, but not limited to, the following: loans among funds, personnel freezes or layoffs, capital project reversions, program eliminations, and use of reserves. However, if the Committee fails to meet within 10 calendar days of a request by the Governor for its consultation, the Governor may proceed to take the actions he feels are appropriate and necessary and shall then report those actions at the next meeting of the Commission.

e.   Approves a new capital improvement project funded from gifts, grants, receipts, special funds, self-liquidating indebtedness, and other funds or any combination of funds for the project not specifically authorized by the General

Assembly. The budget for each capital project must include projected revenues in an amount not less than projected expenditures.

(9)   To examine, on a continuing basis, capital improvements approved and undertaken for State facilities and institutions and to have oversight over implementation of the six-year capital improvements plan developed pursuant to G.S. 143C-8-5.

(10)   To establish a subcommittee to evaluate the need for any new licensing board by establishing criteria and procedures for reviewing proposed licensing boards. To assure that no new licensing board shall be established unless the following criteria are met:

a.   The unregulated practice of the profession or occupation can substantially harm or endanger the public health, safety, or welfare, and the potential for such harm is recognizable and not remote or dependent upon tenuous argument.

b.   The profession or occupation possesses qualities that distinguish it from ordinary labor.

c.   Practice of the profession or occupation requires specialized skill or training.

d.   A substantial majority of the public does not have the knowledge or experience to evaluate whether the practitioner is competent.

e.   The public is not effectively protected by other means.

f.   Licensure will not have a substantial adverse economic impact upon consumers of the practitioner's goods or services.

(11)   To evaluate the North Carolina Utilities Commission, by doing the following:

a.   Reviewing the actions of the North Carolina Utilities Commission, including the review of its interim and final orders, to the end that the members of the General Assembly may better judge whether these actions serve the best interest of the citizens of North Carolina, individual and corporate.

b.   Inquiring into the role of the North Carolina Utilities Commission, the Public Staff, and the several utility companies in the development of alternate sources of energy.

c.   Submitting evaluations to the General Assembly, from time to time, of the performance of the North Carolina Utilities Commission, the Public Staff, and the various utilities operating in the State. A proposed draft of such evaluations shall be submitted to the North Carolina Utilities Commission, the Public Staff, and the affected public utilities prior to submission to the General Assembly, and the affected entity shall be given an opportunity to be heard before the Commission prior to the completion of the evaluation and its submission to the General Assembly.

(12)   To make reports and recommendations to the General Assembly, from time to time, on matters relating to the powers and duties set out in this section.

(13)   To review and evaluate changes in federal law and regulations, relevant court decisions, and changes in technology affecting any of the duties of the Commission.

(14)   To review and evaluate changes in federal law and regulation, or changes brought about by court actions, as well as changes in technology affecting any of the duties of the Commission, to determine whether the State's laws require modification as a result of those changes.

(15)   With regard to seafood and aquaculture:

a.   To monitor and study the seafood industry in North Carolina, including studies of the feasibility of increasing the State's production, processing, and marketing of seafood.

b.   To study the potential for increasing the role of aquaculture in all regions of the State.

c.   To evaluate the feasibility of creating a central permitting office for fishing and aquaculture matters.

d.   To evaluate actions of the Division of Marine Fisheries of the Department of Environment and Natural Resources, the Wildlife Resources Commission of the Department of Environment and Natural Resources and of any other State or local government agency as such actions relate to the seafood and aquaculture industries.

e.   To make recommendations regarding regulatory matters relating to the seafood and aquaculture industries including, but not limited to evaluating the necessity to substantially increase penalties for trespass and theft of shellfish and other aquaculture products.

f.   To review and evaluate changes in federal law and regulations, relevant court decisions, and changes in technology affecting the seafood and aquaculture industries.

g.   To review existing and proposed State law and rules affecting the seafood and aquaculture industries and to determine whether any modification of law or rules is in the public interest. (1975, c. 490; 1981, c. 859, s. 87; 1996, 2nd Ex. Sess., c. 18, s. 7.4(a); 1997-443, s. 7.8(e); 2005-276, s. 6.7(a); 2006-203, s. 62; 2007-117, s. 2; 2011-291, s. 1.2(d).)

§ 120-76.1. Prior consultation with the Commission; reporting requirements.

(a)   Consultation by Governor. - Notwithstanding the provisions of G.S. 120-76(8) or any other provision of law requiring prior consultation by the Governor with the Commission, whenever an expenditure is required because of an emergency that poses an imminent threat to public health or public safety, and is either the result of a natural event, such as a hurricane or a flood, or an accident, such as an explosion or a wreck, the Governor may take action without consulting the Commission if the action is determined by the Governor to be related to the emergency. The Governor shall report to the Commission on any expenditures made under this subsection no later than 30 days after making the expenditure and shall identify in the report the emergency, the type of action taken, and how it was related to the emergency.

(b)   Consultation by Agencies, Boards, and Commission. - Any agency, board, commission, or other entity required under G.S. 120-76(8) or any other provision of law to consult with the Commission prior to taking an action shall submit a detailed report of the action under consideration to the Chairs of the Commission, the Commission Assistant, and the Fiscal Research Division of the General Assembly. If the Commission does not hold a meeting to hear the consultation within 90 days of receiving the submission of the detailed report, the consultation requirement is satisfied. With regard to capital improvement projects of The University of North Carolina, if the Commission does not hold a meeting to hear the consultation within 30 days of receiving the submission of the detailed report, the consultation requirement of G.S. 120-76(8)e. is satisfied.

(c)   Exemptions. - Consultations regarding the establishment of new fees and charges and the increase of existing fees and charges are governed by G.S. 12-3.1, and this section does not apply to those consultations. (1996, 2nd Ex. Sess., c. 18, s. 7.4(a); 2005-276, s. 6.7(a); 2007-322, s. 10; 2011-291, s. 1.2(e).)

§ 120-77. Additional powers.

The Commission, while in the discharge of official duties, shall have access to any paper or document, and may compel the attendance of any State official or employee before the Commission or secure any evidence under the provisions of G.S. 120-19. In addition, the provisions of G.S. 120-19.1 through 120-19.4 shall apply to the proceedings of the Commission as if it were a joint committee of the General Assembly. (1975, c. 490; 1977, c. 344, s. 1.)

§ 120-78. Compensation and expenses of Commission members.

Members of the Commission, who are also members of the General Assembly, shall receive subsistence and travel expenses at the rates set forth in G.S. 120-3.1 for General Assembly members. The Commission shall be funded by the Legislative Services Commission from appropriations made to the General Assembly for that purpose. (1975, c. 490; 1977, c. 988, s. 3; 1991, c. 72, s. 3.)

§ 120-79. Commission staffing.

(a)   The Commission shall use available secretarial employees of the General Assembly, or may employ, and may remove, such professional and clerical employees as the Commission deems proper. The chairmen may assign and direct the activities of the employees of the Commission, subject to the advice of the Commission.

(b)   The employees of the Commission shall receive salaries that shall be fixed by the Legislative Services Commission and shall receive travel and subsistence allowances fixed by G.S. 138-6 and 138-7 when such travel is approved by either chairman, subject to the advice of the Commission. The employees of the Commission shall not be subject to the Executive Budget Act or to the North Carolina Human Resources Act.

(c)   The Commission may use employees of the Fiscal Research Division of the Legislative Services Commission.

(d)   The Commission shall assure that sufficient funds are available within its appropriations before employing professional and clerical employees. (1975, c. 490; 1981, c. 859, ss. 88, 89; 2013-382, s. 9.1(c).)

§§ 120-80 through 120-84. Reserved for future codification purposes.

Article 13A.

Joint Legislative Committee to Review Federal Block Grant Funds.

§§ 120-84.1 through 120-84.5: Repealed by Session Laws 1987, c. 738, s. 120(d).

Article 13B.

Joint Legislative Commission on Future Strategies for North Carolina.

§ 120-84.6: Repealed by Session Laws 2011-266, s. 1.28(a), effective July 1, 2011 and Session Laws 2011-291, s. 1.2(b), effective June 24, 2011.

§ 120-84.7: Repealed by Session Laws 2011-266, s. 1.28(a), effective July 1, 2011 and Session Laws 2011-291, s. 1.2(b), effective June 24, 2011.

§ 120-84.8: Repealed by Session Laws 2011-266, s. 1.28(a), effective July 1, 2011 and Session Laws 2011-291, s. 1.2(b), effective June 24, 2011.

§ 120-84.9: Repealed by Session Laws 2011-266, s. 1.28(a), effective July 1, 2011 and Session Laws 2011-291, s. 1.2(b), effective June 24, 2011.

§ 120-84.10: Repealed by Session Laws 2011-266, s. 1.28(a), effective July 1, 2011 and Session Laws 2011-291, s. 1.2(b), effective June 24, 2011.

§ 120-84.11: Repealed by Session Laws 2011-266, s. 1.28(a), effective July 1, 2011 and Session Laws 2011-291, s. 1.2(b), effective June 24, 2011.

§ 120-84.12: Repealed by Session Laws 2011-266, s. 1.28(a), effective July 1, 2011 and Session Laws 2011-291, s. 1.2(b), effective June 24, 2011.

Article 14.

Legislative Ethics Act.

Part 1. Code of Legislative Ethics.

§ 120-85: Repealed by Session Laws 2006-201, s. 4, effective January 1, 2007.

§ 120-85.1. Definitions.

As used in this Article, the following terms mean:

(1)   Business with which associated. - As defined in G.S. 138A-3.

(2)   Confidential information. - As defined in G.S. 138A-3.

(3)   Economic interest. - As defined in G.S. 138A-3.

(4)   Immediate family. - As defined in G.S. 138A-3.

(5)   Legislator. - As defined in G.S. 138A-3.

(6)   Nonprofit corporation or organization with which associated. - As defined in G.S. 138A-3.

(7)   Vested trust. - As defined in G.S. 138A-3. (2006-201, s. 5.)

§ 120-86. Bribery, etc.

(a)   No person shall offer or give to a legislator or a member of a legislator's immediate family, or to a business with which the legislator is associated, and no legislator shall solicit or receive, anything of monetary value, including a gift, favor or service or a promise of future employment, based on any understanding that the legislator's vote, official actions or judgment would be influenced thereby, or where it could reasonably be inferred that the thing of value would influence the legislator in the discharge of the legislator's duties.

(b)   It shall be unlawful for the partner, client, customer, or employer of a legislator or the agent of that partner, client, customer, or employer, directly or indirectly, to threaten economically that legislator with the intent to influence the legislator in the discharge of the legislator's duties.

(b1)   It shall be unlawful for any person, directly or indirectly, to threaten economically another person in order to compel the threatened person to attempt to influence a legislator in the discharge of the legislator's duties.

(c)   It shall be unethical for a legislator to contact the partner, client, customer, or employer of another legislator if the purpose of the contact is to cause the partner, client, customer, or employer, directly or indirectly, to threaten economically that legislator with the intent to influence that legislator in the discharge of the legislator's duties.

(d)   Repealed by Session Laws 2006-201, s. 6, effective January 1, 2007.

(e)   Violation of subsection (a), (b), or (b1) is a Class F felony. Violation of subsection (c) is not a crime but is punishable under G.S. 120-103.1. (1975, c. 564, s. 1; 1983, c. 780, s. 2; 1993, c. 539, s. 1302; 1994, Ex. Sess., c. 24, s. 14(c); 1997-443, s. 19.27(a); 2006-201, s. 6.)

§ 120-86.1. Personnel-related action unethical.

It shall be unethical for a legislator to take, promise, or threaten any legislative action, as defined in G.S. 120C-100(5), for the purpose of influencing or in retaliation for any action regarding State employee hirings, promotions, grievances, or disciplinary actions subject to Chapter 126 of the General Statutes. (1997-520, s. 7; 2006-201, s. 20(a).)

§ 120-87. Disclosure of confidential information.

(a)   No legislator shall use or disclose in any way confidential information gained in the course of the legislator's official activities or by reason of the legislator's official position that could result in financial gain for: (i) the legislator; (ii) a business with which the legislator is associated; (iii) a nonprofit corporation or organization with which the legislator is associated; (iv) a member of the legislator's immediate family; or (v) any other person.

(b)   Repealed by Session Laws 2006-201, s. 4, effective January 1, 2007. (1975, c. 564, s. 1; 2004-199, s. 31(b); 2006-201, s. 4; 2007-347, s. 1; 2007-484, s. 16.)

§ 120-88: Repealed by Session Laws 2006-201, s. 4, effective January 1, 2007.

Part 2. Statement of Economic Interest.

§ 120-89: Repealed by Session Laws 2006-201, s. 4, effective January 1, 2007.

§ 120-90: Repealed by Session Laws 2001-119, s. 2.

§ 120-91: Repealed by 1987 (Reg. Sess., 1988), c. 1028, s. 3.

§§ 120-92 through 120-94: Repealed by Session Laws 2006-201, s. 4, effective January 1, 2007.

§ 120-95: Repealed by 1987 (Reg. Sess., 1988), c. 1028, s. 3.

§ 120-96: Repealed by Session Laws 2006-201, s. 4, effective January 1, 2007.

§ 120-97: Repealed by 1987 (Reg. Sess., 1988), c. 1028, s. 3.

§ 120-98: Repealed by Session Laws 2006-201, s. 4, effective January 1, 2007.

Part 3. Legislative Ethics Committee.

§ 120-99. Creation; composition.

(a)   The Legislative Ethics Committee is created and shall consist of 12 members, six Senators appointed by the President Pro Tempore of the Senate, and six members of the House of Representatives appointed by the Speaker of the House. The President Pro Tempore of the Senate shall appoint three members from a list of nominees submitted by the majority leader of the Senate and three members from a list of nominees submitted by the minority leader of the Senate. The Speaker of the House shall appoint three members from a list of nominees submitted by the majority leader of the House and three members from a list of nominees submitted by the minority leader of the House. The nominating majority or minority leader shall submit to the person making the appointment a list of twice the number of vacancies on the Committee that are to be filled from that leader's nominees.

(b)   The President Pro Tempore of the Senate and the Speaker of the House as the appointing officers shall each designate a cochair of the Legislative Ethics Committee from the respective officer's appointees to serve as cochair for the current General Assembly, and until the cochair's successor is designated. The cochair appointed by the President Pro Tempore of the Senate shall preside over the Legislative Ethics Committee during the odd-numbered year, and the cochair appointed by the Speaker of the House shall preside in the even-numbered year. A cochair may preside at anytime during the absence of the presiding cochair or upon the presiding cochair's designation. In the event a cochair is unable to act as cochair on a specific matter before the Legislative Ethics Committee, and so indicates in writing to the appointing officer and the Legislative Ethics Committee, the respective officer shall designate from that officer's appointees a member to serve as cochair for that specific matter.

(c)   Repealed by Session Laws 2006-201, s. 8, effective January 1, 2007.

(d)   The appointments of the President Pro Tempore of the Senate and the Speaker of the House shall ensure that the composition of the Legislative Ethics Committee is bipartisan in equal numbers. (1975, c. 564, s. 1; 1985, c. 790, s. 6; 1991, c. 739, s. 15; 1995, c. 180, s. 1; 2004-199, s. 31(d); 2006-201, ss. 7, 8; 2009-10, s. 1.)

§ 120-100. Term of office; vacancies.

(a)   Appointments to the Legislative Ethics Committee shall be made immediately after the convening of the regular session of the General Assembly in odd-numbered years. The term of office for members of the Legislative Ethics Committee shall be four years from the date of the convening of the General Assembly in which the member is appointed to the Committee. Members shall not serve two consecutive full terms.

(b)   A vacancy occurs on the Legislative Ethics Committee when a member resigns or is no longer a member of the General Assembly. A vacancy occurring for any reason during a term shall be filled for the unexpired term by the authority making the appointment which caused the vacancy, and the person appointed to fill the vacancy shall, if possible, be a member of the same political party as the member who caused the vacancy, from a list of two nominees submitted by that party's leader.

(c)   In the event a member of the Legislative Ethics Committee is unable to act on a specific matter before the Legislative Ethics Committee, and so indicates in writing to the appointing officer and the Legislative Ethics Committee, the appointing officer may appoint another member of the respective chamber from a list of two members submitted by the majority leader or minority leader who nominated the member who is unable to act on the matter to serve as a member of the Legislative Ethics Committee for the specific matter only. If on any specific matter, the number of members of the Legislative Ethics Committee who are unable to act on a specific matter exceeds four members, the appropriate appointing officer shall appoint other members of the General Assembly to serve as members of the Legislative Ethics Committee for that specific matter only. (1975, c. 564, s. 1; 1995, c. 180, s. 2; 2004-199, s. 31(e); 2009-10, s. 2.)

§ 120-101. Quorum; expenses of members.

(a)   Eight members constitute a quorum of the Committee. A vacancy on the Committee does not impair the right of the remaining members to exercise all the powers of the Committee.

(b)   The members of the Committee, while serving on the business of the Committee, are performing legislative duties and are entitled to the subsistence and travel allowances to which members of the General Assembly are entitled when performing legislative duties. (1975, c. 564, s. 1; 1995, c. 180, s. 3; 2006-201, s. 9.)

§ 120-102. Powers and duties of Committee.

(a)   In addition to the other powers and duties specified in this Article, the Committee may:

(1)   through (4) Repealed by Session Laws 2006-201, s. 10, effective January 1, 2007.

(5)   Prepare a list of ethical principles and guidelines to be used by legislators and legislative employees to identify potential conflicts of interest and prohibited behavior, prepare advisory memoranda to legislators and legislative employees on specific ethical concerns, and suggest rules of conduct that shall be adhered to by legislators and legislative employees.

(5a)   Advise each General Assembly committee of specific danger areas where conflicts of interest may exist and to suggest rules of conduct that should be adhered to by committee members in order to avoid conflict.

(6)   Advise General Assembly members or render written opinions if so requested by the member about questions of ethics or possible points of conflict and suggested standards of conduct of members upon ethical points raised.

(6a)   Review, modify, or overrule advisory opinions issued to legislators by the State Ethics Commission under G.S. 138A-13.

(7)   Propose rules of legislative ethics and conduct. The rules, when adopted by the House of Representatives and the Senate, shall be the standards adopted for that term.

(8)   Upon receipt of information that a legislator owes money to the State and is delinquent in making repayment of such obligation, investigate and dispose of the matter according to the terms of this Article.

(9)   Investigate alleged violations in accordance with G.S. 120-103.1 and hire separate legal counsel, through the Legislative Services Commission, for these purposes.

(10)   Adopt procedures to implement this Article.

(11)   Perform other duties as may be necessary to accomplish the purposes of this Article.

(b)   G.S. 120-19.1 through G.S. 120-19.8 shall apply to the proceedings of the Legislative Ethics Committee as if it were a joint committee of the General Assembly, except that both cochairs shall sign all subpoenas on behalf of the Committee. Notwithstanding any other law, every State agency, local governmental agency, and units and subdivisions thereof shall make available to the Committee any documents, records, data, statements or other information, except tax returns or information relating thereto, which the Committee designates as being necessary for the exercise of its powers and duties. (1975, c. 564, s. 1; 1979, c. 864, s. 3; 1991, c. 700, s. 1; 2006-201, s. 10; 2007-348, s. 1.)

§ 120-103: Repealed by Session Laws 2006-201, s. 11, effective January 1, 2007.

§ 120-103.1. Investigations by the Committee.

(a)   Institution of Proceedings. - On its own motion, upon receipt by the Committee of a signed and sworn allegation of unethical conduct by a legislator, or upon receipt of a referral of a complaint from the State Ethics Commission under Chapter 138A of the General Statutes, the Committee shall conduct an investigation into any of the following:

(1)   The application or alleged violation of Chapter 138A of the General Statutes and of this Article.

(2)   Repealed by Session Laws 2007-348, s. 2, effective August 9, 2007.

(3)   The alleged violation of the criminal law by a legislator while acting in the legislator's official capacity as a participant in the lawmaking process.

(a1)   Complaints on Its Own Motion. - An investigation initiated by the Committee on its own motion instituted under subsection (a) of this section shall be treated as a complaint for purposes of this section and need not be sworn or verified. Any requirements under this section that require the Committee to notify the complainant shall not apply to complaints taken up by the Committee on its own motion. If the Committee is acting on a complaint referred to the Committee by the Commission where the Commission was acting on its own motion, the Committee shall be deemed to have satisfied the notice requirements by providing notice to the Commission. Any notice provided to the Commission under this section is confidential and shall not be disclosed by the Commission.

(a2)   Notice of Allegation. - Upon receipt by the Committee of a complaint or the referral of a complaint, or upon the initiation by the Committee of an inquiry under subsection (a1) of this section, the Committee shall immediately provide written notice to the legislator who is the subject of the allegation or inquiry.

(b)   Initial Consideration of a Complaint. - All of the following shall apply to the Committee's initial consideration of a complaint:

(1)   The Committee may, in its sole discretion, request additional information to be provided by the complainant within a specified period of time of no less than seven business days.

(2)   The Committee may decline to accept or further investigate a complaint if it determines that any of the following apply:

a.   The complaint is frivolous or brought in bad faith.

b.   The individuals and conduct complained of have already been the subject of a prior complaint.

c.   The conduct complained of is primarily a matter more appropriately and adequately addressed and handled by other federal, State, or local agencies or authorities, including law enforcement authorities. If other agencies or authorities are conducting an investigation of the same actions or conduct involved in a complaint filed under this section, the Committee may stay its complaint investigation pending final resolution of the other investigation.

(3)   Repealed by Session Laws 2009-549, s. 1, effective August 28, 2009.

(4)   Notwithstanding any other provisions of this section, complaints filed with the Committee concerning the conduct of the Lieutenant Governor shall be referred to the State Ethics Commission under Chapter 138A of the General Statutes without investigation by the Committee.

(c)   Investigation of Complaints. - The Committee shall investigate all complaints properly before the Committee in a timely manner. If the Committee receives a complaint or a referral of a complaint while the General Assembly is in Regular Session, the Committee shall proceed under this subsection within 10 business days of receiving the complaint or the referral. If the Committee receives a complaint or a referral of a complaint at any other time, the Committee shall proceed under this subsection within 20 business days of receiving the complaint or the referral. Within the applicable time period, the Committee shall do at least one of the following:

(1)   Dismiss the complaint.

(2)   Initiate a preliminary investigation of the complaint.

(3)   Refer the complaint for further investigation and a hearing in accordance with subsection (i) of this section.

(4)   Make recommendations to the house in which the legislator who is the subject of the complaint is a member without further investigation, if either of the following apply:

a.   The referral is from the State Ethics Commission.

b.   The referral alleges conduct that may be unethical but the Committee determines it does not have jurisdiction under subsection (a) of this section.

(c1)   Preliminary Investigation. - The Committee may initiate a preliminary investigation if it determines that the complaint alleges facts sufficient to constitute a violation of matters over which the Committee has jurisdiction as set forth in subsection (a) of this section. In determining whether there is reason to believe that a violation has or may have occurred, a member of the Committee may take general notice of available information even if not formally provided to the Committee in the form of a complaint. The Committee may utilize the services of a hired investigator when conducting investigations. The Committee shall provide written notification of the initiation of a preliminary investigation under this subsection to the legislator who is the subject of the complaint within 10 days of the date of the Committee's decision to initiate an investigation. The Committee shall conclude the preliminary inquiry within 20 business days of initiating the preliminary investigation but may extend the amount of time if the Committee determines it does not have sufficient information to proceed under subsection (g) or (h) of this section.

(d)   Repealed by Session Laws 2009-549, s. 1, effective August 28, 2009.

(e)   Investigation by the Committee of Matters Other Than Complaints. - The Committee may investigate matters other than complaints properly within the jurisdiction of the Committee under subsection (a) of this section. For any investigation initiated under this subsection, the Committee may take any action it deems necessary or appropriate to further compliance with this Article, including the initiation of a complaint, the issuance of an advisory opinion under G.S. 120-104, or referral to appropriate law enforcement or other authorities pursuant to subdivision (j)(2) of this section.

(f)   Legislator Cooperation with Investigation. - Legislators shall promptly and fully cooperate with the Committee in any Committee-related investigation. Failure to cooperate fully with the Committee in any investigation shall be grounds for sanctions under this section.

(g)   Dismissal of Complaint After Preliminary Investigation. - If the Committee determines at the end of its preliminary investigation that the complaint does not allege facts sufficient to constitute a violation of matters over which the Committee has jurisdiction as set forth in subsection (a) of this section, the Committee shall dismiss the complaint and provide written notice of

91

the dismissal to the individual who filed the complaint and to the legislator against whom the complaint was filed.

(h)   Probable Cause Determination and Notice of Hearing. - If at the end of its preliminary investigation, the Committee determines that probable cause exists to proceed with further investigation into the conduct of a legislator, the Committee shall determine the charges that will be the basis for further investigation of the complaint and provide written notice to the legislator that the Committee will conduct further investigation and the charges against the legislator. The legislator shall be given an opportunity to file a written response to the charges with the Committee.

The Committee shall give full and fair consideration to the complaint and to the legislator's response to the complaint. Except as provided in subsection (h2) of this section, if the Committee determines that the complaint cannot be resolved without further investigation and a hearing, or if the legislator requests a public hearing, the Committee shall hold a hearing on the charges against the legislator. The Committee shall send a notice of the hearing to the complainant and to the legislator. The notice shall contain the charges against the legislator and the time and place for the hearing. The Committee shall begin the hearing no sooner than 15 days and no later than 90 days after the date of the notice of hearing.

(h1)   Repealed by Session Laws 2013-146, s. 1, effective June 19, 2013.

(h2)   Private Admonishment. - The Committee may issue a private admonishment without holding a hearing, subject to the requirements of subsection (k) of this section.

(i)   Hearing. - All the following shall apply to any hearing on a complaint held by the Committee:

(1)-(3) Repealed by Session Laws 2009-549, s. 1, effective August 28, 2009.

(4)   Oral evidence shall be taken only on oath or affirmation.

(5)   The hearing shall be open to the public, except for matters that could otherwise be considered in closed session under G.S. 143-318.11, matters involving minors, or matters involving a personnel record. In any event, the deliberations by the Committee on a complaint may be held in closed session.

(6)   The legislator being investigated shall have the right to present evidence, call and examine witnesses, cross-examine witnesses, introduce exhibits, and be represented by counsel.

(j)   Disposition of Investigations After Hearing. - Except as permitted under subsections (b) and (g) of this section, after the hearing, the Committee shall dispose of the matter before the Committee under this section, in any of the following ways:

(1)   If the Committee finds that the alleged violation is not established by clear and convincing evidence, the Committee shall dismiss the complaint.

(2)   If the Committee finds that the alleged violation is established by clear and convincing evidence, the Committee shall do one or more of the following:

a.   Issue a public or private admonishment to the legislator.

b.   Refer the matter to the Attorney General for investigation and referral to the district attorney for possible prosecution or the appropriate house for appropriate action, or both, if the Committee finds substantial evidence of a violation of a criminal statute.

c.   Refer the matter to the appropriate house for appropriate action, which may include censure and expulsion.

(3)   If the Committee issues an admonishment as provided in subdivision (2)a. of this subsection, the legislator affected may, upon written request to the Committee, have the matter referred as provided under subdivision (2)c. of this subsection.

(k)   Effect of Dismissal or Private Admonishment. - If the Committee dismisses a complaint or issues a private admonishment prior to commencing a hearing under subsection (i) of this section, the Committee shall retain its records or findings in confidence, unless the legislator under inquiry requests in writing that the records and findings be made public. If the Committee later finds that a legislator's subsequent unethical activities were similar to and the subject of an earlier private admonishment, then the Committee may make public the earlier admonishment and the records and findings related to it.

(l)   Confidentiality. - The complaint, response, records, and findings of the Committee connected to an inquiry under this section shall be confidential and not matters of public record, except as otherwise provided in this section or when the legislator under inquiry requests in writing that the complaint, response, and findings be made public. Once a hearing under subsection (i) of this section commences the complaint, response, Committee's report to the house, and all other documents offered at the hearing in conjunction with the complaint, that are not otherwise privileged or confidential under law, shall be public records. If no hearing is held, at such time as the Committee recommends sanctions to the house of which the legislator is a member, the complaint, response, and Committee's report to the house shall be made public.

(m)   Concurrent Jurisdiction. - Any action or lack of action by the Committee under this section shall not limit the right of each house of the General Assembly to discipline or to expel its members.

(n)   Reports. - The Committee shall publish annual statistics on complaints filed with or considered by the Committee, including the number of complaints filed, the number of complaints dismissed, the number of complaints resulting in admonishment, the number of complaints referred to the appropriate house for appropriate action, the number of complaints referred for criminal prosecution, and the number and age of complaints pending action by the Committee. (2006-201, s. 12; 2007-347, s. 2; 2007-348, ss. 2-4; 2008-187, s. 20; 2008-213, ss. 1(a), 3; 2009-549, s. 1; 2010-169, s. 23(f), (g); 2013-146, s. 1.)

§ 120-104. Advisory opinions.

(a)   At the request of any member of the General Assembly, the Committee shall render formal advisory opinions on specific questions involving legislative ethics.

(b)   The Committee shall receive and review recommended advisory opinions issued to legislators, except the Lieutenant Governor, by the State Ethics Commission under G.S. 138A-13. The opinion shall not be considered a formal advisory opinion until the advisory opinion is adopted by the Committee. The Committee may modify or overrule the recommended advisory opinions issued to legislators by the State Ethics Commission, and the final action on the opinion by the Committee shall control.

(c)   A legislator who acts in reliance on a formal advisory opinion issued by the Committee under this section shall be entitled to the immunity granted under G.S. 138A-13(b1).

(d)   Staff to the Committee may issue informal, nonbinding advisory opinions under procedures adopted by the Committee.

(e)   The Committee may interpret this Article and Chapter 138A of the General Statutes as it applies to legislators, except the Lieutenant Governor, and these interpretations are binding on all legislators upon publication.

(f)   The Committee shall submit its formal advisory opinions to the State Ethics Commission, and the State Ethics Commission shall publish the Committee's opinions under G.S. 138A-13(d). The Committee shall edit for publication purposes as necessary to protect the identities of the individuals requesting opinions prior to submission to the State Ethics Commission. The Committee may distribute the edited formal advisory opinion to members of the General Assembly prior to publication by the State Ethics Commission.

(g)   Except as provided under subsection (f) of this section, a request made by a legislator to the Committee for an advisory opinion, advisory opinions issued under this section, recommended advisory opinions received from the State Ethics Commission, and any supporting documents submitted or caused to be submitted to the Committee in connection with requests for advisory opinions or recommended advisory opinions are confidential. Neither the identity of the legislator making the request nor the existence of the request may be revealed to any person without the consent of the legislator. A legislator requesting or receiving an advisory opinion may authorize the release to any other person, the State, or any governmental unit of the request, the recommended advisory opinion, the advisory opinion, or any supporting documents.

For purposes of this section, "document" is as defined in G.S. 120-129. Requests for advisory opinions, recommended advisory opinions, advisory opinions issued by the Committee, and any supporting documents are not "public records" as defined in G.S. 132-1.

(h)   Requests for advisory opinions may be withdrawn by the requestor at any time prior to the issuance of an advisory opinion. (1975, c. 564, s. 1; 2006-201, s. 13; 2007-347, s. 3; 2007-348, ss. 5, 6; 2008-213, s. 2(a); 2010-169, s. 22(e); 2013-146, s. 2.)

§ 120-105. Continuing study of ethical questions.

The Committee shall conduct continuing studies of questions of legislative ethics including revisions and improvements of this Article and Chapter 138A and Chapter 120C of the General Statutes. The Committee shall report to the General Assembly from time to time recommendations for amendments to the statutes and legislative rules which the Committee deems desirable in promoting, maintaining and effectuating high standards of ethics in the legislative branch of State government. (1975, c. 564, s. 1; 2006-201, s. 14.)

§ 120-106. Article applicable to presiding officers.

The provisions of this Article shall apply to the presiding officers of the General Assembly. (1975, c. 564, s. 2.)

§§ 120-107 through 120-111. Reserved for future codification purposes.

Article 14A.

Committees on Pensions and Retirement.

§ 120-111.1. Creation.

A standing committee is hereby created in the House of Representatives to be known as the Committee on Pensions and Retirement, to consist of a minimum of four members to be appointed by the Speaker of the House of Representatives. A standing committee is hereby created in the Senate to be known as the Committee on Pensions and Retirement, to consist of the following members at the minimum: the Chairmen of the Senate Committees on Appropriations, Finance and Ways and Means. (1979, 2nd Sess., c. 1250, s. 1; 1981, c. 85, s. 2; 1989 (Reg. Sess., 1990), c. 899.)

§ 120-111.2. Duties.

With respect to public officers and public employees to whom State-administered retirement benefit or pension plans are applicable, the Senate and House Committees on Pensions and Retirement shall:

(1)   Study the benefits, including those available under Social Security and any other federal programs available to the public officers and employees.

(2)   Consider all aspects of retirement and pension financing, planning and operation, including the financing of accrued liabilities of each retirement or pension fund, health program, and other fringe benefits.

(3)   Request the Governor, the State Treasurer, the State Auditor and any other agency or department head which has information relevant to these committees' study to prepare any reports deemed necessary by the committee.

(4)   Recommend legislation which will insure and maintain sound retirement and pension policy for all funds.

(5)   Analyze each item of proposed pension and retirement legislation in accordance with Article 15 of Chapter 120 of the General Statutes.

(6)   Study, analyze, and report on related subjects directed to be studied by joint resolution, resolution of either house of the General Assembly, or by direction of the Speaker of the House or President of the Senate. (1979, 2nd Sess., c. 1250, s. 1; 1981, c. 85, s. 3; 1987, c. 1091, s. 4; 1989, c. 261, s. 2.)

§ 120-111.3. Analysis of legislation.

Every bill, which creates or modifies any provision for the retirement of public officers or public employees or for the payment of retirement benefits or of pensions to public officers or public employees, shall, upon introduction in either house of the General Assembly, be referred to the Committee on Pensions and Retirement of each house. When the bill is reported out of committee it shall be accompanied by a written report by the Committee on Pensions and Retirement containing, among other matters which the Committee deems relevant, the actuarial note required by Article 15 of Chapter 120 of the General Statutes, and pursuant to the Rules of the General Assembly, and an evaluation of the proposed legislation's actuarial soundness and adherence to sound retirement and pension policy. Any bill referred to the Committee on Pensions and

Retirement cannot be further considered by that house until such bill has received a favorable report, a report without prejudice, or has been recalled from that committee.

Whenever a bill is considered by the Committee on Pensions and Retirement that proposes changes in the benefits of any State-administered retirement or pension plan to be financed by unencumbered actuarial experience gains generated either through a change in actuarial assumptions adopted by the plan for the previous budget year or through a continuation of the actuarial assumptions adopted by the plan for the previous budget year, the Committee shall give equal consideration to the effects that such unencumbered actuarial gains would have upon annual employer or State contributions to the plan and to the amount by which the plan's unfunded accrued liabilities, if any, might be reduced. If such unencumbered actuarial experience gains could be used to modify annual employer or State contributions to the plan resulting in a corresponding effect upon State appropriations, the Committee on Pensions and Retirement shall, upon a favorable report, refer the bill to the Committee on Appropriations of the same house before the bill is considered by that house. (1979, 2nd Sess., c. 1250, s. 1; 1981, c. 85, s. 4; 1985, c. 187; c. 400, s. 10; 1987 (Reg. Sess., 1988), c. 1110, s. 11.1.)

§ 120-111.4. Staff and actuarial assistance.

Upon application of the chairman of the Senate or House Committee on Pensions and Retirement, the Legislative Services Commission shall provide staff, including actuarial assistance, to aid the committee in its work. (1979, 2nd Sess., c. 1250, s. 1; 1981, c. 85, s. 5.)

§ 120-111.5. House Standing Committee on State Personnel.

If the House of Representatives does not have a Committee on Pensions and Retirement but does have a Committee on State Personnel, then any reference to the "Committee on Pensions and Retirement" in the remainder of this Article shall, as to the House of Representatives, be construed as a reference to the "Committee on State Personnel." (2011-14, s. 1.)

Article 15.

Legislative Actuarial Note Act.

§ 120-112. Title.

This Article may be cited as the "Legislative Actuarial Note Act". (1977, c. 503, s. 1; 1987 (Reg. Sess., 1988), c. 1091, s. 1; 1993, c. 553, s. 35.)

§ 120-113. Duties and functions of Fiscal Research Division.

(a)   The Fiscal Research Division of the Legislative Services Commission of the General Assembly shall have authority to evaluate on a continuing basis all aspects of any State, municipal, or other retirement system, funded in whole or in part out of public funds, and all aspects of any program of hospital, medical, disability, or related benefits provided for teachers and State employees, funded in whole or in part by State funds, as to actuarial soundness. The Fiscal Research Division shall make periodic detailed reports to the General Assembly specifically setting forth the findings of such evaluations. In conducting its evaluations the division shall have complete access without charge to all books, accounts, and personnel of the retirement systems, and to all books, accounts, and personnel of agencies and contractors charged with providing programs of hospital, medical, disability, or related benefits for teachers and State employees.

(b)   No provision of this Article shall be deemed or in any way construed to preclude the authority of any retirement system funded in whole or in part out of public funds to hire an actuary for any such retirement system. No provision of this Article shall be deemed or in any way construed to preclude the authority of any program of hospital, medical, disability, or related benefits provided for teachers and State employees, funded in whole or in part by State funds, to hire an actuary for any such program.

(c)   The Fiscal Research Division shall, in addition to the powers and functions conferred by this Article, render such assistance as the Legislative Services Commission may require with respect to any other matter requiring actuarial evaluations. (1977, c. 503, s. 2; 1987 (Reg. Sess., 1988), c. 1091, s. 2.)

§ 120-114. Actuarial notes.

(a)   Every bill, joint resolution, and simple or concurrent resolution introduced in the General Assembly proposing any change in the law relative to any State, municipal, or other retirement system, funded in whole or in part out of public funds, or any program of hospital, medical, disability, or related benefits provided for teachers and State employees, funded in whole or in part by State funds, shall have attached to it at the time of its consideration by any committee of either house of the General Assembly a brief explanatory statement or note which shall include a reliable estimate of the financial and actuarial effect of the proposed change in any such retirement system or program of hospital, medical, disability, or related benefits. This actuarial note shall be attached to the original of each proposed bill or resolution which is reported favorably by any committee of either house of the General Assembly, but shall be separate therefrom, shall be clearly designated as an actuarial note and shall not constitute a part of the law or other provisions or expression of legislative intent proposed by the bill or resolution.

(b)   The author of each bill or resolution shall present a copy of the bill or resolution, with his request for an actuarial note, to the Fiscal Research Division which shall have the duty to prepare said actuarial note as promptly as possible. Actuarial notes shall be prepared and transmitted to the author or authors no later than two weeks after the request for the actuarial note is made, unless an extension of time is agreed to by the author or authors as being necessary in preparation of the note. Any person who signs an actuarial note knowing it to contain false information shall be fined not more than five hundred dollars ($500.00) or imprisoned not more than six months, or both.

(c)   The author of each bill or resolution shall also present a copy of the bill or resolution to any actuary employed by the retirement system, or to any actuary employed by a program of hospital, medical, disability, or related benefits provided for teachers and State employees, affected by the bill or resolution in question. Actuarial notes shall be prepared and transmitted to the author or authors of the measure no later than two weeks after the request for the actuarial note is received, unless an extension of time is agreed to by the author or authors as being necessary in preparation of the note. Any person who signs an actuarial note knowing it to contain false information shall be fined not more than five hundred dollars ($500.00) or imprisoned not more than six months, or both. The provisions of this subsection may be waived for any local government retirement or pension plans not administered by the State, and for any local government program of hospital, medical, disability, or related benefits for local government employees not administered by the State.

(d)   The note shall be factual and shall, if possible, provide a reliable estimate of both the immediate effect and, if determinable or reasonably foreseeable, the long range fiscal and actuarial effect of the measure. If, after careful investigation, it is determined that no dollar estimate is possible, the note shall contain a statement to that effect, setting forth the reasons why no dollar estimate can be given. No comment or opinion shall be included in the actuarial note with regard to the merits of the measure for which the note is prepared. However, technical and mechanical defects may be noted.

(e)   At any time any committee of either house reports any legislative instrument, to which an actuarial note or notes are attached at the time of committee consideration, with any amendment of such nature as would substantially affect the cost to or the revenues of any retirement system, or program of hospital, medical, disability, or related benefits for teachers and State employees, as stated in the actuarial note or notes attached to the measure at the time of such consideration, it shall be the responsibility of the chairman of the committee reporting such instrument to obtain from the Fiscal Research Division an actuarial note of the fiscal and actuarial effect of the change proposed by the amendment reported. Such actuarial note shall be attached to the report of the committee on the measure as a supplement thereto. A floor amendment to a bill or resolution to which an actuarial note was attached at the time of committee consideration of the bill or resolution shall not be in order, if the amendment affects the costs to or the revenues of a retirement system, or program of hospital, medical, disability, or related benefits provided for teachers and State employees, unless the amendment is accompanied by an actuarial note, prepared by the Fiscal Research Division, as to the actuarial effect of the amendment. (1977, c. 503, s. 3; 1985, c. 189; 1987 (Reg. Sess., 1988), c. 1091, s. 3; 1989, c. 261.)

§§ 120-115 through 120-120. Reserved for future codification purposes.

Article 16.

Legislative Appointments to Boards and Commissions.

101

§ 120-121. Legislative appointments.

(a) In any case where the General Assembly is called upon by law to appoint a member to any board or commission, that appointment shall be made by enactment of a bill.

(b) A bill may make more than one appointment.

(c) The bill shall state the name of the person being appointed, the board or commission to which the appointment is being made, the effective date of the appointment, the date of expiration of the term, the county of residence of the appointee, and whether the appointment is made upon the recommendation of the Speaker of the House of Representatives, President Pro Tempore of the Senate, or the President of the Senate.

(d) Nothing in this section or any other statute precludes any member of the General Assembly from proposing an amendment to any bill making an appointment to a board or commission, or from introducing a bill to make an appointment to a board or commission, where an appointment by the General Assembly is authorized by law. (1981 (Reg. Sess., 1982), c. 1191, s. 2; 1983, c. 717, s. 111; 1985, c. 290, s. 9.)

§ 120-122. Vacancies in legislative appointments.

When a vacancy occurs in any office subject to appointment by the General Assembly upon the recommendation of the Speaker of the House of Representatives, upon the recommendation of the President Pro Tempore of the Senate, or upon the recommendation of the President of the Senate, and the vacancy occurs either: (i) after election of the General Assembly but before convening of the regular session; (ii) when the General Assembly has adjourned to a date certain, which date is more than 20 days after the date of adjournment; (iii) after sine die adjournment of the regular session; or (iv) when the term of office expires and a successor has not been appointed, then the Governor may appoint a person to serve until the expiration of the term or until the General Assembly fills the vacancy, whichever occurs first. The General Assembly may fill the vacancy in accordance with G.S. 120-121 during a regular or extra session. When a person is holding over in office after the expiration of the term, for the purpose of this section that office may be filled as if it were vacant. Before making an appointment, the Governor shall consult the officer who recommended the original appointment to the General Assembly (the Speaker of the House of Representatives, the President Pro Tempore of the Senate, or the President of the Senate), and ask for a written recommendation. After receiving the written recommendation, the Governor must within 30 days either appoint the person recommended or inform the officer who made the recommendation that he is rejecting the recommendation. Failure to act within 30 days as required under the provisions of the preceding sentence shall be deemed to be approval of the candidate, and the candidate shall be eligible to enter the office in as full and ample extent as if the Governor had executed the appointment. The Governor shall not appoint a person other than the person so recommended. Any position subject to initial appointment by the General Assembly but not filled prior to sine die adjournment of the Session at which the position was created or adjournment to a date certain which date is more than 20 days after the date of adjournment of the session at which the position was created may be filled by the Governor under this section as if it were a vacancy occurring after the General Assembly had made an appointment. (1981 (Reg. Sess., 1982), c. 1191, s. 2; 1983, c. 717, ss. 112, 113; 1985, c. 752, ss. 1, 2; 1993, c. 563, s. 13; 2004-187, s. 5; 2004-195, s. 7.)

§ 120-123. Service by members of the General Assembly on certain boards and commissions.

No member of the General Assembly may serve on any of the following boards or commissions:

(1)   The Board of Agriculture, as established by G.S. 106-2.

(1a)   Not effectuated.

(1b)   The Rules Review Commission as established by G.S. 143B-30.1.

(2)   Repealed by Session Laws 2007-484, s. 17, effective August 30, 2007.

(3)   Repealed by Session Laws 2007-323, s. 19.1(c), effective July 1, 2007.

(3a)   The State Banking Commission, as established by Article 2 of Chapter 53C of the General Statutes.

(4)   The Board of Public Telecommunications Commissioners, as established by G.S. 143B-426.9.

(5)   The Board of Transportation, as established by G.S. 143B-350.

(6)   The Board of Trustees Teachers' and State Employees' Retirement System, as established by G.S. 135-6.

(6a)   Repealed by Session Laws 1991 (Regular Session, 1992), c. 1030, s. 33.

(7)   The Coastal Resources Commission, as established by G.S. 113A-104.

(8)   The Environmental Management Commission, as established by G.S. 143B-283.

(8a)   The Genetic Engineering Review Board, as created by G.S. 106-769.

(9)   The State Fire and Rescue Commission, as established by G.S. 58-78-1.

(10)   The Public Officers and Employees Liability Insurance Commission, as established by G.S. 58-32-1.

(11)   Repealed by Session Laws 1983 (Regular Session, 1984), c. 995, s. 4.

(12)   Repealed by Session Laws 1987, c. 71, s. 4.

(13)   The North Carolina Criminal Justice Education and Training Standards Commission, as established by G.S. 17C-3.

(14)   The North Carolina Housing Finance Agency Board of Directors, as established by G.S. 122A-4.

(15)   The North Carolina Seafood Industrial Park Authority, as established by G.S. 113-315.25.

(16)   Repealed by Session Laws 1985, c. 479, s. 153(b).

(17)   The Board of Trustees of the North Carolina School of Science and Mathematics, as established by G.S. 116-233.

(18)   The North Carolina Board of Science and Technology, as established by G.S. 143B-426.30.

(19)   Repealed by Session Laws 1989, c. 500, s. 107(b).

(20)   Repealed by Session Laws 1989 (Regular Session, 1990), c. 1024, s. 23(a).

(21)   The Board of Trustees of the University of North Carolina Center for Public Television, as established by G.S. 116-37.1.

(22)   The Commission for Mental Health, Developmental Disabilities, and Substance Abuse Services, as established by G.S. 143B-147.

(23)   Repealed by Session Laws 1993, c. 501, s. 12.

(24)   The North Carolina Alcoholism Research Authority, as established by G.S. 122C-431.

(25)   Repealed by Session Laws 2002-126, s. 6.6(b), effective November 12, 2002.

(25a)   The North Carolina Global TransPark Authority as established under G.S. 63A-3.

(26)   The North Carolina State Ports Authority, as established by G.S. 136-260.

(27)   The Property Tax Commission, as established by G.S. 105-288.

(28)   The Social Services Commission, as established by G.S. 143B-154.

(29)   The North Carolina State Commission of Indian Affairs, as established by G.S. 143B-407.

(30)   The Wildlife Resources Commission, as established by G.S. 143-240.

(31)   The North Carolina Council for Women, as established by G.S. 143B-393.

(31a)   The North Carolina Structural Pest Control Committee, as established by G.S. 106-65.23.

(32)   The Board of Trustees of North Carolina Museum of Art, established by G.S. 140-5.13.

(33)   The North Carolina Sheriffs' Education and Training Standards Commission, established by G.S. 17E.

(33a)   Repealed by Session Laws 1987, c. 738, s. 41(d).

(34)   The Board of Trustees of the North Carolina Public Employee Deferred Compensation Plan, as established by G.S. 143B-426.24.

(34a)   Repealed by Session Laws 1989 (Regular Session, 1990), c. 1024, s. 23(b).

(34b)   The North Carolina Housing Partnership, as established by G.S. 122E-4.

(35)   The Board of Trustees of the State Health Plan for Teachers and State Employees, as established by G.S. 135-39.

(36)   Repealed by Session Laws 2004-199, s. 27(b), effective August 17, 2004.

(37)   The State Board of Chiropractic Examiners as established by G.S. 90-139.

(38)   The North Carolina Manufactured Housing Board, as established by G.S. 143-143.10.

(39)   Repealed by Session Laws 1987, c. 71, s. 4.

(40)   The Alarm System Licensing Board, as established by G.S. 74D-4.

(41)   Repealed by Session Laws 1985 (Regular Session, 1986), c. 1011, s. 2.1(c).

(42)   The Crime Victims Compensation Commission, as established by G.S. 15B-3.

(43)   The North Carolina Council on Ocean Affairs, as established by G.S. 143B-390.10.

(44)   The Child Care Commission, as established by G.S. 143B-168.3.

(45)   Repealed by Session Laws 1995, c. 517, s. 39, effective October 1, 1995.

(45a)   (Repealed effective July 1, 2015) The North Carolina Teaching Fellows Commission, as established by G.S. 115C-363.22.

(46)   The Board of Directors of the North Carolina Arboretum, as established in G.S. 116-240.

(47)   The North Carolina Agricultural Finance Authority, as established by G.S. 122D-4.

(48)   Reserved for future codification purposes.

(49)   The Northeastern North Carolina Farmers Market Commission as established by G.S. 106-720.

(50)   The Southeastern North Carolina Farmers Market Commission as established by G.S. 106-727.

(50a)   The North Carolina Board of Dieteticsutrition as created by Article 25 of Chapter 90 of the General Statutes.

(51)   The State Building Commission, as established by G.S. 143-135.25.

(52)   The Commission on School Facility Needs, established by G.S. 115C-489.4.

(53)   (Effective retroactively to September 1, 1997) The North Carolina Marine Fisheries Commission as established by G.S. 143B-289.51.

(54)   Repealed by Session Laws 2001-474, s. 13, effective November 29, 2001.

(55)   Repealed by Session Laws 1998-217, s. 45, effective October 31, 1998.

(56)	Repealed by Session Laws 2001-474, s. 13, effective November 29, 2001.

(57)	Repealed by Session Laws 2004-129, s. 35, effective July 1, 2004.

(58)	The Appraisal Board created in G.S. 93E-1-5.

(59)	Repealed by Session Laws 1997-286, s. 7.

(59a)	The North Carolina Principal Fellows Commission established by G.S. 116-74.41.

(60)	Repealed by Session Laws 1997-443, s. 8.26b.

(61)	The State Health Plan Purchasing Alliance Board, as established by G.S. 143-625.

(62)	(Repealed effective June 30, 2014) The North Carolina's Northeast Commission, as established by G.S. 158-8.2.

(63)	Repealed by Session Laws 2011-145, s. 7.31(b), as added by Session Laws 2011-391, s. 17, effective July 1, 2011 and Session Laws 2011-266, s. 1.37(b), effective July 1, 2011.

(63a)	The North Carolina Code Officials Qualification Board, as established by G.S. 143-151.9.

(64)	A facility authority established under Part 4 of Article 20 of Chapter 160A of the General Statutes.

(64a)	The North Carolina Educational Facilities Finance Agency, as established by G.S. 115E-4.

(65)	Repealed by Session Laws 1998-217, s. 45.

(66)	The Local Government Commission, as established by G.S. 159-3.

(67)	Repealed by Session Laws 2013-360, s. 14.3(i), effective August 1, 2013.

(68)	The State Human Resources Commission.

(69)   The North Carolina Partnership for Children, Inc., established pursuant to Part 10B of Article 3 of Chapter 143B of the General Statutes, and all local partnerships established pursuant to this Part.

(70)   The Tobacco Trust Fund Commission established in Article 75 of Chapter 143 of the General Statutes.

(71)   The Health and Wellness Trust Fund Commission established in Article 21 of Chapter 130A of the General Statutes.

(72)   Repealed by Session Laws 2008-134, s. 73(c), effective July 28, 2008.

(73)   Repealed by Session Laws 2000-149, s. 5, as amended by Session Laws 2003-425, s. 3, effective December 31, 2003.

(74)   The North Carolina Respiratory Care Board as created by Article 37 of Chapter 90 of the General Statutes.

(75)   The North Carolina Turnpike Authority.

(76)   The Economic Investment Committee established under G.S. 143B-437.54.

(77)   Repealed by Session Laws 2003-425, s. 4, as amended by Session Laws 2006-66, s. 12.3(a), effective December 31, 2011.

(78)   The North Carolina State Lottery Commission, as established in Chapter 18C of the General Statutes.

(79)   Expired pursuant to 2010-31, s. 13.5(e), as amended by 2013-360, s. 14.2, effective July 1, 2013.

(80)   The Rural Infrastructure Authority, as created by G.S. 143B-472.128. (1981 (Reg. Sess., 1982), c. 1191, s. 2; 1983, c. 328, s. 1.1; c. 558, s. 5; c. 559, s. 4; c. 717, ss. 2, 3, 43.2, 99, 105, 110; c. 761, s. 179; c. 778, s. 2; c. 786, s. 9; c. 789, s. 2; c. 832, ss. 2, 6; c. 871, s. 3; c. 899, s. 3; 1983 (Reg. Sess., 1984), c. 995, ss. 4, 19; 1985, c. 202, s. 5; c. 479, s. 153(b); c. 589, s. 37; c. 666, s. 80; c. 746, s. 6; c. 757, ss. 155(b), 167(h), 179(e), 206(f), 208(c); 1985 (Reg. Sess., 1986), c. 1011, ss. 2, 2.1(c); c. 1014, ss. 63(h), 99; c. 1028, s. 33; c. 1029, s. 14.3; 1987, c. 71, ss. 4, 5; c. 622, s. 15; c. 641, s. 21; c. 738, s. 41(d); c. 765, s. 2; c. 841, s. 4; c. 850, s. 18; 1987 (Reg. Sess., 1988), c. 993, s. 27; 1989, c.

139, s. 2; c. 168, s. 8; c. 239, s. 7; c. 500, ss. 107(b), 109(g); c. 625, s. 24; c. 727, s. 140; c. 750, s. 4; c. 752, s. 148(c); 1989 (Reg. Sess., 1990), c. 827, s. 14; c. 1024, s. 23(a)-(d); c. 1074, s. 32(a)-(c); 1991, c. 134, s. 1; c. 301, s. 1; c. 668, s. 2; c. 749, s. 6; 1991 (Reg. Sess., 1992), c. 900, s. 14(f); c. 1007, s. 37; c. 1030, ss. 33, 51.14; c. 1044, s. 10(b); 1993, c. 321, ss. 85(d), 135(b), 309.1(b); c. 405, s. 18.1; c. 419, s. 13.1; c. 501, s. 12; c. 529, s. 3.9; 1993 (Reg. Sess., 1994), c. 777, s. 4(f); 1995, c. 324, s. 17.9(i); c. 458, s. 2; c. 490, ss. 12(b), 17(b), 21(b), 30(b), 37(b); c. 517, s. 39(d); 1997-286, s. 7; 1997-443, s. 8.26; 1997-506, s. 42; 1998-181, s. 3; 1998-212, s. 12.37B(e); 1998-217, s. 45; 1998-224, s. 19(c); 1998-225, s. 1.2; 2000-147, s. 5; 2000-148, s. 2; 2000-149, ss. 2, 5; 2000-162, s. 2; 2001-474, s. 13; 2001-487, s. 21(b); 2002-126, s. 6.6(b); 2002-133, s. 5; 2002-172, s. 2.5; 2003-416, s. 2; 2003-425, ss. 2, 3; 2004-129, s. 35; 2004-199, s. 27(b); 2005-344, s. 8; 2006-66, s. 12.3(a); 2007-93, s. 1; 2007-323, ss. 19.1(c), 28.22A(o); 2007-345, s. 12; 2007-484, s. 17; 2008-134, s. 73(c); 2010-31, s. 13.5(b); 2011-145, ss. 7.31(b), 14.6(c); 2011-266, ss. 1.37(b), 1.38(c); 2011-391, s. 17; 2012-56, s. 47; 2013-360, ss. 14.2, 14.3(i), 15.10(c), 15.28(c); 2013-382, s. 9.1(c).)

§§ 120-124 through 120-128. Reserved for future codification purposes.

Article 17.

Confidentiality of Legislative Communications.

§ 120-129. Definitions.

As used in this Article:

(1)   "Document" means all records, papers, letters, maps, books, photographs, films, sound recordings, magnetic or other tapes, electronic data-processing records, artifacts, or other documentary material regardless of physical form or characteristics.

(1a)   "Legislative commission" means any commission or committee which the Legislative Services Commission is directed or authorized to staff by law or resolution and which it does, in fact, staff.

(2)   "Legislative employee" means employees and officers of the General Assembly, consultants and counsel to members and committees of either house of the General Assembly or of legislative commissions who are paid by State funds, students at an accredited law school while in an externship program at the General Assembly approved by the Legislative Services Commission, and employees of the School of Government at the University of North Carolina at Chapel Hill; but does not mean legislators and members of the Council of State.

(3)   "Legislator" means a member-elect, member-designate, or member of the North Carolina Senate or House of Representatives. (1983, c. 900, s. 1; 1983 (Reg. Sess., 1984), c. 1038, ss. 1-3; 2006-264, s. 29(i); 2009-129, s. 1; 2010-96, s. 20; 2010-169, s. 24(a).)

§ 120-130. Drafting and information requests to legislative employees.

(a)   A drafting request made to a legislative employee from a legislator is confidential. Neither the identity of the legislator making the request nor, except to the extent necessary to answer the request, the existence of the request may be revealed to any person who is not a legislative employee without the consent of the legislator.

(b)   An information request made to a legislative employee from a legislator is confidential. Neither the identity of the legislator making the request nor, except to the extent necessary to answer the request, the existence of the request may be revealed to any person who is not a legislative employee without the consent of the legislator. Notwithstanding the preceding sentences of this subsection, the periodic publication by the Fiscal Research Division of the Legislative Services Office of a list of information requests is not prohibited, if the identity of the legislator making the request is not revealed.

(c)   Any supporting documents submitted or caused to be submitted to a legislative employee by a legislator in connection with a drafting or information request are confidential. Except to the extent necessary to answer the request, neither the document nor copies of it, nor the identity of the person, firm, or

111

association producing it, may be provided to any person who is not a legislative employee without the consent of the legislator.

(d)   Drafting or information requests or supporting documents are not "public records" as defined by G.S. 132-1. (1983, c. 900, s. 1.)

§ 120-131. Documents produced by legislative employees.

(a)   Documents prepared by legislative employees upon the request of legislators are confidential. Except as provided in subsection (b) of this section, the existence of the document may not be revealed nor may a copy of the document be provided to any person who is not a legislative employee without the consent of the legislator.

(b)   A document prepared by a legislative employee upon the request of a legislator becomes available to the public when the document is a:

(1)   Bill or resolution and it has been introduced;

(2)   Proposed amendment or committee substitute for a bill or resolution and it has been offered at a committee meeting or on the floor of a house;

(3)   Proposed conference committee report and it has been offered at a joint meeting of the conference committees; or

(4)   Bill, resolution, memorandum, written analysis, letter, or other document resulting from a drafting or information request and it has been distributed at a legislative commission or standing committee or subcommittee meeting not held in executive session, closed session, or on the floor of a house.

A document prepared by a legislative employee upon the request of any legislator, that pursuant to this Article does not become available to the public, is not a "public record," as defined by G.S. 132-1.

(c)   This section does not prohibit the dissemination of information or language contained in any document which has been prepared by a legislative employee in response to a substantially similar request from another legislator, provided that the identity of the requesting legislator and the fact that he had made such a request not be divulged. (1983, c. 900, s. 1; 1983 (Reg. Sess., 1984), c. 1038, s. 4; 1993 (Reg. Sess., 1994), c. 570, s. 9.)

§ 120-131.1. Requests from legislative employees for assistance in the preparation of fiscal notes and evaluation reports.

(a)   A request, including any accompanying documents, made to an agency employee by a legislative employee of the Fiscal Research Division for assistance in the preparation of a fiscal note is confidential. An agency employee who receives such a request or who learns of such a request made to another agency employee of his or her agency shall reveal the existence of the request only to other agency employees of the agency to the extent that it is necessary to respond to the request, and to the agency employee's supervisor and to the Office of State Budget and Management. All documents prepared by the agency employee in response to the request of the Fiscal Research Division are also confidential and shall be kept confidential in the same manner as the original request, except that documents submitted to the Fiscal Research Division in response to the request cease to be confidential under this section when the Fiscal Research Division releases a fiscal note based on the documents.

(a1)   A request, and any accompanying documents, made to an agency employee by a legislative employee of the Program Evaluation Division for assistance in the preparation of an evaluation report is confidential. The request and any accompanying documents are not "public records" as defined by G.S. 132-1. An agency employee who receives a request under this subsection or who learns of such a request made to another agency employee of his or her agency may reveal the existence of the request to other agency employees to the extent that it is necessary to respond to the request and to the agency employee's supervisor. All documents prepared by the agency employee in response to the request of a legislative employee of the Program Evaluation Division are confidential, shall be kept confidential in the same manner as the original request, and are not "public records" as defined in G.S. 132-1.

(b)   As used in this section, "agency employee" means an employee or officer of every agency of North Carolina government or its subdivisions, including every public office, public officer or official (State or local, elected or appointed), institution, board, commission, bureau, council, department,

113

authority, or other unit of government of the State or of any county, unit, special district, or other political subdivision of government.

(c)   Violation of this section may be grounds for disciplinary action. (1995, c. 324, s. 8.1(a); c. 507, s. 8.2; 2000-140, s. 93.1(a); 2001-424, s. 12.2(b); 2008-196, s. 1(b).)

§ 120-132. Testimony by legislative employees.

(a)   Except as provided in subsections (b) and (c) of this section, no present or former legislative employee may disclose any information that the individual, while employed or retained by the State, may have acquired:

(1)   In a standing, select, or conference committee or subcommittee of either house of the General Assembly or a legislative commission;

(2)   On the floor of either house of the General Assembly, in any office of a legislator, or at any other location of the State legislative buildings and grounds as defined in G.S. 120-32.1(d);

(3)   As a result of communications that are confidential under G.S. 120-130 and G.S. 120-131.

(b)   A present or former legislative employee may disclose information acquired under subsection (a) of this section that would be reflected in the official public record or was otherwise publicly disseminated.

(c)   Subject to G.S. 120-9, G.S. 120-133, and the common law of legislative privilege and legislative immunity, the presiding judge may compel disclosure of information acquired under subsection (a) of this section if in the judge's opinion, the disclosure is necessary to a proper administration of justice. (1983, c. 900, s. 1; 1983 (Reg. Sess., 1984), c. 1038, s. 5; 2010-169, s. 24(b).)

§ 120-133. Redistricting communications.

(a)   Notwithstanding any other provision of law, all drafting and information requests to legislative employees and documents prepared by legislative employees for legislators concerning redistricting the North Carolina General Assembly or the Congressional Districts are no longer confidential and become public records upon the act establishing the relevant district plan becoming law. Present and former legislative employees may be required to disclose information otherwise protected by G.S. 120-132 concerning redistricting the North Carolina General Assembly or the Congressional Districts upon the act establishing the relevant district plan becoming law.

(b)   Nothing in this Chapter nor in Chapter 132 of the General Statutes shall be construed as a waiver of the common law attorney-client privilege nor of the common law work product doctrine with respect to legislators as defined in G.S. 120-129. (1983, c. 900, s. 1; 1995, c. 20, s. 13; 2013-410, s. 36.7.)

§ 120-134. Penalty.

Violation of any provision of this Article shall be grounds for disciplinary action in the case of employees, for referral to the academic institution for appropriate discipline in the case of law student externs, and for removal from office in the case of public officers. No criminal penalty shall attach for any violation of this Article. (1983, c. 900, s. 1; 1983 (Reg. Sess., 1984), c. 1038, s. 6; 2009-129, s. 2.)

§§ 120-135 through 120-139. Reserved for future codification purposes.

Article 18.

Review of Proposals to License New Occupations and Professions.

§§ 120-140 through 120-149: Expired.

Article 18A.

Review of Proposals to License New Occupations and Professions.

§ 120-149.1: Repealed by Session Laws 2011-291, s. 1.2(b), effective June 24, 2011.

§ 120-149.2: Repealed by Session Laws 2011-291, s. 1.2(b), effective June 24, 2011.

§ 120-149.3: Repealed by Session Laws 2011-291, s. 1.2(b), effective June 24, 2011.

§ 120-149.4: Repealed by Session Laws 2011-291, s. 1.2(b), effective June 24, 2011.

§ 120-149.5: Repealed by Session Laws 2011-291, s. 1.2(b), effective June 24, 2011.

§ 120-149.6: Repealed by Session Laws 2011-291, s. 1.2(b), effective June 24, 2011.

Article 19.

Agriculture and Forestry Awareness Study Commission.

§ 120-150. Creation; appointment of members.

There is created an Agriculture and Forestry Awareness Study Commission. Members of the Commission shall be citizens of North Carolina who are interested in the vitality of the agriculture and forestry sectors of the State's economy. Members shall be as follows:

(1)   Three appointed by the Governor.

(2)   Three appointed by the President Pro Tempore of the Senate.

(3)   Three appointed by the Speaker of the House.

(4)   The chairs of the House Agriculture Committee.

(5)   The chairs of the Senate Committee on Agriculture, Environment, and Natural Resources.

(6)   The Commissioner of Agriculture or the Commissioner's designee.

(7)   A member of the Board of Agriculture designated by the chair of the Board of Agriculture.

(8)   The President of the North Carolina Farm Bureau Federation, Inc., or the President's designee.

(9)   The President of the North Carolina State Grange or the President's designee.

(10)   The Secretary of Environment and Natural Resources or the Secretary's designee.

(11)   The President of the North Carolina Forestry Association, Inc., or the President's designee.

Members shall be appointed for two-year terms beginning October 1 of each odd-numbered year. The Chairs of the House Agriculture Committee and the Chairs of the Senate Committee on Agriculture, Environment, and Natural Resources shall serve as cochairs. (1985, c. 792, s. 20.1; 1989, c. 727, s. 218(81); 1989 (Reg. Sess., 1990), c. 1004, s. 19(b); 1991 (Reg. Sess., 1992), c. 785, s. 1; 1993, c. 23, s. 1; 1995, c. 490, s. 5; 1997-443, s. 11A.119(a); 2001-474, s. 14; 2010-142, s. 9.)

§ 120-151. Advisory Committee.

Upon proper motion and by a vote of a majority of the members present, the Commission may appoint an Advisory Committee. Members of the Advisory Committee should be from the various organizations, commodity groups, associations, and councils representing agriculture and forestry. The purpose of the Advisory Committee shall be to render technical advice and assistance to the Commission. The Advisory Committee shall consist of no more than 20 members plus a chairman who shall be appointed by the cochairmen of the Commission. (1985, c. 792, s. 20.1; 1991 (Reg. Sess., 1992), c. 785, s. 2.)

§ 120-152. Subsistence and travel expenses.

The members of the Commission who are members of the General Assembly shall receive subsistence and travel allowances at the rate set forth in G.S. 120-3.1. Members who are officials or employees of the State of North Carolina shall receive subsistence and travel allowances at the rate set forth in G.S. 138-6. All other members plus the Chairman of the Advisory Committee shall be paid the per diem allowances at the rates set forth in G.S. 138-5. Other members of the Advisory Committee shall serve on a voluntary basis and not receive subsistence and travel expenses. (1985, c. 792, s. 20.1.)

§ 120-153. Facilities and staff.

The Commission may hold its meetings in the State Legislative Building with the approval of the Legislative Services Commission. The Legislative Services Commission shall provide necessary professional and clerical assistance to the Commission. (1985, c. 792, s. 20.1.)

§ 120-154. Duties.

The Commission shall bring to the attention of the General Assembly the influence of agriculture and forestry on the economy of the State, develop alternatives for increasing the public awareness of agriculture and forestry, study the present status of agriculture and forestry, identify problems limiting future growth and development of the industry, develop an awareness of the importance of science and technological development to the future of agriculture and forestry industries, and formulate plans for new State initiatives and support for agriculture and forestry and for the expansion of opportunities in these sectors.

In conducting its study the Commission may hold public hearings and meetings across the State.

The Commission shall report to the General Assembly at least one month prior to the first regular session of each General Assembly. (1985, c. 792, s. 20.1; 1991 (Reg. Sess., 1992), c. 785, s. 3.)

118

§ 120-155. Reserved for future codification purposes.

§ 120-156. Reserved for future codification purposes.

§ 120-157. Reserved for future codification purposes.

Article 20.

Joint Legislative Committee on Local Government.

Part 1. Organization.

§ 120-157.1. Committee established.

(a)   The Joint Legislative Committee on Local Government is established. The Committee shall consist of 14 members, appointed as follows:

(1)   Seven members of the Senate appointed by the President Pro Tempore of the Senate, at least two of whom shall be members of the minority party. At least one member shall be a former city or county commissioner, city or county manager, or other city or county elected official.

(2)   Seven members of the House of Representatives appointed by the Speaker of the House of Representatives, at least two of whom shall be members of the minority party. At least one member shall be a former city or county commissioner, city or county manager, or other city or county elected official.

(b)   Terms on the Committee are for two years and begin on the convening of the General Assembly in each odd-numbered year. Members may complete a term of service on the Committee even if they do not seek reelection or are not reelected to the General Assembly, but resignation or removal from service in the General Assembly constitutes resignation or removal from service on the Committee.

(c)   A member continues to serve until a successor is appointed. A vacancy shall be filled within 30 days by the officer who made the original appointment. (2011-291, s. 1.8(a).)

119

§ 120-157.2. Purpose and powers of Committee.

(a)   The Joint Legislative Committee on Local Government shall review and monitor local government capital projects that are required to go before the Local Government Commission and require debt to be issued over one million dollars ($1,000,000), with the exception of schools, jails, courthouses, and administrative buildings. Any project that fits these criteria must be reported to the Committee Chairs, Committee Assistant, and the Fiscal Research Division at least 45 days prior to presentation before the Local Government Commission.

(b)   The Committee may make interim reports to the General Assembly on matters for which it may report to a regular session of the General Assembly. A report to the General Assembly shall include the purpose, scope, debt requirements, financing methods, and repayment plans of any local governmental capital project reviewed pursuant to subsection (a) of this section and may contain any legislation needed to implement a recommendation of the Committee. (2011-291, s. 1.8(a).)

§ 120-157.3. Organization of Committee.

(a)   The President Pro Tempore of the Senate and the Speaker of the House of Representatives shall each designate a cochair of the Joint Legislative Committee on Local Government. The Committee may meet on days when the members of the General Assembly are entitled to subsistence pursuant to G.S. 120-3.1 and may meet at other times upon the joint call of the cochairs.

(b)   A quorum of the Committee is eight members. No action may be taken except by a majority vote at a meeting at which a quorum is present. While in the discharge of its official duties, the Committee has the power of a joint committee under G.S. 120-19 and G.S. 120-19.1 thorough G.S. 120-19.4.

(c)   Members of the Committee may receive subsistence and travel expenses as provided in G.S. 120-3.1. The Committee may contract for consultants or hire employees in accordance with G.S. 120-32.02. The Legislative Services Commission, through the Legislative Services Officer, shall assign professional staff to assist the Committee in its work. Upon the direction of the Legislative Services Commission, the Supervisors of Clerks of the Senate and of the House of Representatives shall assign clerical staff to the Committee.

The expenses for clerical employees shall be borne by the Committee. (2011-291, s. 1.8(a).)

§ 120-157.4. Additional powers.

The Joint Legislative Committee on Local Government, while in discharge of official duties, shall have access to any paper or document, and may compel the attendance of any State official or employee before the Committee or secure any evidence under G.S. 120-19. In addition, G.S. 120-19.1 through G.S. 120-19.4 shall apply to the proceedings of the Committee as if it were a joint committee of the General Assembly. (2011-291, s. 1.8(a).)

§ 120-158. Creation of Municipal Incorporations Subcommittee.

(a)   There is created the Municipal Incorporations Subcommittee of the Joint Legislative Committee on Local Government.

(b)   The Subcommittee shall consist of six members, appointed as follows:

(1)   Three Senators appointed by the President Pro Tempore of the Senate, at least one of whom shall be a former city or county commissioner, city or county manager, or other local elected official.

(2)   Three House members appointed by the Speaker of the House of Representatives, at least one of whom shall be a former city or county commissioner, city or county manager, or other local elected official.

(3),   (4) Repealed by Session Laws 2011-291, s. 1.8(a), effective June 24, 2011. (1985 (Reg. Sess., 1986), c. 1003, s. 1; 1991, c. 739, s. 17; 2011-291, s. 1.8(a).)

§ 120-159. Terms; meetings.

(a)   Members shall be appointed for terms ending June 30, 1987, and subsequently for two-year terms beginning July 1, 1987, and biennially thereafter. A member eligible when appointed may continue for the remainder of the term regardless of the member's continued eligibility for the category. The Municipal Incorporations Subcommittee shall elect a chair from its membership for a one-year term.

(b)   The Subcommittee may meet on days when the members of the General Assembly are entitled to subsistence pursuant to G.S. 120-3.1 and may meet at other times upon the joint call of the cochairs. (1985 (Reg. Sess., 1986), c. 1003, s. 1; 2011-291, s. 1.8(a).)

§ 120-160: Repealed by Session Laws 2011-291, s. 1.8(a), effective June 24, 2011.

§ 120-161: Repealed by Session Laws 2011-291, s. 1.8(a), effective June 24, 2011.

§ 120-162. Reserved for future codification purposes.

Part 2. Procedure for Incorporation Review.

§ 120-163. Petition.

(a)   The process of seeking the recommendation of the Municipal Incorporations Subcommittee is commenced by filing with the Municipal Incorporations Subcommittee a petition signed by fifteen percent (15%) of the registered voters of the area proposed to be incorporated, but by not less than 25 registered voters of that area, asking for incorporation. The voter shall sign the petition and also clearly print that voter's name adjacent to the signature. The petition must also contain the voter's residence address and date of birth.

(b)   The petition must be verified by the county board of elections of the county where the voter is alleged to be registered. The board of elections shall cause to be examined the signature, shall place a check mark beside the name of each signer who is qualified and registered to vote in that county in the area proposed to be incorporated, and shall attach to the petition a certificate stating the number of voters registered in that county in the area proposed to be incorporated, and the total number of registered voters who have been verified. The county board of elections shall return the petition to the person who presented it within 15 working days of receipt. That period of 15 working days shall be tolled for any period of time that is also either two weeks before or one week after a primary or election being conducted by the county board of elections.

(c)   The petition must include a proposed name for the city, a map of the city, a list of proposed services to be provided by the proposed municipality, the names of three persons to serve as interim governing board, a proposed charter, a statement of the estimated population, assessed valuation, degree of development, population density, and recommendations as to the form of government and manner of election. The petition must contain a statement that the proposed municipality will have a budget ordinance with an ad valorem tax levy of at least five cents (5¢) on the one hundred dollar ($100.00) valuation upon all taxable property within its corporate limits. The petition must contain a statement that the proposed municipality will offer four of the following services no later than the first day of the third fiscal year following the effective date of the incorporation: (i) police protection; (ii) fire protection; (iii) solid waste collection or disposal; (iv) water distribution; (v) street maintenance; (vi) street construction or right-of-way acquisition; (vii) street lighting; and (viii) zoning. In order to qualify for providing police protection, the proposed municipality must propose either to provide police service or to have services provided by contract with a county or another municipality that proposes that the other government be compensated for providing supplemental protection. The proposed municipality may not contain any noncontiguous areas.

(d)   The petitioners must present to the Municipal Incorporations Subcommittee the verified petition from the county board of elections.

(e)   A petition must be submitted to the Municipal Incorporations Subcommittee at least 60 days prior to convening of the next regular session of the General Assembly in order for the Municipal Incorporations Subcommittee to make a recommendation to that session. (1985 (Reg. Sess., 1986), c. 1003, s. 1; 1999-458, s. 1; 2001-353, s. 6; 2011-291, s. 2.32.)

§ 120-164. Notification.

(a)   Not later than five days before submitting the petition to the Municipal Incorporations Subcommittee, the petitioners shall notify:

(1)   The board or boards of county commissioners of the county or counties where the proposed municipality is located;

(2)   All cities within that county or counties; and

(3)   All cities in any other county that are within five miles of the proposed municipality of the intent to present the petition to the Municipal Incorporations Subcommittee.

(b)   The petitioners shall also publish, one per week for two consecutive weeks, with the second publication no later than seven days before submitting the petition to the Municipal Incorporations Subcommittee notice in a newspaper of general circulation in the area proposed to be incorporated of the intent to present the petition to the Municipal Incorporations Subcommittee. (1985 (Reg. Sess., 1986), c. 1003, s. 1; 2011-291, s. 2.33.)

§ 120-165. Initial inquiry.

(a)   The Municipal Incorporations Subcommittee shall, upon receipt of the petition, determine if the requirements of G.S. 120-163 and G.S. 120-164 have been met. If it determines that those requirements have not been met, it shall return the petition to the petitioners. The Municipal Incorporations Subcommittee shall also publish in the North Carolina Register notice that it has received the petition.

(b)   If it determines that those requirements have been met, it shall conduct further inquiry as provided by this Part. (1985 (Reg. Sess., 1986), c. 1003, s. 1; 2011-291, s. 2.34.)

§ 120-166. Additional criteria; nearness to another municipality.

(a)   The Municipal Incorporations Subcommittee may not make a positive recommendation if the proposed municipality is located within one mile of a municipality of 5,000 to 9,999, within three miles of a municipality of 10,000 to 24,999, within four miles of a municipality of 25,000 to 49,999, or within five miles of a municipality of 50,000 or over, according to the most recent decennial federal census, or according to the most recent annual estimate of the Office of State Budget and Management if the municipality was incorporated since the return of that census. For purposes of this section, "municipality" means a city as defined by G.S. 160A-1(2) or a county that has exercised its authority under Article 24 of Chapter 153A of the General Statutes.

(b)   Subsection (a) of this section does not apply in the case of proximity to a specific municipality if:

(1)   The proposed municipality is entirely on an island that the nearby city is not on;

(2)   The proposed municipality is separated by a major river or other natural barrier from the nearby city, such that provision of municipal services by the nearby city to the proposed municipality is infeasible or the cost is prohibitive, and the Municipal Incorporations Subcommittee shall adopt policies to implement this subdivision;

(3)   The municipalities within the distances described in subsection (a) of this section by resolution express their approval of the incorporation; or

(4)   An area of at least fifty percent (50%) of the proposed municipality has petitioned for annexation to the nearby city under G.S. 160A-31 within the previous 12 months before the incorporation petition is submitted to the Municipal Incorporations Subcommittee but the annexation petition was not approved. (1985 (Reg. Sess., 1986), c. 1003, s. 1; 1989 (Reg. Sess., 1990), c. 1024, s. 25; 1998-150, s. 2; 2000-140, s. 93.1(a); 2001-424, s. 12.2(b); 2005-35, s. 2; 2011-291, s. 2.35.)

§ 120-167. Additional criteria; population.

The Commission may not make a positive recommendation unless the proposed municipality has a permanent population of at least 100 and a population density (either permanent or seasonal) of at least 250 persons per square mile. (1985 (Reg. Sess., 1986), c. 1003, s. 1; 1999-458, s. 2.)

§ 120-168. Additional criteria; development.

The Municipal Incorporations Subcommittee may not make a positive recommendation unless forty percent (40%) of the area is developed for residential, commercial, industrial, institutional, or governmental uses, or is dedicated as open space under the provisions of a zoning ordinance, subdivision ordinance, conditional or special use permit, or recorded restrictive covenants. (1985 (Reg. Sess., 1986), c. 1003, s. 1; 1999-458, s. 3; 2011-291, s. 2.36.)

§ 120-169. Additional criteria; area unincorporated.

The Municipal Incorporations Subcommittee may not make a positive recommendation if any of the proposed municipality is included within the boundary of another incorporated municipality, as defined by G.S. 153A-1(1), or if any of the proposed municipality is included within the boundary of a county that has exercised its authority under Article 24 of Chapter 153A of the General Statutes. (1985 (Reg. Sess., 1986), c. 1003, s. 1; 2005-35, s. 3; 2011-291, s. 2.37.)

§ 120-169.1. Additional criteria; level of development, services; financial impact on other local governments.

(a)   Repealed by Session Laws 1999-458, s. 4.

(b)   Services. - The Municipal Incorporations Subcommittee may not make a positive recommendation unless the area to be incorporated submits a plan for providing a reasonable level of municipal services. This plan shall be based on the proposed services stated in the petition under G.S. 120-163(c).

(c)   The Municipal Incorporations Subcommittee in its report shall indicate the impact on other municipalities and counties of diversion of already levied local taxes or State-shared revenues from existing local governments to support services in the proposed municipality. (1998-150, s. 3; 1999-458, s. 4; 2011-291, s. 2.38.)

§ 120-170. Findings as to services.

The Commission may not make a positive recommendation unless it finds that the proposed municipality can provide at a reasonable tax rate the services requested by the petition, and finds that the proposed municipality can provide at a reasonable tax rate the types of services usually provided by similar municipalities. In making findings under this section, the Commission shall take into account municipal services already being provided. (1985 (Reg. Sess., 1986), c. 1003, s. 1.)

§ 120-171. Procedures if findings made.

(a)   If the Commission finds that it may not make a positive recommendation because of the provisions of G.S. 120-166 through G.S. 120-170, it shall make a negative recommendation to the General Assembly. The report to the General Assembly shall list the grounds on which a negative recommendation is made, along with specific findings. If a negative recommendation is made, the Commission shall notify the petitioners of the need for a legally sufficient description of the proposed municipality if the proposal is to be considered by the General Assembly. At the request of a majority of the members of the interim board named in the petition, the Commission may conduct a public hearing and forward any comments or findings made as a result of that hearing along with the negative recommendation.

(b)   If the Commission determines that it will not be barred from making a positive recommendation by G.S. 120-166 through G.S. 120-170, it shall require that petitioners have a legally sufficient description of the proposed municipality prepared at their expense as a condition of a positive recommendation.

(c)   If the Commission determines that it is not barred from making a positive recommendation, it shall make a positive recommendation to the General Assembly for incorporation.

(d)   The report of the Commission on a petition shall be in a form determined by the Commission to be useful to the General Assembly. (1985 (Reg. Sess., 1986), c. 1003, s. 1.)

§ 120-172. Referendum.

Based on information received at the public hearing, the Commission may recommend that any incorporation act passed by the General Assembly shall be submitted to a referendum, except if the petition contained the signatures of fifty percent (50%) of registered voters the Commission shall not recommend a referendum. (1985 (Reg. Sess., 1986), c. 1003, s. 1.)

§ 120-173. Modification of petition.

With the agreement of the majority of the persons designated by the petition as an interim governing board, the Commission may submit to the General Assembly recommendations based on deletion of areas from the petition, as long as there are no noncontiguous areas. (1985 (Reg. Sess., 1986), c. 1003, s. 1.)

§ 120-174. Deadline for recommendations.

If the petition is timely received under G.S. 120-163(e), the Commission shall make its recommendation to the General Assembly no later than 60 days after convening of the next regular session after submission of the petition. (1985 (Reg. Sess., 1986), c. 1003, s. 1.)

§§ 120-175 through 120-179. Reserved for future codification purposes.

Article 21.

The North Carolina Study Commission on Aging.

§ 120-180: Repealed by Session Laws 2011-291, s. 1.6, effective June 24, 2011.

§ 120-181: Repealed by Session Laws 2011-291, s. 1.6, effective June 24, 2011.

§ 120-182: Repealed by Session Laws 2011-291, s. 1.6, effective June 24, 2011.

§ 120-183: Repealed by Session Laws 2011-291, s. 1.6, effective June 24, 2011.

§ 120-184: Repealed by Session Laws 2011-291, s. 1.6, effective June 24, 2011.

§ 120-185: Repealed by Session Laws 2011-291, s. 1.6, effective June 24, 2011.

§ 120-186: Repealed by Session Laws 2011-291, s. 1.6, effective June 24, 2011.

§ 120-186.1: Repealed by Session Laws 2011-291, s. 1.6, effective June 24, 2011.

§ 120-187: Repealed by Session Laws 2011-291, s. 1.6, effective June 24, 2011.

§ 120-188: Repealed by Session Laws 2011-291, s. 1.6, effective June 24, 2011.

§§ 120-189 through 120-194. Reserved for future codification purposes.

Article 22.

The Public Health Study Commission.

§ 120-195: Repealed by Session Laws 2011-266, s. 1.16(a), effective July 1, 2011 and Session Laws 2011-291, s. 1.6(b), effective June 24, 2011.

§ 120-196: Repealed by Session Laws 2011-266, s. 1.16(a), effective July 1, 2011 and Session Laws 2011-291, s. 1.6(b), effective June 24, 2011.

§ 120-197: Repealed by Session Laws 2011-266, s. 1.16(a), effective July 1, 2011 and Session Laws 2011-291, s. 1.6(b), effective June 24, 2011.

§ 120-198: Repealed by Session Laws 2011-266, s. 1.16(a), effective July 1, 2011 and Session Laws 2011-291, s. 1.6(b), effective June 24, 2011.

§ 120-199: Repealed by Session Laws 2011-266, s. 1.16(a), effective July 1, 2011 and Session Laws 2011-291, s. 1.6(b), effective June 24, 2011.

§ 120-200: Repealed by Session Laws 2011-266, s. 1.16(a), effective July 1, 2011 and Session Laws 2011-291, s. 1.6(b), effective June 24, 2011.

§ 120-201: Repealed by Session Laws 2011-266, s. 1.16(a), effective July 1, 2011 and Session Laws 2011-291, s. 1.6(b), effective June 24, 2011.

§ 120-202: Repealed by Session Laws 2011-266, s. 1.16(a), effective July 1, 2011 and Session Laws 2011-291, s. 1.6(b), effective June 24, 2011.

§ 120-203: Repealed by Session Laws 2011-266, s. 1.16(a), effective July 1, 2011 and Session Laws 2011-291, s. 1.6(b), effective June 24, 2011.

Article 23.

The Legislative Study Commission on Mental Health, Developmental Disabilities, and Substance Abuse Services.

§§ 120-204 through 120-207: Repealed by Session Laws 2006-32, s. 2, effective June 29, 2006.

Article 23A.

Joint Legislative Oversight Committee on Health and Human Services.

§ 120-208. Creation and membership of Joint Legislative Oversight Committee on Health and Human Services.

(a)   The Joint Legislative Oversight Committee on Health and Human Services is established. The Committee consists of 22 members as follows:

(1)   Eleven members of the Senate appointed by the President Pro Tempore of the Senate, at least three of whom are members of the minority party; and

(2)   Eleven members of the House of Representatives appointed by the Speaker of the House of Representatives, at least three of whom are members of the minority party.

(b)   Terms on the Committee are for two years and begin on the convening of the General Assembly in each odd-numbered year. Members may complete a term of service on the Committee even if they do not seek reelection or are not reelected to the General Assembly, but resignation or removal from service in the General Assembly constitutes resignation or removal from service on the Committee.

(c)   A member continues to serve until a successor is appointed. A vacancy shall be filled within 30 days by the officer who made the original appointment. (2011-291, s. 1.6(c).)

§ 120-208.1. Purpose and powers of Committee.

(a)   The Joint Legislative Oversight Committee on Health and Human Services shall examine, on a continuing basis, the systemwide issues affecting the development, budgeting, financing, administration, and delivery of health and human services, including issues relating to the governance, accountability, and quality of health and human services delivered to individuals and families in this State. The Committee shall make ongoing recommendations to the General Assembly on ways to improve the quality and delivery of services and to maintain a high level of effectiveness and efficiency in system administration at the State and local levels. In conducting its examination, the Committee shall do all of the following:

(1)   Study the budgets, programs, and policies of each Division within the Department of Health and Human Services, to determine ways in which the

General Assembly may encourage improvement in the budgeting and delivery of health and human services provided to North Carolinians;

(2)   Examine, in particular, issues relating to services provided by the following Divisions within the Department of Health and Human Services:

a.   Aging and Adult Services.

b.   Medical Assistance.

c.   Mental Health, Developmental Disabilities, and Substance Abuse Services.

d.   Public Health.

e.   Social Services;

(3)   Study other states' health and human services initiatives, in order to provide an ongoing commentary to the General Assembly on these initiatives and to make recommendations for implementing similar initiatives in North Carolina; and

(4)   Study any other health and human services matters that the Committee considers necessary to fulfill its mandate.

(b)   The Committee may make interim reports to the General Assembly on matters for which it may report to a regular session of the General Assembly. A report to the General Assembly may contain any legislation needed to implement a recommendation of the Committee. (2011-291, s. 1.6(c).)

§ 120-208.2. Organization of Committee.

(a)   The President Pro Tempore of the Senate and the Speaker of the House of Representatives shall each designate a cochair of the Joint Legislative Oversight Committee on Health and Human Services. The Committee shall meet at least once per quarter, except while the General Assembly is in regular session, and may meet at other times upon the joint call of the cochairs.

(b)   A quorum of the Committee is 10 members. No action may be taken except by a majority vote at a meeting at which a quorum is present. While in the discharge of its official duties, the Committee has the powers of a joint committee under G.S. 120-19 and G.S. 120-19.1 through G.S. 120-19.4.

(c)   Members of the Committee receive subsistence and travel expenses as provided in G.S. 120-3.1. The Committee may contract for consultants or hire employees in accordance with G.S. 120-32.02. The Legislative Services Commission, through the Legislative Services Officer, shall assign professional staff to assist the Committee in its work. Upon the direction of the Legislative Services Commission, the Supervisors of Clerks of the Senate and of the House of Representatives shall assign clerical staff to the Committee. The expenses for clerical employees shall be borne by the Committee.

(d)   The Committee cochairs may establish subcommittees for the purpose of examining issues relating to services provided by particular Divisions within the Department of Health and Human Services. (2011-291, s. 1.6(c).)

§ 120-208.3. Additional powers.

The Joint Legislative Oversight Committee on Health and Human Services, while in discharge of official duties, shall have access to any paper or document, and may compel the attendance of any State official or employee before the Committee or secure any evidence under G.S. 120-19. In addition, G.S. 120-19.1 through G.S. 120-19.4 shall apply to the proceedings of the Committee as if it were a joint committee of the General Assembly. (2011-291, s. 1.6(c).)

§ 120-208.4. Reports to the Committee.

(a)   Whenever a Division within the Department of Health and Human Services is required by law to report to the General Assembly or to any of its permanent, study, or oversight committees or subcommittees on matters affecting that Division, the Department shall transmit a copy of the report to the cochairs of the Joint Legislative Oversight Committee on Health and Human Services.

(b)   Beginning no later than November 1, 2012, and annually thereafter, the Department of Health and Human Services shall submit a report to the Joint Legislative Oversight Committee on Health and Human Services and the Fiscal Research Division on the use of lapsed salary funds by each Division within the Department. For each Division, the report shall include the following information about the preceding State fiscal year:

(1)   The total amount of lapsed salary funds.

(2)   The number of full-time equivalent positions comprising the lapsed salary funds.

(3)   The Fund Code for each full-time equivalent position included in the number reported pursuant to subdivision (2) of this section.

(4)   The purposes for which the Department expended lapsed salary funds. (2011-291, s. 1.6(c); 2012-142, s. 10.20; 2013-360, s. 12A.11.)

§ 120-209: Reserved for future codification purposes.

§ 120-210: Reserved for future codification purposes.

§ 120-211: Reserved for future codification purposes.

§ 120-212: Reserved for future codification purposes.

§ 120-213: Reserved for future codification purposes.

§ 120-214: Reserved for future codification purposes.

Article 24.

The Legislative Study Commission on Children and Youth.

§ 120-215: Repealed by Session Laws 2011-291, s. 1.5(b), effective June 24, 2011.

§ 120-216: Repealed by Session Laws 2011-291, s. 1.5(b), effective June 24, 2011.

§ 120-217: Repealed by Session Laws 2011-291, s. 1.5(b), effective June 24, 2011.

§ 120-218: Repealed by Session Laws 2011-291, s. 1.5(b), effective June 24, 2011.

§ 120-219: Repealed by Session Laws 2011-291, s. 1.5(b), effective June 24, 2011.

§ 120-220: Repealed by Session Laws 2011-291, s. 1.5(b), effective June 24, 2011.

§ 120-221: Repealed by Session Laws 2011-291, s. 1.5(b), effective June 24, 2011.

§ 120-222: Reserved for future codification purposes.

§ 120-223: Reserved for future codification purposes.

§ 120-224: Reserved for future codification purposes.

Article 25.

Joint Legislative Public Assistance Commission.

§ 120-225: Repealed by Session Laws 2001-424, s. 21.13(a).

Article 25A.

Legislative Commission on Methamphetamine Abuse.

§ 120-226. Commission established; purpose; reports.

(a)   Establishment. - The Legislative Commission on Methamphetamine Abuse is established.

(b)   Purpose. - The purpose of the Commission is to study: (i) issues regarding the abuse of methamphetamine precursors used to make methamphetamine and any other issues that are relevant to that topic; (ii) the cost, feasibility, and advisability of developing and implementing data-tracking mechanisms related to the sale of pseudoephedrine products; (iii) development of programs to curb the use of and access to methamphetamine in North Carolina; (iv) development of training and education programs targeted for employees of establishments where pseudoephedrine products are available for sale; (v) development of programs to educate the citizens of the State on the issues of detection and prevention of clandestine methamphetamine laboratories in the State and to educate the citizens of the State of the restrictions on the sale of pseudoephedrine products set forth in Article 5D of Chapter 90 of the General Statutes.

(c)   Membership. - The Commission shall consist of 22 members to be appointed as follows:

(1)   Two members of the Senate appointed by the President Pro Tempore of the Senate.

(2)   Two members of the House of Representatives appointed by the Speaker of the House of Representatives.

(3)   The Attorney General or the Attorney General's designee.

(4)   The Governor or the Governor's designee.

(5)   One representative from the North Carolina Association of County Directors of Social Services, as appointed by the President Pro Tempore of the Senate.

(6)   One representative from the North Carolina Retail Merchants Association, as appointed by the Speaker of the House of Representatives.

(7)   One representative from the North Carolina Association of Community Pharmacists, as appointed by the President Pro Tempore of the Senate.

(8)   One representative from the Conference of District Attorneys of North Carolina, as appointed by the Speaker of the House of Representatives.

(9)   One representative from the Consumer Healthcare Products Association, as appointed by the President Pro Tempore of the Senate.

(10)   One representative from the North Carolina Sheriffs' Association, Inc., as appointed by the Speaker of the House of Representatives.

(11)   The Secretary of Health and Human Services or the Secretary's designee.

(12)   The Director of the State Bureau of Investigation or the Director's designee.

(13)   One representative from the North Carolina Narcotic Enforcement Officers' Association, as appointed by the President Pro Tempore of the Senate.

(14)   One representative from the North Carolina Association of Chiefs of Police, as appointed by the Speaker of the House of Representatives.

(15)   The Commissioner of Agriculture or the Commissioner's designee.

(16)   The Chair of the Commission on Mental Health or the Chair's designee.

(17)   The Director of the National Drug Intelligence Center or the Director's designee.

(18)   The Administrator of the United States Drug Enforcement or the Administrator's designee.

(19)   One representative from the National Association of Chain Drug Stores, as appointed by the President Pro Tempore of the Senate.

(20)   One representative from a child advocacy organization in the State, as appointed by the Speaker of the House of Representatives.

(d)   Terms. - Members shall serve for two-year terms, with no prohibition against being reappointed, except initial appointments shall be for terms as follows:

(1)   The President Pro Tempore of the Senate shall initially appoint three members for a term of two years and four members for a term of three years.

(2)　The Speaker of the House of Representatives shall initially appoint three members for a term of two years and four members for a term of three years.

Initial terms shall commence on September 1, 2005.

(e)　Cochairs. - The Commission shall have two Cochairs, one senator designated by the President Pro Tempore of the Senate and one representative designated by the Speaker of the House of Representatives from among their respective appointees. The initial terms shall commence on September 1, 2005.

(f)　Vacancies. - A vacancy on the Commission shall be filled in the same manner in which the original appointment was made, and the term shall be for the balance of the unexpired term.

(g)　Compensation. - The Commission members shall receive no salary as a result of serving on the Commission but shall receive per diem, subsistence, and travel expenses in accordance with the provisions of G.S. 120-3.1, 138-5, and 138-6, as applicable. When approved by the Commission, members may be reimbursed for subsistence and travel expenses in excess of the statutory amount.

(h)　Meetings. - The Cochairs shall convene the Commission. Meetings shall be held as often as necessary, but not less than four times a year.

(i)　Quorum. - A majority of the members of the Commission shall constitute a quorum for the transaction of business.

(j)　Staff. - Upon the prior approval of the Legislative Services Commission, the Legislative Services Officer shall assign professional staff to the Commission to aid in its work.

(k)　Reports. - The Commission shall annually report on its activities and recommendations, including any legislative proposals, to the General Assembly. The Commission shall make its first report on or before November 1, 2005.

(l)　Funding. - From funds appropriated to the General Assembly, the Legislative Services Commission shall allocate funds for the purpose of conducting the study provided for in this section. (2005-434, s. 7.)

§ 120-227. Reserved for future codification purposes.

§ 120-228. Reserved for future codification purposes.

§ 120-229. Reserved for future codification purposes.

Article 26.

Joint Legislative Oversight Committee on Information Technology.

§ 120-230. Creation and purpose of the Joint Legislative Oversight Committee on Information Technology.

There is established the Joint Legislative Oversight Committee on Information Technology. The Committee shall review current information technology that impacts public policy, including electronic data processing and telecommunications, software technology, and information processing. The goals and objectives of the Committee shall be to develop electronic commerce in the State and to coordinate the use of information technology by State agencies in a manner that assures that the citizens of the State receive quality services from all State agencies and that the needs of the citizens are met in an efficient and effective manner. The Committee shall examine, on a continuing basis, systemwide issues affecting State government information technology, including, but not limited to, State information technology operations, infrastructure, development, financing, administration, and service delivery. The Committee may examine State agency or enterprise-specific information technology issues. The Committee shall make ongoing recommendations to the General Assembly on ways to improve the effectiveness, efficiency, and quality of State government information technology. (1999-237, s. 22(a); 2004-129, s. 7A(b).)

§ 120-231. Committee duties; reports.

(a)   The Joint Legislative Oversight Committee on Information Technology may:

(1)   Evaluate the current technological infrastructure of State government and information systems use and needs in State government and determine

139

potential demands for additional information staff, equipment, software, data communications, and consulting services in State government during the next 10 years. The evaluation may include an assessment of ways technological infrastructure and information systems use may be leveraged to improve State efficiency and services to the citizens of the State, including an enterprise-wide infrastructure and data architecture.

(2)   Evaluate information technology governance, policy, and management practices, including policies and practices related to personnel and acquisition issues, on both a statewide and project level.

(3)   Study, evaluate, and recommend changes to the North Carolina General Statutes relating to electronic commerce.

(4)   Study, evaluate, and recommend action regarding reports received by the Committee.

(5)   Study, evaluate, and recommend any changes proposed for future development of the information highway system of the State.

(b)   The Committee may consult with the State Chief Information Officer on statewide technology strategies and initiatives and review all legislative proposals and other recommendations of the State Chief Information Officer.

(c)   The Committee shall submit annual reports to the General Assembly on or before the convening of the regular session of the General Assembly each year. The Committee may submit interim reports at any time it deems appropriate. (1999-237, s. 22(a); 2004-129, ss. 7A(c), 36; 2006-264, s. 10.)

§ 120-232. Committee membership; terms; organization; vacancies.

(a)   The Committee shall consist of 16 members as follows:

(1)   Eight members of the Senate at the time of their appointment, appointed by the President Pro Tempore of the Senate. At least two appointees shall be members of the Senate Appropriations Committee.

(2)   Eight members of the House of Representatives at the time of their appointment, appointed by the Speaker of the House of Representatives. At

least two appointees shall be members of the House of Representatives Appropriations Committee.

(3),   (4) Repealed by Session Laws 2004-129, s. 7A(d), effective July 1, 2004.

(b)   Members of the Committee shall serve terms of two years beginning at the convening of the General Assembly in each odd-numbered year, with no prohibition against being reappointed, except initial appointments shall begin on appointment and end on the day of convening of the 2005 General Assembly.

(c)   Members may complete a term of service on the Committee even if they do not seek reelection or are not reelected, but resignation or removal from service constitutes resignation or removal from service on the Committee.

(d)   The President Pro Tempore of the Senate and the Speaker of the House of Representatives shall each select a legislative member from their appointees to serve as cochair of the Committee.

(e)   The Committee shall meet at least once a quarter and may meet at other times upon the call of the cochairs. A majority of the members of the Committee shall constitute a quorum for the transaction of business. The affirmative vote of a majority of the members present at meetings of the Committee shall be necessary for action to be taken by the Committee.

(f)   All members shall serve at the will of their appointing officer. A member continues to serve until the member's successor is appointed. A vacancy shall be filled within 30 days by the officer who made the original appointment. (1999-237, s. 22(a); 2001-486, s. 2.7; 2004-129, s. 7A(d).)

§ 120-233. Assistance; per diem; subsistence; and travel allowances.

(a)   The Committee may contract for consulting services as provided by G.S. 120-32.02. Upon approval of the Legislative Services Commission, the Legislative Services Officer shall assign professional and clerical staff to assist in the work of the Committee. The professional staff shall include the appropriate staff from the Fiscal Research, Research, Legislative Drafting, and Information Systems Divisions of the Legislative Services Office of the General Assembly. Clerical staff shall be furnished to the Committee through the offices of the Senate and the House of Representatives Supervisors of Clerks. The expenses of employment of the clerical staff shall be borne by the Committee. The Committee may meet in the Legislative Building or the Legislative Office Building upon the approval of the Legislative Services Commission.

(b)   Members of the Committee shall receive per diem, subsistence, and travel allowances as follows:

(1)   Committee members who are members of the General Assembly, at the rate established in G.S. 120-3.1.

(2)   Committee members who are officials or employees of the State or of local government agencies, at the rate established in G.S. 138-6.

(3)   All other Committee members, at the rate established in G.S. 138-5. (1999-237, s. 22(a).)

§ 120-234. Committee authority.

The Committee may obtain information and data from all State officers, agents, agencies, and departments, while in discharge of its duties, under G.S. 120-19, as if it were a committee of the General Assembly. The provisions of G.S. 120-19.1 through G.S. 120-19.4 shall apply to the proceedings of the Committee as if it were a committee of the General Assembly. Any cost of providing information to the Committee not covered by G.S. 120-19.3 may be reimbursed by the Committee from funds appropriated to it for its continuing study. (1999-237, s. 22(a).)

§ 120-235. Committee subcommittees; noncommittee membership.

The Committee cochairs may establish subcommittees for the purpose of making special studies pursuant to its duties, and may appoint noncommittee members to serve on each subcommittee as resource persons. Resource persons shall be voting members of the subcommittee and shall receive subsistence and travel expenses in accordance with G.S. 138-5 and G.S. 138-6. (1999-237, s. 22(a).)

§ 120-236. Report on use of mobile devices by executive-branch agencies.

Beginning October 1, 2012, each agency shall report annually to the Chairs of the House of Representatives Committee on Appropriations and the House of Representatives Subcommittee on General Government, the Chairs of the Senate Committee on Appropriations and the Senate Appropriations Committee on General Government and Information Technology, the Joint Legislative Oversight Committee on Information Technology, the Fiscal Research Division, and the Office of State Budget and Management on the following:

(1)   Any changes to agency policies on the use of mobile devices.

(2)   The number and types of new devices issued since the last report.

(3)   The total number of mobile devices issued by the agency.

(4)   The total cost of mobile devices issued by the agency.

(5)   The number of each type of mobile device issued, with the total cost for each type. (2011-145, s. 6A.14(a); 2011-391, s. 11(f); 2012-142, s. 6A.7.)

§ 120-237. Reserved for future codification purposes.

§ 120-238. Reserved for future codification purposes.

§ 120-239. Reserved for future codification purposes.

Article 27.

The Joint Legislative Oversight Committee On Mental Health, Developmental Disabilities, and Substance Abuse Services.

§ 120-240: Repealed by Session Laws 2011-291, s. 1.6(b), effective June 24, 2011.

§ 120-241: Repealed by Session Laws 2011-291, s. 1.6(b), effective June 24, 2011.

§ 120-242: Repealed by Session Laws 2011-291, s. 1.6(b), effective June 24, 2011.

§ 120-243: Repealed by Session Laws 2011-291, s. 1.6(b), effective June 24, 2011.

§ 120-244: Repealed by Session Laws 2011-291, s. 1.6(b), effective June 24, 2011.

Article 28.

Future of the North Carolina Railroad Study Commission.

§ 120-245: Repealed by Session Laws 2011-266, s. 1.22, effective July 1, 2011, and Session Laws 2011-291, s. 1.7(b), effective June 24, 2011.

§ 120-246: Repealed by Session Laws 2011-266, s. 1.22, effective July 1, 2011, and Session Laws 2011-291, s. 1.7(b), effective June 24, 2011.

§ 120-247: Repealed by Session Laws 2011-266, s. 1.22, effective July 1, 2011, and Session Laws 2011-291, s. 1.7(b), effective June 24, 2011.

§ 120-248: Repealed by Session Laws 2011-266, s. 1.22, effective July 1, 2011, and Session Laws 2011-291, s. 1.7(b), effective June 24, 2011.

§ 120-249: Repealed by Session Laws 2011-266, s. 1.22, effective July 1, 2011, and Session Laws 2011-291, s. 1.7(b), effective June 24, 2011.

§ 120-250: Repealed by Session Laws 2011-266, s. 1.22, effective July 1, 2011, and Session Laws 2011-291, s. 1.7(b), effective June 24, 2011.

§ 120-251: Repealed by Session Laws 2011-266, s. 1.22, effective July 1, 2011, and Session Laws 2011-291, s. 1.7(b), effective June 24, 2011.

§ 120-252: Repealed by Session Laws 2011-266, s. 1.22, effective July 1, 2011, and Session Laws 2011-291, s. 1.7(b), effective June 24, 2011.

§ 120-253: Repealed by Session Laws 2011-266, s. 1.22, effective July 1, 2011, and Session Laws 2011-291, s. 1.7(b), effective June 24, 2011.

§ 120-254: Repealed by Session Laws 2011-266, s. 1.22, effective July 1, 2011, and Session Laws 2011-291, s. 1.7(b), effective June 24, 2011.

§ 120-255: Repealed by Session Laws 2011-266, s. 1.22, effective July 1, 2011, and Session Laws 2011-291, s. 1.7(b), effective June 24, 2011.

§ 120-256. Reserved for future codification purposes.

§ 120-257. Reserved for future codification purposes.

Article 29.

Joint Legislative Oversight Committee on Capital Improvements.

§ 120-258: Repealed by Session Laws 2011-291, s. 1.2(b), effective June 24, 2011.

§ 120-259: Repealed by Session Laws 2011-291, s. 1.2(b), effective June 24, 2011.

§ 120-260: Repealed by Session Laws 2011-291, s. 1.2(b), effective June 24, 2011.

§ 120-261. Reserved for future codification purposes.

§ 120-262. Reserved for future codification purposes.

§ 120-263. Reserved for future codification purposes.

§ 120-264. Reserved for future codification purposes.

Article 30.

Joint Legislative Committee on Domestic Violence.

§ 120-265: Repealed by Session Laws 2011-291, s. 1.4(b), effective June 24, 2011.

§ 120-266: Repealed by Session Laws 2011-291, s. 1.4(b), effective June 24, 2011.

§ 120-267: Repealed by Session Laws 2011-291, s. 1.4(b), effective June 24, 2011.

§ 120-268. Reserved for future codification purposes.

§ 120-269. Reserved for future codification purposes.

Article 31.

Miscellaneous.

§ 120-270. Report by State agencies to the General Assembly on ways to reduce incidence of identity theft.

Agencies of the State shall evaluate the agency's efforts to reduce the dissemination of personal identifying information, as defined in G.S. 14-113.20(b). The evaluation shall include the review of public forms, the use of random personal identification numbers, restriction of access to personal identifying information, and reduction of use of personal identifying information when it is not necessary. Special attention shall be given to the use, collection, and dissemination of social security numbers. If the collection of a social security number is found to be unwarranted, the State agency shall immediately discontinue the collection of social security numbers for that purpose. Any agency that determines that an act of the General Assembly or other provision of law impedes the agency's ability to reduce the incidence of identity theft shall report such findings to the General Assembly by January 1 of the year following such a determination. (2005-414, s. 5; 2012-187, s. 10.2.)

§ 120-271. Use of likenesses of any seal or coat of arms of the Senate.

(a)   Whoever, except as directed by the Senate or the Principal Clerk of the Senate on its behalf, knowingly uses, manufactures, reproduces, sells, or purchases for resale, either separately or appended to any article manufactured or sold, any likeness of any seal or coat of arms of the Senate, or any substantial part thereof, except for manufacture or sale of the article for the official use of the State of North Carolina, shall be guilty of a Class 2 misdemeanor.

(b)   A violation of this section may be enjoined at the suit of the Attorney General. (2007-354, s. 1.)

§ 120-272: Reserved for future codification purposes.

§ 120-273: Reserved for future codification purposes.

§ 120-274: Reserved for future codification purposes.

Article 32.

Joint Legislative Commission on the Department of Transportation Disadvantaged Minority-Owned and Women-Owned Businesses Program.

§ 120-275. (Effective until June 30, 2015) Commission established.

There is established the Joint Legislative Commission on the Department of Transportation Disadvantaged Minority-Owned and Women-Owned Businesses Program. (2006-261, s. 5.)

§ 120-276. (Effective until June 30, 2015) Membership; terms.

(a)   Membership. - The Commission shall be composed of 12 members as follows:

(1)   Five members of the House of Representatives appointed by the Speaker of the House.

(2)   Five members of the Senate appointed by the President Pro Tempore of the Senate.

(3)   The Senate and House cochairs of the Joint Legislative Transportation Oversight Committee, or their designees, shall serve as ex officio members.

147

(b)   Terms. - Members of the Commission shall serve two-year terms, beginning July 1 of each odd-numbered year. Members shall serve at the pleasure of the appointing authority. Members may complete a term of service on the Commission even if they do not seek reelection or are not reelected to the General Assembly, but resignation or removal from service in the General Assembly constitutes resignation or removal from the Commission.

(c)   Vacancies. - Vacancies on the Commission shall be filled by the appointing authority. (2006-261, s. 5.)

§ 120-277. (Effective until June 30, 2015) Duties of the Commission.

The Commission shall:

(1)   Monitor the implementation, and assess and evaluate the effectiveness, of the Department of Transportation program under G.S. 136-28.4.

(2)   Review the strategies the Department of Transportation plans to use to implement the requirements of G.S. 136-28.4.

(3)   Develop recommendations for submittal to the Department of Transportation or the General Assembly to improve the program under G.S. 136-28.4. (2006-261, s. 5.)

§ 120-278. (Effective until June 30, 2015) Department of Transportation reporting.

The Department of Transportation shall report quarterly to the Commission on the status of the program under G.S. 136-28.4 and efforts made to achieve the goals of the program. (2006-261, s. 5.)

§ 120-279. (Effective until June 30, 2015) Organization of Commission.

(a)   The President Pro Tempore of the Senate and the Speaker of the House of Representatives shall each designate a cochair of the Joint Legislative

Commission on the Department of Transportation Disadvantaged Minority-Owned and Women-Owned Businesses Program. The Commission shall meet upon the joint call of the cochairs.

(b)   A quorum of the Commission is seven members. No action may be taken except by a majority vote at a meeting at which a quorum is present. While in the discharge of its official duties, the Commission has the powers of a joint commission under G.S. 120-19 and G.S. 120-19.1 through G.S. 120-19.4.

(c)   Members of the Commission receive subsistence and travel expenses as provided in G.S. 120-3.1. The Commission may contract for consultants or hire employees in accordance with G.S. 120-32.02. The Legislative Services Commission, through the Legislative Services Officer, shall assign professional staff to assist the Commission in its work. Upon the direction of the Legislative Services Commission, the Directors of Legislative Assistants of the Senate and of the House of Representatives shall assign clerical staff to the Commission. The expenses for clerical employees shall be borne by the Commission. (2006-261, s. 5.)

Article 33.

Joint Legislative Commission on Energy Policy.

§ 120-285. Creation and membership of Joint Legislative Commission on Energy Policy.

(a)   The Joint Legislative Commission on Energy Policy is established.

(b)   The Commission shall consist of 10 members as follows:

(1)   Five members of the Senate appointed by the President Pro Tempore of the Senate, at least one of whom is a member of the minority party.

(2)   Five members of the House of Representatives appointed by the Speaker of the House of Representatives, at least one of whom is a member of the minority party.

(c)   Terms on the Commission are for two years and begin on the convening of the General Assembly in each odd-numbered year. Members may complete a term of service on the Commission even if they do not seek reelection or are not reelected to the General Assembly, but resignation or removal from service in the General Assembly constitutes resignation or removal from service on the Commission. A member continues to serve until the member's successor is appointed. (2012-143, s. 6(a).)

§ 120-286. Purpose and powers and duties of Commission.

(a)   The Joint Legislative Commission on Energy Policy shall exercise legislative oversight over energy policy in the State. In the exercise of this oversight, the Commission may do any of the following:

(1)   Monitor and evaluate the programs, policies, and actions of the Mining and Energy Commission established pursuant to G.S. 143B-293.1, the Energy Policy Council established pursuant to G.S. 113B-2, the Energy Division in the Department of Commerce, the Utilities Commission and Public Staff established pursuant to Chapter 62 of the General Statutes, and of any other board, commission, department, or agency of the State or local government with jurisdiction over energy policy in the State.

(2)   Review and evaluate existing and proposed State statutes and rules affecting energy policy and determine whether any modification of these statutes or rules is in the public interest.

(3)   Monitor changes in federal law and court decisions affecting energy policy.

(4)   Monitor and evaluate energy-related industries in the State and study measures to promote these industries.

(5)   Study any other matters related to energy policy that the Commission considers necessary to fulfill its mandate.

(b)   The Commission may make reports and recommendations, including proposed legislation, to the General Assembly from time to time as to any matter relating to its oversight and the powers and duties set out in this section. (2012-143, s. 6(a).)

§ 120-287. Organization of Commission.

(a)   The President Pro Tempore of the Senate and the Speaker of the House of Representatives shall each designate a cochair of the Joint Legislative Commission on Energy Policy. The Commission may meet at any time upon the call of either cochair, whether or not the General Assembly is in session.

(b)   A quorum of the Commission is six members.

(c)   While in the discharge of its official duties, the Commission has the powers of a joint committee under G.S. 120-19 and G.S. 120-19.1 through G.S. 120-19.4. The Commission may contract for consultants or hire employees in accordance with G.S. 120-32.02.

(d)   From funds available to the General Assembly, the Legislative Services Commission shall allocate monies to fund the Joint Legislative Commission on Energy Policy. Members of the Commission receive subsistence and travel expenses as provided in G.S. 120-3.1. The Legislative Services Commission, through the Legislative Services Officer, shall assign professional staff to assist the Commission in its work. Upon the direction of the Legislative Services Commission, the Supervisors of Clerks of the Senate and of the House of Representatives shall assign clerical staff to the Commission. The expenses for clerical employees shall be borne by the Commission. (2012-143, s. 6(a).)

Chapter 120C.

Lobbying.

Article 1.

General Provisions.

§§ 120C-1 through 120C-99: Reserved for future codification purposes.

§ 120C-100. Definitions.

(a)   As used in this Article, the following terms mean:

(1)   Commission. - The State Ethics Commission under Chapter 138A of the General Statutes.

(2)   Designated individual. - A legislator, legislative employee, or public servant.

(3)   Executive action. - The preparation, research, drafting, development, consideration, modification, amendment, adoption, approval, tabling, postponement, defeat, or rejection of a policy, guideline, request for proposal, procedure, regulation, or rule by a public servant purporting to act in an official capacity. This term does not include any of the following:

a.   Present, prior, or possible proceedings of a contested case hearing under Chapter 150B of the General Statutes, of a judicial nature, or of a quasi-judicial nature.

b.   A public servant's communication with a person, or another person on that person's behalf, with respect to any of the following:

1.   Applying for a permit, license, determination of eligibility, or certification.

2.   Making an inquiry about or asserting a benefit, claim, right, obligation, duty, entitlement, payment, or penalty.

3.   Making an inquiry about or responding to a request for proposal made under Chapter 143 of the General Statutes.

4.   Ratemaking.

c.   Internal administrative functions, including those functions exempted from the definition of "rule" in G.S. 150B-2(8a).

d.   Ministerial functions.

e.   A public servant's communication with a person or another person on that person's behalf with respect to public comments made at an open meeting, or submitted as written comment, on a proposed executive action in response to a request for public comment, provided the identity of the person on whose behalf the comments are made is disclosed as part of the public participation, and no reportable expenditure is made.

(4)	In session. - One of the following:

a.	The General Assembly is in extra session from the date the General Assembly convenes until the General Assembly:

1.	Adjourns sine die.

2.	Recesses or adjourns for more than 10 days.

b.	The General Assembly is in regular session from the date set by law or resolution that the General Assembly convenes until the General Assembly:

1.	Adjourns sine die.

2.	Recesses or adjourns for more than 10 days.

(5)	Legislative action. - The preparation, research, drafting, introduction, consideration, modification, amendment, approval, passage, enactment, tabling, postponement, defeat, or rejection of a bill, resolution, amendment, motion, report, nomination, appointment, or other matter, whether or not the matter is identified by an official title, general title, or other specific reference, by a legislator or legislative employee acting or purporting to act in an official capacity. It also includes the consideration of any bill by the Governor for the Governor's approval or veto under Article II, Section 22(1) of the Constitution or for the Governor to allow the bill to become law under Article II, Section 22(7) of the Constitution.

(6)	Legislative employee. - Employees and officers of the General Assembly, consultants and counsel to committees of either house of the General Assembly or of legislative commissions, who are paid by State funds, and students at an accredited law school while in an externship program at the General Assembly approved by the Legislative Services Commission, but not including legislators, members of the Council of State, nonsupervisory employees of the Administrative Division's Facility Maintenance and Food Services staff, or pages.

(7)	Legislator. - As defined in G.S. 138A-3 and G.S. 120C-104.

(8)	Liaison personnel. - Any State employee, counsel employed under G.S. 147-17, or officer whose principal duties, in practice or as set forth in that individual's job description, include lobbying legislators or legislative employees.

153

(9)   Lobby or Lobbying. - Any of the following:

a.   Influencing or attempting to influence legislative or executive action, or both, through direct communication or activities with a designated individual or that designated individual's immediate family.

b.   Developing goodwill through communications or activities, including the building of relationships, with a designated individual or that designated individual's immediate family with the intention of influencing current or future legislative or executive action, or both.

The terms "lobby" or "lobbying" do not include communications or activities as part of a business, civic, religious, fraternal, personal, or commercial relationship which is not connected to legislative or executive action, or both.

(10)   Lobbyist. - An individual who engages in lobbying for payment and meets any of the following criteria:

a.   Repealed by Session Laws 2007-348, s. 8(a), effective October 10, 2007.

b.   Represents another person or governmental unit, but is not directly employed by that person or governmental unit.

c.   Contracts for payment for lobbying.

d.   Is employed by a person and a significant part of that employee's duties include lobbying. In no case shall an employee be considered a lobbyist if in no 30-day period less than five percent (5%) of that employee's actual duties include engaging in lobbying as defined in subdivision (9)a. of this section or if in no 30-day period less than five percent (5%) of that employee's actual duties include engaging in lobbying as defined in subdivision (9)b. of this section.

The term "lobbyist" shall not include individuals who are specifically exempted from this Chapter by G.S. 120C-700 or registered as liaison personnel under Article 5 of this Chapter.

(11)   Lobbyist principal and principal. - The person or governmental unit on whose behalf the lobbyist lobbies and who makes payment for the lobbying. In the case where a lobbyist is paid by a law firm, consulting firm, or other entity retained by a person or governmental unit for lobbying, the principal is the

154

person or governmental unit whose interests the lobbyist represents in lobbying. In the case of a lobbyist employed or retained by an association or other organization, the lobbyist principal is the association or other organization, not the individual members of the association or other organization.

The term "lobbyist principal" shall not include those designating registered liaison personnel under Article 5 of this Chapter.

(11a)   through (11j) Reserved for future codification purposes.

(11k)   Payment. - Any money, thing of value, or economic benefit conveyed to the lobbyist for lobbying, other than reimbursement of actual travel, administrative expenses, or subsistence.

(12)   Reportable expenditure. - Any of the following that directly or indirectly is made to, at the request of, for the benefit of, or on the behalf of a designated individual or that individual's immediate family member:

a.   Any advance, contribution, conveyance, deposit, distribution, payment, gift, retainer, fee, salary, honorarium, reimbursement, loan, pledge, or thing of value greater than ten dollars ($10.00) per designated individual per single calendar day.

b.   A contract, agreement, promise, or other obligation whether or not legally enforceable.

(13)   Solicitation of others. - A solicitation of members of the public to communicate directly with or contact one or more designated individuals to influence or attempt to influence legislative or executive action to further the solicitor's position on that legislative or executive action, when that request is made by any of the following methods:

a.   A broadcast, cable, or satellite transmission.

b.   An e-mail communication or a Web site posting.

c.   A communication delivered by print media as defined in G.S. 163-278.38Z.

d.   A letter or other written communication delivered by mail or by comparable delivery service.

155

e.   Telephone.

f.   A communication at a conference, meeting, or similar event.

The term "solicitation of others" does not include communications made by a person or by the person's agent to that person's stockholders, employees, board members, officers, members, subscribers, or other recipients who have affirmatively assented to receive the person's regular publications or notices.

(b)   Except as otherwise defined in this section, the definitions in Article 1 of Chapter 138A of the General Statutes apply in this Chapter. (1933, c. 11, s. 1; 1975, c. 820, s. 1; 1991, c. 740, s. 1.1; 2001-424, s. 6.10(b); 2005-456, s. 1.; 2006-201, s. 18; 2007-347, s. 6(b); 2007-348, ss. 7, 8(a), (b); 2008-213, ss. 4-8, 90; 2009-129, s. 3; 2010-169, s. 17(a)-(e).)

§ 120C-101. Rules and forms.

(a)   The Commission shall adopt any rules or definitions necessary to interpret the provisions of this Chapter and adopt any rules necessary to administer the provisions of this Chapter, except for Articles 2, 4 and 8 of this Chapter. The Secretary of State shall adopt any rules, orders, and forms as are necessary to administer the provisions of Articles 2, 4 and 8 of this Chapter. The Secretary of State may appoint a council to advise the Secretary in adopting rules under this section.

(b)   With respect to the forms adopted under subsection (a) of this section, the Secretary of State shall adopt rules to protect from disclosure all confidential information under Chapter 132 of the General Statutes related to economic development initiatives or to industrial or business recruitment activities. The information shall remain confidential until the State, a unit of local government, or the business has announced a commitment by the business to expand or locate a specific project in this State or a final decision not to do so, and the business has communicated that commitment or decision to the State or local government agency involved with the project.

(c)   In adopting rules under this Chapter, the Commission is exempt from the requirements of Article 2A of Chapter 150B of the General Statutes, except that the Commission shall comply with G.S. 150B-21.2(d). At least 30 business days prior to adopting a rule, the Commission shall:

(1)   Publish the proposed rules in the North Carolina Register.

(2)   Submit the rule and a notice of public hearing to the Codifier of Rules, and the Codifier of Rules shall publish the proposed rule and the notice of public hearing on the Internet to be posted within five business days.

(3)   Notify those on the mailing list maintained in accordance with G.S. 150B-21.2(d) and any other interested parties of its intent to adopt a rule and of the public hearing.

(4)   Accept written comments on the proposed rule for at least 15 business days prior to adoption of the rule.

(5)   Hold at least one public hearing on the proposed rule no less than five days after the rule and notice have been published.

A rule adopted under this subsection becomes effective the first day of the month following the month the final rule is submitted to the Codifier of Rules for entry into the North Carolina Administrative Code, and applies prospectively. A rule adopted by the Commission that does not comply with the procedural requirements of this subsection shall be null, void, and without effect. For purposes of this subsection, a rule is any Commission regulation, standard, or statement of general applicability that interprets an enactment by the General Assembly or Congress, or a regulation adopted by a federal agency, or that describes the procedure or practice requirements of the Commission.

(d)   For purposes of G.S. 150B-21.3(b2), a written objection filed by the Commission to a rule adopted by the Secretary of State pursuant to this Chapter shall be deemed written objections from 10 or more persons under that statute. Notwithstanding G.S. 150B-21.3(b2), a rule adopted by the Secretary of State pursuant to this Chapter objected to by the Commission under this subsection shall not become effective until an act of the General Assembly approving the rule has become law. If the General Assembly does not approve a rule under this subsection by the day of adjournment of the next regular session of the General Assembly that begins at least 25 days after the date the Rules Review Commission approves the rule, the permanent rule shall not become effective and any temporary rule associated with the permanent rule expires. If the General Assembly fails to approve a rule by the day of adjournment, the Secretary of State may initiate rulemaking for a new permanent rule, including by the adoption of a temporary rule. (1991, c. 740, s. 1.1; 2005-456, s. 1; 2006-201, s. 18; 2007-348, s. 9; 2008-213, s. 9; 2010-169, s. 16.)

§ 120C-102. Request for advice.

(a)   At the request of any person, State agency, or governmental unit affected by this Chapter, the Commission shall render advice on specific questions involving the meaning and application of this Chapter and that person's, State agency's, or any governmental unit's compliance therewith. Requests for advice and advice rendered in response to those requests shall relate to real or reasonably anticipated fact settings or circumstances.

(a1)   A request for a formal opinion under subsection (a) of this section shall be in writing, electronic or otherwise. The Commission shall issue formal advisory opinions having prospective application only. An individual, State agency, or governmental unit who relies upon the advice provided to that individual, State agency, or governmental unit on a specific matter addressed by a requested formal advisory opinion shall be immune from all of the following:

(1)   Investigation by the Commission.

(2)   Any adverse action by the employing entity.

(3)   Investigation by the Secretary of State.

(b)   Staff to the Commission may issue advice, but not formal advisory opinions, under procedures adopted by the Commission.

(c)   The Commission shall publish its formal advisory opinions within 30 days of issuance, edited as necessary to protect the identities of the individuals requesting opinions.

(d)   Except as provided under subsections (c) and (d1) of this section, a request for advice, any advice provided by Commission staff, any formal advisory opinions, any supporting documents submitted or caused to be submitted to the Commission or Commission staff, and any documents prepared or collected by the Commission or the Commission staff in connection with a request for advice are confidential. The identity of the individual, State agency, or governmental unit making the request for advice, the existence of the request, and any information related to the request may not be revealed without the consent of the requestor. An individual, State agency, or governmental unit who requests advice or receives advice, including a formal advisory opinion, may authorize the release to any other person, the State, or any governmental unit of the request, the advice, or any supporting documents.

For purposes of this section, "document" is as defined in G.S. 120-129. Requests for advice, any advice, and any documents related to requests for advice are not "public records" as defined in G.S. 132-1.

(d1)   Staff to the Commission may share all information and documents related to requests under subsection (a) and (a1) of this section with staff of the Office of the Secretary of State. The information and documents in the possession of the staff of the Office of the Secretary of State shall remain confidential and not public records. The Commission shall forward an unedited copy of each formal advisory opinion under this section to the Secretary of State at the time the formal advisory opinion is issued to the requestor, and the Secretary of State shall treat that unedited advisory opinion as confidential and not a public record.

(e)   Requests for advisory opinions may be withdrawn by the requestor at any time prior to the issuance of a formal advisory opinion. (2006-201, s. 18; 2007-348, s. 10; 2008-213, s. 2(c); 2009-570, s. 14.)

§ 120C-103. Lobbying education program.

(a)   The Commission shall develop and implement a lobbying education and awareness program designed to instill in all designated individuals, lobbyists, and lobbyists' principals a keen and continuing awareness of their obligations and sensitivity to situations that might result in real or potential violation of this Chapter or other related laws. The Commission shall make basic lobbying education and awareness presentations to all designated individuals upon their election, appointment, or hiring and shall offer periodic refresher presentations as the Commission deems appropriate. Every designated individual shall participate in a lobbying presentation approved by the Commission within six months of the designated individual's election, appointment, or hiring and shall attend refresher lobbying education presentations at least every two years thereafter in a manner the Commission deems appropriate. The Commission shall also make lobbying education and awareness programs available to lobbyists and lobbyists' principals. Upon request, the Commission shall assist each agency in developing in-house education programs and procedures necessary or desirable to meet the agency's particular needs for lobbying education.

(a1)   A designated individual appointed to a board determined and designated as nonadvisory under G.S. 138A-10(a)(3) by the Commission shall attend lobbying education and awareness programs within six months of notification of the designation by the Commission and at least every two years thereafter in a manner as the Commission deems appropriate.

(b)   The Commission shall publish a newsletter containing summaries of the advisory opinions, policies, procedures, and interpretive bulletins as issued from time to time, but no less than once per year. The newsletter shall be distributed to all designated individuals, lobbyists, and lobbyists' principals. Publication under this subsection may be done electronically.

(c)   The Commission shall assemble and maintain a collection of relevant State laws, rules, and regulations that set forth lobbying standards applicable to designated individuals. The collection of laws, rules, and regulations shall be made available electronically as resource material to designated individuals, lobbyists, and lobbyists' principals upon request. (2006-201, s. 18; 2008-213, s. 11; 2009-549, s. 2.)

§ 120C-104. Chapter applies to candidates for certain offices.

For purposes of this Chapter, the term "legislator" as defined in G.S. 120C-100(7) and the term "public servant" as defined in G.S. 138A-3(30)a. shall include an individual having filed a notice of candidacy for such office under G.S. 163-106 or Article 11 of Chapter 163 of the General Statutes or nominated under G.S. 163-114 or G.S. 163-98. (2006-201, s. 18; 2008-213, s. 12.)

§§ 120C-105 through 120C-199. Reserved for future codification purposes.

Article 2.

Registration.

§ 120C-200. Lobbyist registration procedure.

(a)   A lobbyist shall file a separate registration statement for each principal the lobbyist represents with the Secretary of State before engaging in any lobbying. It shall be unlawful for an individual to lobby without registering within one business day of engaging in any lobbying as defined in G.S. 120C-100(9) unless exempted by this Chapter.

(b)   The form of the registration shall be prescribed by the Secretary of State, be filed electronically, and shall include the registrant's full name, firm, complete address, and telephone number; the registrant's place of business; the full name, complete address, and telephone number of each principal the lobbyist represents; and a general description of the matters on which the registrant expects to act as a lobbyist.

(c)   Each lobbyist shall electronically file an amended registration form with the Secretary of State no later than 10 business days after any change in the information supplied in the lobbyist's last registration under subsection (b) of this section. Each supplementary registration shall include a complete statement of the information that has changed.

(d)   Unless a resignation is filed under G.S. 120C-210, each registration statement of a lobbyist required under this Chapter shall be effective from the date of filing until January 1 of the following year. The lobbyist shall file a new registration statement after that date, and the applicable fee shall be due and payable.

(e)   Each lobbyist shall identify himself or herself as a lobbyist prior to engaging in lobbying communications or activities with a designated individual. The lobbyist shall also disclose the identity of the lobbyist principal connected to that lobbying communication or activity.

(f)   In addition to the information required for registration under subsection (b) of this section, former employees of a State agency who register as a lobbyist within six months after voluntary separation or separation for cause from employment with a State agency shall also indicate which State agency with which the former employee was employed. (1933, c. 11, s. 2; 1973, c. 1451; 1975, c. 820, s. 1; 1983, c. 713, s. 51; 1991, c. 740, s. 1.1; 2004-203, s. 50(a); 2006-201, s. 18; 2008-213, ss. 13, 90; 2009-549, s. 3; 2010-169, s. 4(c); 2013-360, s. 27.1(c).)

§ 120C-201. Lobbyist's registration fee.

(a) A fee of two hundred fifty dollars ($250.00) is due and payable to the Secretary of State at the time of each lobbyist registration. Fees so collected shall be deposited in the General Fund of the State. The fees required under this section shall be paid electronically.

(b) Repealed by Session Laws 2013-360, s. 27.1(a), effective August 1, 2013. (1975, c. 852, s. 1; 1983, c. 713, s. 50; 1991, c. 740, s. 1.1; 2002-126, s. 29A.33; 2005-456, s. 1; 2006-201, s. 18; 2013-360, s. 27.1(a), (d).)

§ 120C-202. Reserved for future codification purposes.

§ 120C-203. Reserved for future codification purposes.

§ 120C-204. Reserved for future codification purposes.

§ 120C-205. Reserved for future codification purposes.

§ 120C-206. Lobbyist principal's authorization.

(a) A written authorization signed by the lobbyist principal authorizing the lobbyist to represent the principal shall be filed with the Secretary of State within 20 business days after the lobbyist's registration. If the written authorization is filed more than 20 business days after the lobbyist's registration and before January 1 of the following year, the lobbyist registration is effective from the date of filing of the lobbyist registration and all reports due under Article 4 of this Chapter shall be filed.

(b) The form of the written authorization shall be prescribed by the Secretary of State, be filed electronically, and shall include the lobbyist principal's full name, complete address, and telephone number, name and title of any official authorized to sign for the lobbyist principal, and the name of each lobbyist registered to represent that principal.

(c)   An amended authorization shall be electronically filed with the Secretary of State no later than 10 business days after any change in the information on the principal's authorization. Each supplementary authorization shall include a complete statement of the information that has changed. (1933, c. 11, s. 4; 1961, c. 1151; 1975, c. 820, s. 1; 1991, c. 740, s. 1.1; 2005-456, s. 1; 2006-201, s. 18; 2007-347, s. 4; 2008-213, s. 90; 2009-549, s. 4; 2013-360, s. 27.1(e).)

§ 120C-207. Lobbyist principal's fees.

(a)   A fee of two hundred fifty dollars ($250.00) is due and payable to the Secretary of State at the time the principal's first authorization statement is filed each calendar year for a lobbyist. Fees so collected shall be deposited in the General Fund of the State. The fees required under this section shall be paid electronically.

(b)   Repealed by Session Laws 2013-360, s. 27.1(b), effective August 1, 2013. (1933, c. 11, s. 4; 1961, c. 1151; 1975, c. 820, s. 1; 1991, c. 740, s. 1.1; 2005-456, s. 1; 2006-201, s. 18; 2008-213, s. 90; 2013-360, s. 27.1(b), (f).)

§ 120C-208. Reserved for future codification purposes.

§ 120C-209. Reserved for future codification purposes.

§ 120C-210. Resignation and termination.

(a)   A registration of a lobbyist under G.S. 120C-200 and the written authorization of that lobbyist principal under G.S. 120C-206 are terminated upon the filing of either a lobbyist resignation or a principal termination with the Secretary of State, whichever occurs first.

(b)   Lobbyist resignations and lobbyist principal terminations are effective upon filing. (2009-549, s. 5.)

163

§ 120C-211. Reserved for future codification purposes.

§ 120C-212. Reserved for future codification purposes.

§ 120C-213. Reserved for future codification purposes.

§ 120C-214. Reserved for future codification purposes.

§ 120C-215. Other persons required to register.

(a)   A person not otherwise required to register under this Chapter shall register and report when the total expense incurred for solicitation of others exceeds three thousand dollars ($3,000) during any 90-day period. Expenses incurred shall mean the costs of producing and transmitting the communication and, if the communication is made at a conference, meeting, or similar event, the costs of planning, hosting, sponsoring, and attending the conference, meeting, or similar event.

(b)   A person required to register and report under this section shall be referred to as a "solicitor" for purposes of this Chapter.

(c)   No fee shall be charged for registering as a solicitor.

(d)   For purposes of this section, "incur" means the point at which a binding obligation arises. (2006-201, s. 18; 2007-348, s. 11.)

§ 120C-216. Reserved for future codification purposes.

§ 120C-217. Reserved for future codification purposes.

§ 120C-218. Reserved for future codification purposes.

§ 120C-219. Reserved for future codification purposes.

§ 120C-220. Publication and availability of registrations.

(a)   The Secretary of State shall make available as soon as practicable the registrations of the lobbyists and liaison personnel in an electronic, searchable format.

(b)   The Secretary of State shall make available as soon as practicable the authorizations of the lobbyists' principals in an electronic, searchable format.

(c)   The Secretary of State shall make available as soon as practicable the registrations of other persons required by this Chapter to file a registration in an electronic, searchable format.

(d)   Within 20 days after the convening of each session of the General Assembly, the Secretary of State shall furnish each designated individual and the State Legislative Library a list of all persons who have registered as lobbyists and whom they represent. A supplemental list of lobbyists shall be furnished periodically every 20 days while the General Assembly is in session and every 60 days thereafter. For each special session of the General Assembly, a supplemental list of lobbyists shall be furnished to the State Legislative Library.

(e)   All lists required by this section may be furnished electronically. (2006-201, s. 18; 2008-213, s. 15.)

§§ 120C-221 through 120C-299. Reserved for future codification purposes.

Article 3.

Prohibitions and Restrictions.

§ 120C-300. Contingency fees prohibited.

(a)   No individual shall act as a lobbyist and receive payment for lobbying that is dependent upon the result or outcome of any legislative or executive action.

(b)   This section shall not apply to an individual doing business with the State who is engaged in sales with respect to that business with the State whose regular remuneration agreement includes commissions based on those sales. For purposes of this subsection, the term "regular remuneration" means

165

any money, thing of value, or economic benefit conferred on or received by the individual in return for services rendered or to be rendered by that individual or another.

(c)   Any payment to a lobbyist in violation of this section is subject to forfeiture and shall be paid into the Civil Penalty and Forfeiture Fund. (1933, c. 11, s. 3; 1975, c. 820, s. 1; 1991, c. 740, s. 1.1; 2005-456, s. 1; 2006-201, s. 18; 2008-213, s. 16; 2010-169, s. 17(f).)

§ 120C-301. Election influence prohibited.

(a)   No person shall attempt to influence the action of any designated individual by the promise of financial support of the designated individual's candidacy, or by threat of financial support in opposition to the designated individual's candidacy in any future election.

(b)   No lobbyist, lobbyist principal, or other person required to register under this Chapter shall attempt to influence the action of any designated individual by the promise of financial support of the designated individual's candidacy, or by threat of financial support in opposition to the designated individual's candidacy in any future election. (1933, c. 11, s. 3; 1975, c. 820, s. 1; 1991, c. 740, s. 1.1; 2005-456, s. 1; 2006-201, s. 18; 2008-213, s. 90.)

§ 120C-302: Recodified as G.S. 163-278.13C, by Session Laws 2007-347, s. 5(a), effective August 9, 2007.

§ 120C-303. Gifts by lobbyists and lobbyist principals prohibited.

(a)   Except as provided in subsection (b) of this section, no lobbyist or lobbyist principal may do any of the following:

(1)   Knowingly give a gift to a designated individual.

(2)   Knowingly give a gift with the intent that a designated individual be an ultimate recipient.

(b)   Subsection (a) of this section shall not apply to gifts as described in G.S. 138A-32(e).

(c)   The offering or giving of a gift in compliance with this Chapter without corrupt intent shall not constitute a violation of the statutes related to bribery under G.S. 14-217, 14-218, or 120-86, but shall be subject to civil fines under G.S. 120C-602(b).

(d)   Gifts made to a nonpartisan state, regional, national, or international legislative organization of which the General Assembly is a member or a legislator or legislative employee is a member or participant of by virtue of that legislator's or legislative employee's public position, or to an affiliated organization of that nonpartisan state, regional, national, or international organization, shall not constitute a violation of subdivision (a)(2) of this section or of G.S. 138A-32(c).

(e)   Gifts made to a nonpartisan state, regional, national, or international organization of which a public servant's agency is a member or a public servant is a member or participant of by virtue of that public servant's public position, or to an affiliated organization of that nonpartisan state, regional, national, or international organization, shall not constitute a violation of subdivision (a)(2) of this section or of G.S. 138A-32(c). (2006-201, s. 18; 2007-348, s. 12(a), (b); 2008-213, ss. 17-19, 90; 2010-169, s. 15(a).)

§ 120C-304. Restrictions.

(a)   No legislator or former legislator may register as a lobbyist under this Chapter:

(1)   While in office.

(2)   Before the later of the close of session as set forth in G.S. 120C-100(a)(4)b.1 in which the legislator served or six months after leaving office.

(b)   No public servant or former public servant as defined in G.S. 138A-3(30)a. may register as a lobbyist under this Chapter while in office or within six months after leaving office.

(c)   No public servant or former public servant as defined in G.S. 138A-3(30)c. may register as a lobbyist under this Chapter within six months after separation from employment as a public servant. No other employee of any State agency may register as a lobbyist under this Chapter to lobby the State agency that previously employed the former employee within six months after voluntary separation or separation for cause from that State agency.

(d)   No individual registered as a lobbyist under this Chapter shall serve as a treasurer as defined in G.S. 163-278.6(19) or an assistant campaign treasurer for a political committee for the election of a member of the General Assembly or a Constitutional officer of the State.

(e)   A lobbyist shall not be eligible for appointment by a State official to, or service on, any body created under the laws of this State that has regulatory authority over the activities of a person or governmental unit that the lobbyist currently represents or has represented within 120 days after the expiration of the lobbyist's registration representing that person or governmental unit. Nothing herein shall be construed to prohibit appointment by any unit of local government.

(f)   Any appointment or registration made in violation of this section shall be void. (2005-456, s. 1; 2006-201, s. 18; 2007-348, s. 13(a); 2008-213, ss. 20, 21; 2010-169, s. 4(a), (b).)

§ 120C-305. Prohibition on the use of cash or credit of the lobbyist.

No lobbyist or another acting on the lobbyist's behalf shall lobby by permitting a designated individual, or that designated individual's immediate family member, to use the cash or credit of the lobbyist unless the lobbyist is in attendance at the time of the reportable expenditure. G.S. 120C-303 applies to this section. (2006-201, s. 18; 2008-213, s. 22; 2010-169, s. 17(g).)

§§ 120C-306 through 120C-399. Reserved for future codification purposes.

Article 4.

168

Reporting.

§ 120C-400. Reporting of reportable expenditures.

(a)   For purposes of this Chapter, all reportable expenditures made for lobbying shall be reported, including the following:

(1)   Reportable expenditures benefiting or made on behalf of a designated individual in the regular course of that designated individual's employment.

(1a)   Reportable expenditures benefiting or made on behalf of a designated individual's immediate family member in the regular course of that immediate family member's employment.

(2)   Contractual arrangements or direct business relationships between a lobbyist or lobbyist principal and a designated individual, or that designated individual's immediate family member, in effect during the reporting period or the previous 12 months.

(3)   Reportable expenditures reimbursed to a lobbyist in the ordinary course of business by the lobbyist principal or other employer.

(b)   This section shall not apply to any reportable expenditure of cash, a cash equivalent, or a fixed asset made directly to a State agency that maintains an accounting of the reportable expenditure that is a public record. (2005-456, s. 1; 2006-201, s. 18; 2007-348, s. 14; 2008-213, ss. 23, 90; 2010-169, s. 17(h).)

§ 120C-401. Reporting generally.

(a)   Reports shall be filed whether or not reportable expenditures are made and shall be due 15 business days after the end of the reporting period.

(b)   For reportable expenditures, each report shall set forth all of the following:

(1)   The fair market value or face value if shown.

(2)   The date of the reportable expenditure.

(3)   A description of the reportable expenditure.

(4)   The name and address of the payee or beneficiary.

(5)   The name of any designated individual or that designated individual's immediate family member connected with the reportable expenditure.

(b1)   For purposes of subdivision (b)(5) of this section, when more than 15 designated individuals benefit from or request a reportable expenditure, no names of individuals need be reported provided that the report identifies the approximate number of designated individuals benefiting or requesting and the basis for their selection, including the name of the legislative body, committee, caucus, or other group whose membership list is a matter of public record in accordance with G.S. 132-1 or including a description of the group that clearly distinguishes its purpose or composition from the general membership of the General Assembly. The approximate number of immediate family members of designated individuals who benefited from the reportable expenditure shall be listed separately.

(b2)   For purposes of subdivision (b)(5) of this section, when the reportable expenditure is a gift given with the intent that a designated individual be the ultimate recipient and the lobbyist or lobbyist principal does not know the name or names of the designated individuals, the lobbyist or lobbyist principal shall report a description of the designated individuals and those designated individuals' immediate family members connected with the reportable expenditure that clearly distinguishes its purpose or composition, and an approximate number, if known.

(c)   Reportable expenditures shall be reported using the following categories:

(1)   Transportation and lodging.

(2)   Entertainment.

(3)   Food and beverages.

(4)   Meetings and events.

(5)   Gifts.

170

(6)   Other reportable expenditures.

(d)   Each report required by this Article shall be in the form prescribed by the Secretary of State and filed electronically.

(e)   When any report as required by this Article is not filed, the Secretary of State shall send a certified letter, return receipt requested, advising the lobbyist, lobbyist principal, or other person required to report of the delinquency and the penalties provided by law. A late filing fee of fifty dollars ($50.00) per day, commencing on the tenth business day after the date the certified letter is received, applies to a report that is not timely filed. The cumulative late filing fee may not exceed five hundred dollars ($500.00). Within 20 days of the receipt of the letter, the report shall be delivered or posted by United States mail to the Secretary of State together with the late filing fee. Filing of the required report and payment of the additional fee within the time extended shall constitute compliance with this section.

(f)   Failure to file a required report in one of the manners prescribed in this section shall void any and all registrations of the lobbyist, lobbyist principal, or solicitor. No lobbyist, lobbyist principal, or solicitor may register or reregister until full compliance with this section has occurred.

(g)   Appeal of a decision by the Secretary of State under this section shall be in accordance with Article 3 of Chapter 150B of the General Statutes.

(h)   The Secretary of State may adopt rules to facilitate complete and timely disclosure of required reporting, including additional categories of information, and to protect the addresses of payees under protective order issued pursuant to Chapter 50B of the General Statutes or participating in the Address Confidentiality Program pursuant to Chapter 15C of the General Statutes. The Secretary of State shall not impose any penalties or late filing fees upon a lobbyist, lobbyist principal, or solicitor for subsequent failures to comply with the requirements of this section if the Secretary of State failed to provide the required notification under subsection (e) of this section.

(i)   Any reportable expenditure promptly paid for at fair market value or promptly returned to a lobbyist or lobbyist principal by a designated individual or a member of the designated individual's immediate family within the reporting period shall not be reported under G.S. 120C-402 or G.S. 120C-403, and if reported, the repayment or return of the expenditure at any time shall be

171

reported by the lobbyist and lobbyist principal on the next report due under this Article.

(j)   The Secretary of State shall make available a report form that may be filed by a designated individual or a member of the designated individual's immediate family who promptly declines, returns, pays fair market value for, or donates a reportable expenditure in accordance with G.S. 138A-32(g). The Secretary of State shall index the filing of this form together with the lobbyist or lobbyist principal who gave the reportable expenditure. (1933, c. 11, s. 5; 1973, c. 108, s. 70; 1975, c. 820, s. 1; 1991, c. 740, s. 1.1; 1991 (Reg. Sess., 1992), c. 1030, s. 51.9; 1999-338, s. 1; 2005-456, s. 1; 2006-201, s. 18; 2007-348, s. 15(a); 2008-213, ss. 24, 25, 90; 2009-477, s. 1; 2009-549, s. 7(a); 2013-360, s. 27.1(g).)

§ 120C-402. Lobbyist's reports.

(a)   Each lobbyist shall file quarterly reports under oath with the Secretary of State with respect to each lobbyist principal.

(b)   The report shall include all of the following for the reporting period:

(1)   All reportable expenditures made for lobbying.

(2)   Solicitation of others when such solicitation involves an aggregate cost of more than three thousand dollars ($3,000).

(3)   Reportable expenditures reimbursed by the lobbyist principal, or another person or governmental unit on the lobbyist principal's behalf.

(4)   All reportable expenditures for gifts given under G.S. 138A-32(e)(1)-(9), 138A-32(e)(11), 138A-32(e)(12), and all gifts given under G.S. 138A-32(e)(10) with a value of more than ten dollars ($10.00).

(c)   In addition to the reports required by this section, each lobbyist incurring reportable expenditures in any month while the General Assembly is in session with respect to lobbying legislators and legislative employees shall file a monthly reportable expenditure report. The monthly reportable expenditure report shall contain information required by this section with respect to all lobbying of legislators and legislative employees, and is due within 10 business days after the end of the month. The information on the monthly reportable expenditure report shall also be included in each quarterly report required by subsection (a) of this section. (1933, c. 11, s. 5; 1973, c. 108, s. 70; 1975, c. 820, s. 1; 1991, c. 740, s. 1.1; 1991 (Reg. Sess., 1992), c. 1030, s. 51.9; 1999-338, s. 1; 2005-456, s. 1; 2006-201, s. 18; 2007-348, s. 41(b); 2008-213, ss. 27, 90; 2010-169, s. 17(i).)

§ 120C-403. Lobbyist principal's reports.

(a)   Each lobbyist principal shall file quarterly reports under oath with the Secretary of State with respect to each lobbyist principal.

(b)   The report shall be filed whether or not reportable expenditures are made, shall be due 15 business days after the end of the reporting period, and shall include all of the following for the reporting period:

(1)   All reportable expenditures made for lobbying.

(2)   Solicitation of others when such solicitation involves an aggregate cost of more than three thousand dollars ($3,000).

(3)   Repealed by Session Laws 2011-393, s. 2, effective October 1, 2011, and applicable to reports filed on or after that date.

(4)   With respect to each lobbyist registered under G.S. 120C-206, reportable expenditures reimbursed or paid to lobbyists for lobbying that are not reported on the lobbyist's report, with an itemized description of those reportable expenditures.

(5)   All reportable expenditures for gifts given under G.S. 138A-32(e)(1)-(9), 138A-32(e)(11), 138A-32(e)(12), and all gifts given under G.S. 138A-32(e)(10) with a value of more than two hundred dollars ($200.00).

(6)   With respect to each lobbyist registered under G.S. 120C-206, the name of each person or governmental unit not otherwise registered as a lobbyist principal for whom the lobbyist principal directs the lobbyist to lobby, whether for pay or not. If the lobbyist principal is an association or other organization, the lobbyist principal shall not be required to report under this subdivision any

173

individual member of the association or other organization for which the lobbyist is directed to lobby by that lobbyist principal.

(c)   In addition to the reports required by this section, each lobbyist principal incurring reportable expenditures in any month while the General Assembly is in session with respect to lobbying legislators and legislative employees shall file a monthly reportable expenditure report. The monthly reportable expenditure report shall contain information required by this section with respect to all lobbying of legislators and legislative employees, and is due within 10 business days after the end of the month. The information on the monthly report shall also be included in each quarterly report required by subsection (a) of this section.

(d)   In addition to the reports required by this section, each lobbyist principal shall annually, in the last report for the registration period under G.S. 120C-200(d), report the cumulative combined total of all payments made during the registration period for all of the following:

(1)   All payments for lobbying.

(2)   Activities as described in subdivision (e)(2) of this section.

(d1)   The cumulative combined total of payments reported under subsection (d) of this section made during the registration period, as applicable:

(1)   If a lobbyist represents the lobbyist principal, but is not directly employed by that lobbyist principal, the portion of the payment that is for lobbying and to whom it was paid.

(2)   If a lobbyist is under contract with the lobbyist principal for lobbying, the portion of the contract that is reasonably allocated for lobbying.

(3)   If a lobbyist is a full-time employee of the principal, or is paid by means of an annual fee or retainer, the principal shall estimate and report the portion of the salary, fee, or retainer salary that is reasonably allocated for lobbying.

(d2)   Notwithstanding any other provision of this Article, the cumulative combined total of all payments for lobbying and other activities made by the principal to all lobbyists registered for that lobbyist principal shall be reported as one cumulative amount with no further division or allocation by individual lobbyist, activity, or any other categorization.

(e)   For purposes of subsection (d) of this section, the following shall apply:

(1)   A lobbyist principal may rely upon a statement by the lobbyist estimating the portion of the salary or other payment that is reasonably allocated for lobbying.

(2)   In addition to reporting any payment to a lobbyist for lobbying under subsection (d) of this section, a lobbyist principal shall report, cumulatively for the year, any payment to a lobbyist for any of the following communications and activities that were used to lobby within the registration period under G.S. 120C-200(d):

a.   Research.

b.   Drafting of written communications.

c.   Monitoring of proposed or pending legislative action or executive action, including time spent preparing communications with the lobbyist principal to relate information on proposed or pending legislative action or executive action.

d.   Time spent advising and rendering opinions to the lobbyist principal as to the construction and effect of proposed or pending legislative action or executive action.

(3)   A lobbyist principal is required to report any payment to a lobbyist for any of the following:

a.   Direct lobbying communications or direct lobbying activities with a designated individual or that designated individual's immediate family.

b.   Communications or activities to develop goodwill, including the building of relationships, with a designated individual or that designated individual's immediate family member. (1933, c. 11, s. 5; 1973, c. 108, s. 70; 1975, c. 820, s. 1; 1991, c. 740, s. 1.1; 1991 (Reg. Sess., 1992), c. 1030, s. 51.10; 1999-338, s. 2; 2005-456, s. 1; 2006-201, s. 18; 2007-348, s. 41(c); 2008-213, ss. 29(a), 90; 2010-169, s. 17(j); 2011-393, s. 2.)

§ 120C-404. Solicitor's reports.

175

(a)   Each solicitor shall file quarterly reports under oath with the Secretary of State.

(b)   The report shall include all of the following:

(1)   All reportable expenditures made for lobbying during the reporting period.

(2)   Solicitation of others when such solicitation involves an aggregate cost of more than three thousand dollars ($3,000). (2006-201, s. 18; 2010-169, s. 17(k).)

§ 120C-405. Report availability.

(a)   All reports filed under this Chapter shall be open to public inspection upon filing.

(b)   The Secretary of State shall coordinate with the State Board of Elections to create a searchable Web-based database of reports filed under this Chapter and reports filed under Subchapter VIII of Chapter 163 of the General Statutes. (2006-201, s. 18.)

§§ 120C-406 through 120C-499. Reserved for future codification purposes.

Article 5.

Liaison Personnel.

§ 120C-500. Liaison personnel.

(a)   All agencies and constitutional officers of the State, including all boards, departments, divisions, constituent institutions of The University of North Carolina, community colleges, and other units of government in the executive branch shall designate liaison personnel to lobby for legislative action. This subsection shall not apply to units of local government, or a State agency or board with no staff.

(b)   No State agency or constitutional officer of the State may contract with individuals who are not employed by the State to lobby legislators and legislative employees. This subsection shall not apply to counsel employed by any agency, board, department, or division authorized to employ counsel under G.S. 147-17.

(c)   No more than two individuals may be designated as liaison personnel for each agency and constitutional officers of the State, including all boards, departments, divisions, constituent institutions of The University of North Carolina, community colleges, and other units of government in the executive branch.

(d)   The Chief Justice of the Supreme Court shall designate at least one, but no more than four, liaison personnel to lobby for legislative action for all offices, conferences, commissions, and other agencies established under Chapter 7A of the General Statutes. This subsection shall not apply to any office created under Article 60 of Chapter 7A of the General Statutes, so long as that office complies with subsection (a) of this section.

(e)   Notwithstanding subsection (c) of this section, the Secretary of Public Safety shall designate at least one, but no more than five, liaison personnel to lobby for legislative action for all offices, commissions, and agencies within the Department of Public Safety, as established by Article 13 of Chapter 143B. (1933, c. 11, s. 7; 1975, c. 820, s. 1; 1977, c. 697; 1991, c. 740, s. 1.1; 1993, c. 553, s. 3; 2001-424, s. 6.10(a); 2005-456, s. 1; 2006-201, s. 18; 2007-347, s. 6(a); 2008-213, ss. 30-32; 2012-83, s. 6.)

§ 120C-501. Applicability of Chapter on liaison personnel.

(a)   Except as otherwise provided in this section, this Chapter shall not apply to liaison personnel.

(b)   G.S. 120C-200 shall apply to liaison personnel. No registration fee shall be required for registration under this subsection.

(c)   Liaison personal designated under this Article shall file reports under G.S. 120C-402.

(d)   G.S. 120C-303 shall apply to liaison personnel with respect to legislators and legislative employees.

(e)   The Board of Governors of the University of North Carolina and its constituent institutions, or the liaison personnel designated by that board or the constituent institutions, shall not give, for lobbying, athletic tickets to any designated individual, except for those who are described in G.S. 138A-3(30)j. or those who are students and receive tickets on the same basis as other students. (2001-424, s. 6.10(a); 2005-456, s. 1; 2006-201, s. 18; 2008-213, s. 33; 2010-169, s. 17(l).)

§ 120C-502. Local government liaison equivalents.

(a)   An individual who is an employee of a governmental unit whose principal duties, in practice or as set forth in that individual's job description, include lobbying for legislative action shall register under G.S. 120C-200.

(b)   G.S. 120C-501 shall apply to an individual required to register under subsection (a) of this section.

(c)   For purposes of publication of the registry under G.S. 120C-220, the Secretary of State shall treat individuals registered under this section as liaison personnel. (2010-169, s. 5(a).)

§§ 120C-503 through 120C-599. Reserved for future codification purposes.

Article 6.

Violations and Enforcement.

§ 120C-600. Powers and duties of the Secretary of State.

(a)   The Secretary of State shall perform systematic reviews of reports required to be filed under Articles 4 and 8 of this Chapter on a regular basis to assure complete and timely disclosure of reportable expenditures. The Secretary of State shall refer to the Commission any complaints of violations of this Chapter other than those related solely to Articles 2, 4, or 8 of this Chapter.

(b)   The Secretary of State may petition the Superior Court of Wake County for the approval to issue subpoenas and subpoenas duces tecum as necessary to conduct investigations of violations of Articles 2, 4, and 8 of this Chapter. The court shall authorize subpoenas under this subsection when the court determines they are necessary for the enforcement of Articles 2, 4, and 8 of this Chapter. Subpoenas issued under this subsection shall be enforceable by the court through contempt powers. Venue shall be with the Superior Court of Wake County for any nonresident person, or that person's agent, who makes a reportable expenditure under this Chapter, and personal jurisdiction may be asserted under G.S. 1-75.4.

(c)   Complaints of violations of Articles 2, 4, and 8 of this Chapter, all other records accumulated in conjunction with the investigation of these complaints, and any records accumulated in the performance of a systematic review shall be considered confidential records and may be released only by order of a court of competent jurisdiction. Any information obtained by the Secretary of State from any law enforcement agency, administrative agency, or regulatory organization on a confidential or otherwise restricted basis in the course of an investigation or systematic review shall be confidential and exempt from G.S. 132-6 to the same extent that it is confidential in the possession of the providing agency or organization.

(d)   The Secretary shall publish annual statistics on complaints received and systematic reviews conducted under this section, including the number of systematic reviews, the number of complaints, the number of apparent violations of this Chapter referred to a district attorney, the number of complaints dismissed, and the number and age of complaints pending. Subject to the provisions of Chapter 132 of the General Statutes, the levy of all civil fines, including the amount of the fine and the identity of the person or governmental unit against whom it was levied, shall be a public record as defined in G.S. 132-1(a). (2005-456, s. 1; 2006-201, s. 18; 2006-259, s. 43.5(a); 2008-213, s. 34; 2010-169, s. 19(a).)

179

§ 120C-601. Powers and duties of the Commission.

(a)   The Commission may investigate complaints of violations of this Chapter and shall refer complaints related solely to Articles 2, 4, or 8 of this Chapter to the Secretary of State.

(b)   The Commission may petition the Superior Court of Wake County for the approval to issue subpoenas and subpoenas duces tecum as necessary to conduct investigations of violations of this Chapter. The court shall authorize subpoenas under this subsection when the court determines they are necessary for the enforcement of this Chapter. Subpoenas issued under this subsection shall be enforceable by the court through contempt powers. Venue shall be with the Superior Court of Wake County for any nonresident person, or that person's agent, who makes a reportable expenditure under this Chapter, and personal jurisdiction may be asserted under G.S. 1-75.4.

(c)   Complaints of violations of this Chapter and all other records accumulated in conjunction with the investigation of these complaints shall be considered confidential records and may be released only by order of a court of competent jurisdiction. Any information obtained by the Commission from any law enforcement agency, administrative agency, or regulatory organization on a confidential or otherwise restricted basis in the course of an investigation shall be confidential and exempt from G.S. 132-6 to the same extent that it is confidential in the possession of the providing agency or organization.

(d)   The Commission shall publish annual statistics on complaints, including the number of complaints, the number of apparent violations of this Chapter referred to a district attorney, the number of dismissals, and the number and age of complaints pending. (2006-201, s. 18; 2006-259, s. 43.5(a); 2008-213, s. 35; 2010-169, s. 19(b).)

§ 120C-602. Punishment for violation.

(a)   Whoever willfully violates any provision of Article 2 or Article 3 of this Chapter shall be guilty of a Class 1 misdemeanor, except as provided in those Articles. In addition, no lobbyist who is convicted of a violation of the provisions of this Chapter shall in any way act as a lobbyist for a period of two years from the date of conviction.

(b)   In addition to the criminal penalties set forth in this section, the Secretary of State may levy civil fines for a violation of any provision of Articles 2, 4, or 8 of this Chapter up to five thousand dollars ($5,000) per violation. In addition to the criminal penalties set forth in this section, the Commission may levy civil fines for a violation of any provision of this Chapter except Article 2, 4, or 8 of this Chapter up to five thousand dollars ($5,000) per violation. (1933, c. 11, s. 8; 1975, c. 820, s. 1; 1991, c. 740, s. 1.1; 1993, c. 539, s. 914; 1994, Ex. Sess., c. 24, s. 14(c); 2005-456, s. 1; 2006-201, s. 18; 2006-259, s. 43.5(a).)

§ 120C-603. Enforcement by district attorney and Attorney General.

(a)   The Commission or the Secretary of State, as appropriate, may investigate complaints of violations of this Chapter and shall report apparent violations of this Chapter to the district attorney of the prosecutorial district as defined in G.S. 7A-60 of which Wake County is a part, who shall prosecute any person or governmental unit who violates any provisions of this Chapter.

(b)   Complaints of violations of this Chapter involving the Commission or any member employee of the Commission shall be referred to the Attorney General for investigation. The Attorney General shall, upon receipt of a complaint, make an appropriate investigation thereof, and the Attorney General shall forward a copy of the investigation to the district attorney of the prosecutorial district as defined in G.S. 7A-60 of which Wake County is a part, who shall prosecute any person or governmental unit who violates any provisions of this Chapter. (1975, c. 820, s. 1; 1987 (Reg. Sess., 1988), c. 1037, s. 112; 2005-456, s. 1; 2006-201, s. 18; 2006-259, s. 43.5(b); 2008-213, s. 36.)

§§ 120C-604 through 120C-699. Reserved for future codification purposes.

Article 7.

Exemptions.

§ 120C-700. Persons exempted from this Chapter.

Except as otherwise provided in Article 8, the provisions of this Chapter shall not be construed to apply to any of the following:

(1)   An individual solely engaged in expressing a personal opinion or stating facts or recommendations on legislative action or executive action to a designated individual and not acting as a lobbyist.

(2)   A person appearing before a committee, commission, board, council, or other collective body whose membership includes one or more designated individuals at the invitation or request of the committee or a member thereof and who does not act in any further activities as a lobbyist with respect to the legislative or executive action for which that person appeared.

(3)   A duly elected or appointed official or employee of the State, the United States, a county, municipality, school district, or other governmental agency, when acting solely in connection with matters pertaining to the office and public duties, except for a person designated as liaison personnel under G.S. 120C-500 or G.S. 120C-502. For purposes of this subdivision, an individual appointed as a county or city attorney under Part 7 of Article 5 of Chapter 153A of the General Statutes or Part 6 of Article 7 of Chapter 160A of the General Statutes, respectively, shall be considered an employee of the county or city.

(4)   A person performing professional services in drafting bills, or in advising and rendering opinions to clients, or to designated individuals on behalf of clients, as to the construction and effect of proposed or pending legislative or executive action where the professional services are not otherwise connected with the legislative or executive action.

(5)   A person who owns, publishes, or is an employee of any recognized news medium, while engaged in the acquisition and publication of news or news and commentary on behalf of that recognized news medium.

(6)   Designated individuals while acting in their official capacity.

(7)   A person responding to inquiries from a designated individual and who does not act in any further activities as a lobbyist in connection with that inquiry.

(8)   A person who is a political committee as defined in G.S. 163-278.6(14), that person's employee, or that person's contracted service provider.

(9)   Anything of value given or received in connection with seeking or hosting a national convention of a political party. (1933, c. 11, s. 7; 1975, c. 820, s. 1; 1977, c. 697; 1991, c. 740, s. 1.1; 1993, c. 553, s. 3; 2005-456, s. 1; 2006-201, s. 18; 2007-348, s. 16; 2010-169, ss. 5(b), 20.)

§§ 120C-701 through 120C-799. Reserved for future codification purposes.

Article 8.

Miscellaneous.

§ 120C-800. Reportable expenditures made by persons exempted or not covered by this Chapter.

(a)   If a designated individual accepts a reportable expenditure made for lobbying with a total value of over two hundred dollars ($200.00) per calendar quarter from a person or group of persons acting together, exempted or not otherwise covered by this Chapter, the person, or group of persons, making the reportable expenditure shall report the date, a description of the reportable expenditure, the name and address of the person, or group of persons, making the reportable expenditure, the name of the designated individual accepting the reportable expenditure, and the estimated fair market value, or face value if shown, of the reportable expenditure.

(b)   If the person making the reportable expenditure in subsection (a) of this section is outside North Carolina, and the designated individual accepting the reportable expenditure is also outside North Carolina at the time the designated individual accepts the reportable expenditure, then the designated individual accepting the reportable expenditure shall be responsible for filing the report or reporting the information in the designated individual's statement of economic interest in accordance with G.S. 138A-24(a)(8).

(c)   If a designated individual accepts a scholarship related to that designated individual's public service or position valued over two hundred dollars ($200.00) from a person, or group of persons, acting together, exempted or not covered by this Chapter, the person, or group of persons, granting the scholarship shall report the date of the scholarship, a description of the event

183

involved, the name and address of the person, or group of persons, granting the scholarship, the name of the designated individual accepting the scholarship, and the estimated fair market value.

(d)   If the person granting the scholarship in subsection (c) of this section is outside North Carolina, the designated individual accepting the scholarship shall be responsible for filing the report or reporting the information in the designated individual's statement of economic interest in accordance with G.S. 138A-24(a)(2).

(e)   This section shall not apply to any of the following:

(1)   Anything of value properly reported as required under Article 22A of Chapter 163 of the General Statutes.

(2)   Any reportable expenditure from a designated individual's extended family member to a designated individual.

(3)   Reportable expenditures associated primarily with the designated individual's employment or that designated individual's immediate family member's employment.

(4)   Reportable expenditures, other than food, beverages, travel, and lodging, which are received from a person who is a citizen of a country other than the United States or a state other than North Carolina and given during a ceremonial presentation or as a custom.

(5)   A thing of value that is paid for by the State.

(6)   A scholarship paid for by a nonpartisan state, regional, national, or international legislative organization of which the General Assembly is a member or a legislator or legislative employee is a member or participant of by virtue of that legislator's or legislative employee's public position, or to an affiliated organization of that nonpartisan state, regional, national, or international organization.

(f)   Within 15 business days after the end of the quarter in which the reportable expenditure was made, reports required by this section shall be filed electronically with the Secretary of State in a form prescribed by the Secretary of State. If the designated individual is required to file a statement of economic interest under G.S. 138A-24, then that designated individual may opt to report any information required by this section in the statement of economic interest.

(g)   For purposes of this section, the term "scholarship" shall mean a grant-in-aid to attend a conference, meeting, or other similar event. For purposes of this section only, the term "person" shall include all persons as defined in G.S. 138A-3(27) and all governmental units as defined in G.S. 138A-3(15d). (2005-456, s. 1; 2006-201, s. 18; 2007-348, s. 17; 2008-213, ss. 37, 38(a), 39; 2009-549, s. 7(b); 2010-169, ss. 17(m), 22(f); 2010-170, s. 15; 2013-360, s. 27.1(h).)

§§ 120C-801 through 120C-899. Reserved for future codification purposes.

Chapter 121.

Archives and History.

Article 1.

General Provisions.

§ 121-1. Short title.

This Article shall be known as the North Carolina Archives and History Act. (1973, c. 476, s. 48.)

§ 121-2. Definitions.

For the purposes of this Article:

(1)   "Agency" shall mean any State, county, or municipal office, department, division, board, commission or separate unit of government created or established by constitution or law.

(2)   "Commission" shall mean the North Carolina Historical Commission.

(3)   "Department" shall mean the Department of Cultural Resources of the State of North Carolina.

(4)   "Historic preservation" shall mean any activity reasonably related to the identification, research, conservation, protection, and restoration, maintenance, or operation of buildings, structures, objects, districts, areas, and sites significant in the history, architecture, archaeology, or culture of this State, its communities, or the nation.

(5)   "Historic property" or "historic properties" shall mean any building, structure, object, district, area, or site that is significant in the history, architecture, archaeology, or culture of this State, its communities, or the nation.

(6)   "North Carolina Museum of History" shall mean an establishment or establishments administered by the Department of Cultural Resources as the official State museum of history for the collection, preservation, and exhibition of artifacts and other materials that have been determined by the Department or by the Commission to have sufficient historical or other cultural value to warrant retention as evidence of the history and culture of the State and its subdivisions.

(7)   "North Carolina State Archives" shall mean an establishment or establishments administered by the Department of Cultural Resources as the State's official repository for the preservation of those public records or other documentary materials that have been determined by the Department in accordance with rules, regulations, and standards of the Historical Commission to have sufficient historical or other value to warrant their continued preservation and have been accepted by the Department for preservation in its custody.

(8)   "Public record" or "public records" shall mean all documents, papers, letters, maps, books, photographs, films, sound recordings, magnetic or other tapes, electronic data processing records, artifacts, or other documentary material, regardless of physical form or characteristics, made or received pursuant to law or ordinance or in connection with the transaction of official business by any agency.

(9)   "Records center" or "records centers" shall mean an establishment or establishments administered by the Department of Cultural Resources primarily for the economical housing, processing, servicing, microfilming or security of public records that must be retained for varying periods of time but which need not be retained in an agency's office equipment and space.

(10)   "Secretary" shall mean the Secretary of Cultural Resources.

(11)   "State historic site" or "state historic sites" shall mean a property or properties acquired by the State and administered by the Department of Cultural Resources because of its or their historical, archaeological, architectural, or cultural value in depicting the heritage of the State. (1973, c. 476, s. 48.)

§ 121-3. Name.

The archival and historical agency of the State of North Carolina shall be the Department of Cultural Resources. (1945, c. 55; 1955, c. 543, s. 1; 1973, c. 476, s. 48.)

§ 121-4. Powers and duties of the Department of Cultural Resources.

The Department of Cultural Resources shall have the following powers and duties:

(1)   To accept gifts, devises, and endowments for purposes which fall within the general legal powers and duties of the Department. Unless otherwise specified by the donor or testator, the Department may either expend both the principal and interest of any gift or devises or may invest such funds in whole or in part, by and with the consent of the State Treasurer.

(2)   To conduct a records management program, including the operation of a records center or centers and a centralized microfilming program, for the benefit of all State agencies, and to give advice and assistance to the public officials and agencies in matters pertaining to the economical and efficient maintenance and preservation of public records.

(3)   To preserve and administer, in the North Carolina State Archives, such public records as may be accepted into its custody, and to collect, preserve, and administer private and unofficial historical records and other documentary materials relating to the history of North Carolina and the territory included therein from the earliest times. The Department shall carefully protect and preserve such materials, file them according to approved archival practices, and permit them, at reasonable times and under the supervision of the Department, to be inspected, examined, or copied: Provided, that any materials placed in the

187

keeping of the Department under special terms or conditions restricting their use shall be made accessible only in accordance with such terms or conditions.

(4)   To have materials on the history of North Carolina properly edited, published as other State printing, and distributed under the direction of the Department. The Department may charge a reasonable price for such publications and devote the revenue arising from such sales to the work of the Department.

(5)   With the cooperation of the State Board of Education and the Department of Public Instruction to develop, conduct, and assist in the coordination of a program for the better and more adequate teaching of State and local history in the public schools and the institutions of the community college system of North Carolina, including, as appropriate, the preparation and publication of suitable histories of all counties and of other appropriate materials, the distribution of such materials to the public schools and community college system for a reasonable charge, and the coordination of this program throughout the State.

(6)   To maintain and administer the North Carolina Museum of History, to collect and preserve therein important historical and cultural materials, and according to approved museum practices to classify, accession, house, and when feasible exhibit such materials and make them available for study.

(7)   To select suitable sites on property owned by the State of North Carolina, or any subdivision of the State, for the erection of historical markers calling attention to nearby historic sites and prepare appropriate inscriptions to be placed on such markers. The Department shall have all markers manufactured, and when completed, each marker shall be delivered to the Department of Transportation for payment and erection under the provisions of G.S. 136-42.2 and 136-42.3. The Secretary is authorized to appoint a highway historical marker advisory committee to approve all proposed highway historical markers and to establish criteria for carrying out this responsibility.

(8)   In accordance with G.S. 121-9 of this Chapter, to acquire real and personal properties that have statewide historical, architectural, archaeological, or other cultural significance, by gift, purchase, or devise; to preserve and administer such properties; and, when necessary, to charge reasonable admission fees to such properties. In the acquisition of such property, the Department shall also have the authority to acquire nearby or adjacent property adjacent to properties having statewide significance deemed necessary for the

proper use, administration, and protection of historic, architectural, archaeological, or cultural properties, or for the protection of the environment thereof.

(9)   To administer and enforce reasonable rules adopted and promulgated by the Historical Commission for the regulation of the use by the public of such historical, architectural, archaeological, or cultural properties under its charge, which regulations, after having been posted in conspicuous places on and adjacent to such State properties and having been filed according to law, shall have the force and effect of law and any violation of such regulations shall constitute a Class 3 misdemeanor.

(10)   To coordinate the objectives of the state-created historical and commemorative commissions with the other policies, objectives, and programs of the Department of Cultural Resources.

(11)   To organize and administer a junior historian program, in cooperation with the Department of Public Education, the public schools, and other agencies or organizations that may be concerned therein.

(12)   With the approval of the Historical Commission, to dispose of any accessioned records, artifacts, and furnishings in the custody of the Department that are determined to have no further use or value for official or administrative purposes or for research and reference purposes.

(13)   To promote and encourage throughout the State knowledge and appreciation of North Carolina history and heritage by encouraging the people of the State to engage in the preservation and care of archives, historical manuscripts, museum items, and other historical materials; the writing and publication of State and local histories of high standard; the display and interpretation of historical materials; the marking and preservation of historic, architectural, or archaeological structures and sites of great importance; the teaching of North Carolina and local history in the schools and colleges; the appropriate observance of events of importance to the State's history; the publicizing of the State's history through media of public information; and other activities in historical and allied fields.

(14)   With the approval of the Historical Commission, to charge and collect fees not to exceed cost for photographs, photocopies of documents, microfilm and other microforms and other audio or visual reproductions of public records or other documentary materials, objects, artifacts, and research materials; and

for the restoration and preservation of documents and other materials important for archival or historical purposes.

(15)   To encourage and develop, in cooperation with the Department of Administration and in consultation with the Department of Transportation, the Department of Commerce, the Department of Environment and Natural Resources, the North Carolina League of Municipalities, the North Carolina Association of County Commissioners, and the Historic Preservation Foundation of North Carolina, Inc., a central clearinghouse for information on historic preservation for the benefit and use of public and private agencies and persons in North Carolina.

(16)   Repealed by Session Laws 2004-203, s. 51, effective August 17, 2004.

(17)   (See Editor's note) To enter into an agreement with a private nonprofit corporation for the management of facilities to provide food and beverages at the North Carolina Museum of History. Any net proceeds received by the private nonprofit corporation shall be devoted to the work of the Department. Any private nonprofit corporation entering into an agreement with the Department with regard to the management of the facilities may enter into further agreements with private persons or corporations concerning the operation of the facilities. The Department may enter into an agreement in regard to obtaining or installing equipment, furniture, and furnishings for such facilities. (Rev., ss. 4540, 4541; 1907, c. 714, s. 2; 1911, c. 211, s. 6; C.S., s. 6142; 1925, c. 275, s. 11; 1943, c. 237; 1945, c. 55; 1955, c. 543, s. 1; 1957, c. 330, s. 1; 1959, c. 68, s. 1; 1971, c. 345, s. 3; 1973, c. 476, s. 48; 1977, c. 464, s. 38; 1981, c. 721; 1989, c. 379; c. 727, s. 218(83); c. 751, s. 11; 1991, c. 757, s. 5; 1991 (Reg. Sess., 1992), c. 959, s. 30; 1993, c. 522, s. 8; c. 539, s. 915; 1994, Ex. Sess., c. 24, s. 14(c); 1997-443, s. 11A.119(a); 2004-203, s. 51; 2011-284, s. 86.)

§ 121-4.1. North Carolina Register of Historic Places.

(a)   The Department of Cultural Resources may establish, expand, and maintain a North Carolina Register of Historic Places composed of districts, sites, buildings, structures, and objects significant in North Carolina history, architecture, archaeology, engineering, and culture. Until such time as the North Carolina Register of Historic Places is established, all references to it in the General Statutes and in the rules adopted pursuant to it shall be construed to mean properties and districts in North Carolina that are listed in the National Register of Historic Places.

(b)   The North Carolina Historical Commission shall establish criteria for properties to be included in the State Register of Historic Places, and, within such criteria, shall provide for levels of significance as necessary and appropriate.

(c)   The North Carolina Historical Commission shall promulgate regulations requiring that before any property or district may be included on the North Carolina Register of Historic Places, the owner or owners of such property, or a majority of the owners of the properties within the district in the case of an historic district, shall be given the opportunity (including a reasonable period of time) to concur in, or object to, the nomination of the property or district for such inclusion or designation. If the owner or owners of any privately owned property, or a majority of the owners of such properties within the district in the case of an historic district, object to such inclusion or designation, such property shall not be included on the North Carolina Register until such objection has been withdrawn. The regulations under this paragraph shall include provisions to carry out the purposes of this paragraph in the case of multiple ownership of a single property. (1989, c. 60.)

§ 121-5. Public records and archives.

(a)   State Archival Agency Designated. - The Department of Cultural Resources shall be the official archival agency of the State of North Carolina with authority as provided throughout this Chapter and Chapter 132 of the General Statutes of North Carolina in relation to the public records of the State, counties, municipalities, and other subdivisions of government.

(b)   Destruction of Records Regulated. - No person may destroy, sell, loan, or otherwise dispose of any public record without the consent of the Department of Cultural Resources, except as provided in G.S. 130A-99. Whoever unlawfully removes a public record from the office where it is usually kept, or alters, mutilates, or destroys it shall be guilty of a Class 3 misdemeanor and upon conviction only fined at the discretion of the court.

When the custodian of any official State records certifies to the Department of Cultural Resources that such records have no further use or value for official and administrative purposes and when the Department certifies that such records appear to have no further use or value for research or reference, then such records may be destroyed or otherwise disposed of by the agency having custody of them.

When the custodian of any official records of any county, city, municipality, or other subdivision of government certifies to the Department that such records have no further use or value for official business and when the Department certifies that such records appear to have no further use or value for research or reference, then such records may be authorized by the governing body of said county, city, municipality, or other subdivision of government to be destroyed or otherwise disposed of by the agency having custody of them. A record of such certification and authorization shall be entered in the minutes of the governing body granting the authority.

The North Carolina Historical Commission is hereby authorized and empowered to make such orders, rules, and regulations as may be necessary and proper to carry into effect the provisions of this section. When any State, county, municipal, or other governmental records shall have been destroyed or otherwise disposed of in accordance with the procedure authorized in this subsection, any liability that the custodian of such records might incur for such destruction or other disposal shall cease and determine.

(c)   Assistance to Public Officers. - The Department of Cultural Resources shall have the right to examine into the condition of public records and shall, subject to the availability of staff and funds, give advice and assistance to public officials and agencies in regard to preserving or disposing of the public records in their custody. When requested by the Department of Cultural Resources, public officials shall assist the Department in the preparation of an inclusive inventory of records in their custody, to which inventory shall be attached a schedule, approved by the head of the governmental unit or agency having custody of the records and the Department of Cultural Resources, establishing a time period for the retention or disposal of each series of records. So long as such approved schedule remains in effect, destruction or disposal of records in accordance with its provisions shall be deemed to have met the requirements of G.S. 121-5(b).

The Department of Cultural Resources is hereby authorized and directed to conduct a program of inventorying, repairing, and microfilming in the counties for security purposes those official records of the several counties which the Department determines have permanent value, and of providing safe storage for microfilm copies of such records. Subject to the availability of funds, such program shall be extended to the records of permanent value of the cities, municipalities, and other subdivisions of government.

(d)   Preservation of Permanently Valuable Records. - Public records certified by the Department of Cultural Resources as being of permanent value shall be preserved in the custody of the agency in which the records are normally kept or of the North Carolina State Archives. Any State, county, municipal, or other public official is hereby authorized and empowered to turn over to the Department of Cultural Resources any State, county, municipal, or other public records no longer in current official use, and the Department of Cultural Resources is authorized in its discretion to accept such records, and having done so shall provide for their administration and preservation in the North Carolina State Archives. When such records have been thus surrendered, photocopies, microfilms, typescripts, or other copies of them shall be made and certified under seal of the Department, upon application of any person, which certification shall have the same force and effect as if made by the official or agency by which the records were transferred to the Department of Cultural Resources; and the Department may charge reasonable fees for these copies. The Department may answer written inquiries for nonresidents of the State and for this service may charge a search and handling fee not to exceed twenty-five dollars ($25.00). The receipts from this fee shall be used to defray the cost of providing this service.

(e)   Archives and Records Management Fund. - The Archives and Records Management Fund is established as a special revenue fund. The Fund consists of the fees credited to it under Chapter 161 of the General Statutes. Revenue in the Fund may be used only to offset the Department's costs in providing essential records management and archival services for public records pursuant to Chapter 121 and Chapter 132 of the General Statutes. (1907, c. 714, s. 5; C.S., s. 6145; 1939, c. 249; 1943, c. 237; 1945, c. 55; 1953, c. 224; 1955, c. 543, s. 1; 1959, c. 1162; 1973, c. 476, s. 48; 1979, c. 361; c. 801, s. 95; 1981, c. 406, ss. 1, 2; 1993, c. 539, s. 916; 1994, Ex. Sess., c. 24, s. 14(c); 1997-309, s. 13; 2001-427, s. 3(a); 2009-451, s. 20B.3(b); 2012-79, s. 2.19(a).)

§ 121-5.1. State Historical Records Advisory Board.

(a)   The State Historical Records Advisory Board, which was constituted in 1975 in accordance with 44 U.S.C. § 2501; 36 C.F.R. § 1206 is continued under

State law and shall be located administratively in the Department of Cultural Resources. The Board shall consist of 10 members. Eight members shall be appointed by the Governor for three-year staggered terms, and each member shall have experience in the administration and use of historical records. All current members shall continue to serve until the expiration of their term unless a member is removed or the position becomes vacant, in which case the vacancy shall be filled in accordance with subsection (c) of this section. The Deputy Secretary of the Office of Archives and History and the State Archivist shall both serve as ex officio members of the Board.

(b)   The Board's primary duty shall be to serve as the central advisory body for historical records coordination within the State and for the National Historical Publications and Records Commission (NHPRC). In addition, subject to the availability of funds, the Board shall:

(1)   Offer assistance, advice, and consultation to State, county, and municipal governments, historic sites, museums, historical societies, and other institutions holding records of historical value concerning the care, preservation, and management of their records.

(2)   Solicit, review, and assess grant proposals in connection with NHPRC grants or grants from other sources.

(3)   Offer educational programs and conferences.

(4)   Conduct statewide studies and surveys of the State's historical records.

(c)   The Governor may remove any member for good cause shown. The Governor shall fill any vacancy on the Board. Appointees to fill vacancies shall serve the remainder of the unexpired term and until their successors have been appointed and qualified.

(d)   Members of the Board shall receive per diem and reimbursement for travel and subsistence as provided in G.S. 138-5 and G.S. 138-6, as appropriate.

(e)   The Governor shall appoint either the Deputy Secretary of the Office of Archives and History or the State Archivist as the State coordinator as required by NHPRC regulations. The State coordinator shall serve a four-year term and may be reappointed. The State coordinator may designate a deputy State coordinator from the Board's membership.

(f)   The Board shall hold at least two meetings each year to conduct business. The Board shall establish the procedures for calling, holding, and conducting regular and special meetings. A majority of the members of the Board constitutes a quorum for the transaction of business. (2007-150, s. 1.)

§ 121-6. Historical publications.

(a)   General Provisions. - It shall be the duty of the Department of Cultural Resources to promote and encourage the writing of North Carolina history and to collect, edit, publish, print, and distribute books, pamphlets, papers, manuscripts, documents, maps, and other materials relating to North Carolina archives and history. The Department of Cultural Resources may establish a reasonable charge for such publications and devote the revenue arising therefrom to such additional publication of materials relating to North Carolina archives and history as may be undertaken by the Department of Cultural Resources. Except for reports, bulletins, and other publications issued for free distribution, professional materials including books and journals published by the Department of Cultural Resources are hereby expressly excluded from provisions of G.S. 147-50.

(b)   Editing and Publishing of Official Messages and Other Papers of Governor. - During the term of office of each Governor of this State, a copy of all official messages delivered to the General Assembly, addresses, speeches, statements, news releases, proclamations, executive orders, weekly calendars, articles, transcripts of news conferences, lists of appointments, and other official releases and papers of the Governor shall be kept in the Governor's office for delivery to the Department of Cultural Resources at the end of each quarter during the Governor's administration. These papers shall be compiled and a selection made therefrom by a skilled and competent editor. The editor shall edit, according to acceptable scholarly standards, the selected materials which shall be published in a documentary volume as soon as practicable after the conclusion of the term of office of each Governor. If, for any reason, a Governor serves less than a full term, a documentary volume shall be edited and published for such portion of a term as he shall have served. If a Governor serves more than one term, a documentary volume shall be edited and published for each term served. Funds for editorial assistance, printing, binding, and distribution shall be paid from the Contingency and Emergency Fund. The number of copies of each volume to be printed shall be determined by the

Department of Cultural Resources in consultation with the Governor whose papers are being published.

(c)   It shall be the duty and the responsibility for the Department of Cultural Resources to edit and publish a second or new series of the most significant records of colonial North Carolina. From records which have been compiled in the North Carolina State Archives concerning the colonial period of North Carolina, a selection of the most significant documents shall be made therefrom by a skilled and competent editor. The editor shall edit, according to acceptable scholarly standards, the selected materials which shall be published in documentary volumes not to exceed approximately 700 pages each in length until full and representative published colonial records of North Carolina shall have been achieved. The number of copies of each volume to be so printed shall be determined by the Department of Cultural Resources, and such determination shall be based on the number of copies the Department can reasonably expect to sell in a period of 10 years from the date of publication. In any year during which the Department of Cultural Resources has completed a volume and has it ready for publication, the Department may include in its continuation budget for that year sufficient funds to pay the estimated costs of publishing the volume. In the event that the volume is not published during that year, the appropriation made, or any unencumbered balance, shall revert to the general fund. (1971, c. 480, s. 6; 1973, c. 476, s. 48; 1979, c. 1010; 1981 (Reg. Sess., 1982), c. 1290.)

§ 121-7. Historical museums.

(a)   The Department of Cultural Resources shall maintain and administer State historic attractions under the management of the Office of Archives and History for the collection, preservation, study, and exhibition of authentic artifacts and other historical materials relating to the history and heritage of North Carolina. The Department, with the approval of the Historical Commission, may acquire, either by purchase, gift, or loan such artifacts and materials, and, having acquired them, shall according to accepted museum practices classify, accession, preserve, and where feasible exhibit such materials and make them available for study. Within available funds, one or more branch museums of history or specialized regional history museums may be established and administered by the Department. The Department of Cultural Resources, subject to the availability of staff and funds, may give financial, technical, and professional assistance to nonstate historical museums sponsored by governmental agencies and nonprofit organizations according to regulations adopted by the North Carolina Historical Commission.

The Department of Cultural Resources may, with the explicit approval of the North Carolina Historical Commission sell, trade, or place on permanent loan any artifact owned by the State of North Carolina and in the custody of and curated by the Office of Archives and History, unless the sale, trade, or loan would be contrary to the terms of acquisition. The net proceeds of any sale, after deduction of the expenses attributable to that sale, shall be deposited to the State treasury to the credit of the Office of Archives and History Artifact Fund and shall be used only for the purchase of other artifacts. No artifact curated by any agency of the Department of Cultural Resources may be pledged or mortgaged.

(b)   Insofar as practicable, the Office of Archives and History shall accession and maintain records showing provenance, value, location, and other pertinent information on such furniture, furnishings, decorative items, and other objects as have historical or cultural importance and which are owned by or to be acquired by the State for use in the State Capitol and the Executive Mansion, and, upon request of the Department of Administration, any other state-owned building. When any such item or object has been entered in the accession records of the Office of Archives and History, the custodian of such item or object shall, upon its removal from the premises upon which it was located or when it is otherwise disposed of, submit to the Office of Archives and History sufficient details concerning its removal or disposition to permit an adequate entry in the accession records to the end that its location or disposition, and authority for such change, shall be shown therein.

(c)   Title to an artifact whose ownership is unknown or whose owner cannot be located passes to the Department of Cultural Resources if:

(1)   The artifact was placed on loan with the Office of Archives and History for a period of time exceeding five years or for an indefinite period of time or the artifact's status with the Office of Archives and History as a loan, gift, purchase, or other arrangement is unknown; and

(2)   The artifact has been a part of the inventory of the Office of Archives and History for more than five years; and

(3)   The Department of Cultural Resources makes a reasonable effort, including a diligent search of its own records, to locate and inform the owner, his

heirs or successors, that the Office of Archives and History is holding the artifact and to clarify the artifact's status with that Office.

To initiate the procedure to clarify title to an artifact, the Department of Cultural Resources shall mail, first class postage prepaid, a notice to the last known address of the owner of the artifact or the last known address of the owner's heirs or successors. The Department need not mail a notice, if after exercising due diligence to find a record within the Department of Cultural Resources indicating the owner of the artifact and his latest address, that information is not available. If no claim is made within 90 days from the date that notice is mailed, the Department of Cultural Resources shall publish a notice in three papers of general circulation once a week for four consecutive weeks. If, at the end of 30 days, no claim of ownership is submitted to the Department of Cultural Resources, the Department may determine that legal title to the artifact is vested in the Office of Archives and History.

(d)   Any person claiming legal title to an artifact to which the North Carolina Office of Archives and History also claims title as provided by subsection (c) may file a claim with the Department of Cultural Resources on a form prescribed by the Department. If the claimant is not the owner from whom the Department originally obtained the artifact, the claimant shall state in addition to any other information required by the Department, the facts surrounding the unavailability of the person who originally loaned or bestowed the property to the Office of Archives and History and the basis for the claim to title of the artifact. If the Department of Cultural Resources is satisfied that the claim is valid and that the claimant is the legal owner of the artifact, the Department shall return the artifact to the owner. If the Department determines that the claim is not valid and rejects the claim to the artifact, the claimant may appeal the determination as provided by Chapter 150B. (1973, c. 476, s. 48; 1979, c. 861, s. 1; 1987, c. 721, s. 1; 1991, c. 689, s. 191(a); c. 757, s. 6; 1993 (Reg. Sess., 1994), c. 769, s. 12.3; 1997-411, s. 4; 2002-159, s. 35(g).)

§ 121-7.1. Maritime Museum; disposition of artifacts.

Notwithstanding Article 3A of Chapter 143 of the General Statutes, G.S. 143-49(4), or any other law pertaining to surplus State property, the Department of Cultural Resources, with the approval of the North Carolina Historical Commission, may sell, trade, or place on permanent loan any artifact from the collection of the North Carolina Maritime Museum unless the sale, trade, or loan would be contrary to the terms of the acquisition. Sales or exchanges shall be conducted in accordance with generally accepted practices for accredited museums. If an artifact is sold, the net proceeds of the sale shall be deposited in the State treasury to the credit of a special fund to be used for the improvement of the Museum's collections or exhibits. (1998-212, s. 21(b).)

§ 121-7.2. Maritime Museum; branch museum.

The Department of Cultural Resources shall assume from the Southport Maritime Museum, Inc., the administration of the Southport Maritime Museum in Brunswick County and shall operate it as a branch of the North Carolina Maritime Museum. (1999-237, s. 26.1(a).)

§ 121-7.3. Admission and related activity fees.

The Department of Cultural Resources may charge a reasonable admission and related activity fee to any historic site or museum administered by the Department. Admission and related activity fees collected under this section are receipts of the Department and shall be deposited in the appropriate special fund. The revenue collected pursuant to this section shall be used only for the individual historic site or museum where the receipts were generated. The Secretary may adopt rules necessary to carry out the provisions of this section. The Department is exempt from the requirements of Chapter 150B of the General Statutes when adopting, amending, or repealing rules for admission fees or related activity fees at historic sites and museums. The Department shall submit a report to the Joint Legislative Commission on Governmental Operations on the amount and purpose of a fee change within 30 days following its effective date. (2003-284, s. 35A.4; 2013-297, s. 2(a); 2013-360, s. 19.2(a).)

§ 121-7.4. Graveyard of the Atlantic Museum.

The Department of Cultural Resources shall assume from the Graveyard of the Atlantic Museum, the administration of the Graveyard of the Atlantic Museum on Hatteras Island and shall designate it as a member of the State History

Museums Division, in accordance with the feasibility study conducted by the Department. (2007-359, s. 1(a).)

§ 121-7.5. Bentonville Battlefield Fund.

(a)   Fund. - The Bentonville Battlefield Fund is created as a special fund in the Department of Cultural Resources, Division of State Historic Sites. The interest earned by the Fund shall be credited to the Fund by the State Treasurer pursuant to G.S. 147-69.2 and G.S. 147-69.3. The Fund shall be used for operation, interpretation, maintenance, preservation, development, and expansion at Bentonville Battlefield State Historic Site.

(b)   Disposition of Fees. - Notwithstanding Chapter 146 of the General Statutes, all receipts derived from donations or the lease, rental, or other disposition of structures or products of the land owned by or under the supervision or control of the Division of Historic Sites in Johnston County shall be credited to the Fund.

(c)   The monies credited to this Fund pursuant to this section are annually appropriated to the Department of Cultural Resources. (2008-107, s. 19A.1.)

§ 121-7.6. North Carolina Transportation Museum special fund.

(a)   Fund Established. - The North Carolina Transportation Museum Fund is created as a special interestbearing, nonreverting enterprise fund in the Department of Cultural Resources. The Fund shall be used to pay all costs associated with the operation and maintenance of the North Carolina Transportation Museum.

(b)   Monies Credited to the Fund. - Notwithstanding Chapter 146 of the General Statutes, all receipts derived from the lease, rental, or other disposition of structures or products of the land, as well as all admissions and fees, gifts, donations, grants, and bequests, shall be credited to the Fund. The Fund shall be credited with interest by the State Treasurer pursuant to G.S. 147-69.2 and G.S. 147-69.3.

(c)   Emergency Reserve. - The Department of Cultural Resources shall establish, out of existing unobligated funds including lapsed salaries and unobligated special funds, an emergency reserve fund in the amount of three hundred thousand dollars ($300,000). Any use of the emergency reserve will require reimbursement from museum receipts.

(d)   Audit. - The Fund shall be subject to the oversight of the State Auditor pursuant to Article 5A of Chapter 147 of the General Statutes. The Fund shall reimburse the State Auditor for the cost of any audit. (2011-145, s. 21.1.)

§ 121-7.7. State Historic Sites and Museums special fund.

(a)   Fund. - The State Historic Sites and Museums Fund is created as a special, interest-bearing revenue fund in the Division of State Historic Sites and the Division of State History Museums. The Fund consists of all receipts derived from the lease or rental of property or facilities, disposition of structures or products of the land, private donations, and admissions and fees collected at the State Historic Sites, State History Museums, and Maritime Museums. The revenues in the Fund may be used only for the operation, interpretation, maintenance, preservation, development, and expansion of the individual State Historic Site, State History Museum, and Maritime Museum where the receipts are generated. The respective Division and the staff from each State Historic Site, State History Museum, and Maritime Museum will determine how the funds will be used at that Historic Site, State History Museum, and Maritime Museum.

(b)   Application. - This section applies to the individual State Historic Sites and State History and Maritime Museums owned by or under the control of the Division of State Historic Sites and the Division of State History Museums, with the exception of the Bentonville Battlefield State Historic Site and the North Carolina Transportation Museum. The Bentonville Battlefield State Historic Site is subject to G.S. 121-7.5. The North Carolina Transportation Museum is subject to G.S. 121-7.6.

(c)   Reports. - The Department of Cultural Resources must submit to the Joint Legislative Commission on Governmental Operations, the House of Representatives and Senate Appropriations Subcommittees on General Government, and the Fiscal Research Division by September 30 of each year a report on the Fund that includes the source and amounts of all funds credited to

201

the Fund and the purpose and amount of all expenditures from the Fund during the prior fiscal year. (2011-213, s. 1; 2012-142, s. 18.2.)

§ 121-8. Historic preservation program.

(a)   Historic Preservation Agency Designated. - The historic preservation agency of the State of North Carolina shall be the Department of Cultural Resources.

(b)   Surveys of Historic Properties. - The Department of Cultural Resources shall conduct a continuing statewide survey to identify, document, and record properties having historical, architectural, archaeological, or other cultural significance to the State, its communities, and the nation. Upon approval of the North Carolina Historical Commission, the Deputy Secretary of Archives and History or his designee as the State Historic Preservation Officer, may nominate appropriate properties for entry in the National Register of Historic Places as established by the National Historic Preservation Act of 1966, Public Law 89-665, 16 U.S.C. section 470. The Department of Cultural Resources shall maintain a permanent file containing research reports, descriptions, photographs, and other appropriate documentation relating to properties deemed worthy of inclusion in the statewide survey.

(c)   Statewide Historic Preservation Plan. - The Department of Cultural Resources shall prepare and revise as needed a State plan for historic preservation, which plan, when approved by the North Carolina Historical Commission, shall constitute official State policy for the preservation, or the encouragement of the preservation, of important historic, architectural, archaeological, and other cultural properties in North Carolina.

(d)   Cooperation with Federal Government. - The Department of Cultural Resources and/or the Department of Administration may enter into and carry out contracts with the federal government or any agency thereof under which said government or agency grants financial or other assistance to the Department of Cultural Resources to further the purposes of this Chapter. Either of the Departments may agree to and comply with any reasonable conditions not inconsistent with State law which are imposed on such grants. Such grants or other assistance may be accepted from the federal government or an agency thereof and expended whether or not pursuant to a contract.

(e)   Cooperation with Local Governments. - The Department shall, within the limits of staff and available funds, cooperate with and assist counties, cities, municipalities, and other subdivisions of government, and, where appropriate, private individuals and organizations, in promoting historic preservation to the end that important properties which are not owned by the State may be preserved or encouraged to be preserved. Such cooperation and assistance may include but not be limited to reviewing historic preservation plans, evaluating historic properties, and providing technical, financial and professional assistance. The Department may further enter into and carry out contracts with local governments or their agencies and with any private party to further the purposes of this Article.

(f)   Continuing Programs. - The Department of Cultural Resources shall develop a continuing program of historical, architectural, archaeological, and cultural research and development to include surveys, excavation, salvage, preservation, scientific recording, interpretation, and publication of the State's historical, architectural, archaeological, and cultural resources. A reasonable charge may be made for publications resulting therefrom and the income from such sales may be devoted to the work of the Department.

(g)   Abandoned Cemeteries. - The Department of Cultural Resources is authorized to take appropriate measures to record and permanently preserve information of significant historical genealogical or archaeological value when, in the opinion of the Department, any such information located within an abandoned cemetery is in imminent danger of loss or destruction because of the condition or circumstances of the cemetery. The Department may obtain access to any abandoned cemetery for the purpose of recording and preserving information of significant historical, genealogical or archaeological value pursuant to Chapter 15, Article 4A of the General Statutes: Provided, that prior to the requesting of the administrative warrant, the Department shall contact the affected landowners and request their consent for access to their lands for the purpose of gathering such information. If consent is not granted, the Department shall give reasonable notice of the time, place and before whom the administrative warrant will be requested so that the owner or owners may have an opportunity to be heard. Service of this notice may be in any manner prescribed by N.C.G.S. 1A-1 Rule 4(j). Any measures taken by the Department pursuant to this subsection shall be effected in such a manner as to cause as little inconvenience or disruption as possible to the owners of the land upon which the abandoned cemetery is located and of land necessary to obtain access to the cemetery. (1973, c. 476, s. 48; 1981, c. 215; 1989, c. 65; 2002-159, s. 35(h).)

203

§ 121-9. Historic properties.

(a)   Administration of Properties Acquired by State. - Historic or archaeological properties acquired by the State for administration by the State of North Carolina shall be under the control and administration of the Department of Cultural Resources. Upon approval of the North Carolina Historical Commission and the Secretary of Cultural Resources, the Department of Cultural Resources may, in its discretion, make a contract with any county or municipality within the State or with any nonprofit corporation or organization for the administration of any portion of such property.

(b)   Acquisition of Historic Properties. - For the purpose of protecting or preserving any property of historical, architectural, archaeological, or other cultural importance to the people of North Carolina, and subject to the provisions of Subchapter II of Chapter 146 of the General Statutes, the Department may, with the approval of the North Carolina Historical Commission and after consultation with the Joint Legislative Commission on Governmental Operations, acquire, preserve, restore, hold, maintain, operate, and dispose of such properties, together with such adjacent lands as may be necessary for their protection, preservation, maintenance, and operation. Such property may be real or personal in nature, and in the case of real property, the acquisition may include the fee or any lesser interest therein. Property may be acquired by gift, grant, devise, lease, purchase, or condemnation pursuant to the provisions of Chapter 40A of the General Statutes, or otherwise. Property may be acquired by the Department, using such funds as may be appropriated for the purpose or monies available to it from any other source.

(b1)   In the case of real property, the North Carolina Historical Commission shall report the following information to the Joint Legislative Commission on Governmental Operations before acquiring the property:

(1)   The statewide historical significance of the site.

(2)   The potential uses of the site.

(3)   The capital requirements of the site over a 20-year period of time.

(4)   The annual operating costs of the site.

(5)   The expected levels of visitation at the site.

(6)   Any other information that would assist in determining the full cost of maintaining, operating, and administering the site as State property.

(c)   Interests Which May Be Acquired. - In the case of real property, the interest acquired shall be limited to that estate, interest, or term deemed by the Department to be reasonably necessary for the continued protection or preservation of the property. The Department may acquire the fee simple title, but where it finds that a lesser interest, including any development right, negative or affirmative easement in gross or appurtenant, covenant, lease, or other contractual right of or to any real property to be the most practical and economical method of protecting and preserving historic property, the lesser interest may be acquired.

(d)   Conveyance of Property for Preservation Purposes. - In appropriate cases, the Department may acquire or dispose of the fee or lesser interest to any such property for the specific purpose of conveying or leasing the property back to its original owner or of conveying or leasing it to such other person, firm, association, corporation, or other organization under such covenants, deed restrictions, lease, or other contractual arrangements as will limit the future use of the property in such a way as to insure its preservation. Where such action is taken, the property may be conveyed or leased by private sale. In all cases where property is conveyed, it shall be subjected by covenant or otherwise to such rights of access, public visitation, and other conditions or restrictions of operation, maintenance, restoration, and repair as the Department may prescribe, or to such conditions as may be agreed upon between the Department and the grantee or lessee to accomplish the purposes of this section.

(e)   Use of Property so Acquired. - Any historic property acquired, whether in fee or otherwise, may be used, maintained, improved, restored, or operated by the Department for any public purpose within its powers and not inconsistent with the purpose of the continued preservation of the property. The property shall not be subject to condemnation by the State of North Carolina or any of its agencies or political subdivisions at any time, unless such method of acquisition is first approved by the Governor and Council of State.

(f)   Emergency Acquisition Where Funds Not Immediately Available. - If funds or contributions for the acquisition of needed historic property are not available, the Governor and Council of State may, upon the recommendation of the Secretary of Cultural Resources and approval of the North Carolina Historical Commission, allocate from the Contingency and Emergency Fund an amount sufficient to acquire an option on the property or properties, which option shall continue until 90 days after the adjournment sine die of the next General Assembly. Upon recommendation of the Secretary and approval of the Historical Commission, the Governor and Council of State may allocate funds from the Contingency and Emergency Fund for the immediate acquisition, preservation, restoration, or operation of historically, archaeologically, architecturally, or culturally important properties. All funds hereinafter appropriated to purchase, restore, maintain, develop, or operate historic or archaeological or other important property shall be administered subject to the provisions of Chapter 143C and G.S. 143B-53.1 of the General Statutes unless the statute making the appropriation shall in specific and express terms provide otherwise.

(g)   Power to Acquire Property by Condemnation. - In the event that a property which has been found by the Department of Cultural Resources to be important for public ownership or assistance is in danger of being sold, used, or neglected to such an extent that its historical or cultural importance will be destroyed or seriously impaired, or that the property is otherwise in danger of destruction or serious impairment, the Department of Cultural Resources, after receiving the approval of the North Carolina Historical Commission and of the Governor and Council of State, may acquire the historic property or any interest therein by condemnation under the provisions of Chapter 40A of the General Statutes. The Department of Cultural Resources, upon finding that destruction or serious impairment of the value of the property is imminent, shall file with the Governor and Council of State a report on the importance of the property and the desirability of ownership of the property, or the ownership of an interest therein, by the State of North Carolina. Upon giving their approval, the Governor and Council of State shall cause to have filed such approval with the clerk of the superior court in the county or counties where the property is situated. Until the approval is filed, the power of condemnation may not be exercised. All condemnation proceedings shall be instituted and prosecuted in the name of the State of North Carolina.

(h)   Preservation and Custodial Care of State Capitol. - The rotunda, corridors, and stairways of the first floor of the State Capitol and all portions of the second, third, and loft floors of the said building shall be placed in the custody of the Department of Cultural Resources; and the Department shall, subject to the availability of funds for the purpose, care for and administer these areas for the edification of present and future generations. The aforesaid areas shall be preserved as historic shrines and shall be maintained insofar as practicable as they shall appear following the restoration of the Capitol. The

Department of Cultural Resources is authorized to deny the use of the legislative chambers for meetings in order that they, with their historic furnishings, may be better preserved for posterity; provided, however, that the General Assembly may hold therein such sessions as it may by resolution deem proper.

The Department of Cultural Resources is hereby entrusted with the responsibilities herein specified as being the agency with the experience best qualified to preserve and administer historic properties in a suitable manner. However, for the purposes of carrying out the provisions of this section, it is hereby directed that such cooperation and assistance shall be made available to the said Department of Cultural Resources and such labor supplied, as may be feasible, by the Department of Administration.

The offices and working areas of the first floor as well as all washrooms and the exterior of the Capitol shall remain under the jurisdiction of the Department of Administration: Provided, however, that the Department of Administration shall seek the advice of the Department of Cultural Resources in matters relating to any alteration, renovation, and furnishing of said offices and areas. (1955, c. 543, s. 1; 1961, c. 724; 1963, c. 210, s. 1; 1965, c. 1129; 1971, c. 480, ss. 1-3, 5; 1973, c. 476, s. 48; 1991 (Reg. Sess., 1992), c. 1030, s. 34; 1993 (Reg. Sess., 1994), c. 682, s. 2; 1995, c. 507, s. 12(b); 1996, 2nd Ex. Sess., c. 18, s. 7.7(a); 2006-203, s. 64; 2011-284, s. 87.)

§ 121-9.1. Lake Mattamuskeet Lodge Preservation.

(a)   Notwithstanding G.S. 121-9, the State of North Carolina accepts the transfer of the Mattamuskeet Lodge and surrounding property to the State under the Lake Mattamuskeet Lodge Preservation Act, P.L. 109-358. After completion of repairs and renovations by the Department of Cultural Resources, the property shall be transferred to and managed by the Wildlife Resources Commission.

(b)   Any plans for repair and renovation of the Mattamuskeet Lodge from the Repairs and Renovations Reserve Account under G.S. 143C-4-3 are subject to review by the Wildlife Resources Commission. (2007-13, ss. 1, 2.)

§ 121-10. Security of historic properties.

(a)   Designated Employees Commissioned Special Peace Officers by Governor. - Upon application by the Secretary of Cultural Resources, the Governor is hereby authorized and empowered to commission as special peace officers such employees of the Department of Cultural Resources as the Secretary may designate for the purpose of enforcing the laws, rules, and regulations enacted or adopted for the protection, preservation and government of State historic or archaeological properties under the control or supervision of the Department of Cultural Resources. Such employees shall receive no additional compensation for performing the duties of special peace officers under this section.

(b)   Powers of Arrest. - Any employee of the Department of Cultural Resources commissioned as a special peace officer shall have the right to arrest with warrant any person violating any law, rule, or regulation on or relating to the State historic or archaeological properties under the control or supervision of the Department of Cultural Resources, and shall have power to pursue and arrest without warrant any person violating in his presence any law, rule, or regulation on or relating to said historic and archaeological properties under the control or supervision of the Department of Cultural Resources.

(c)   Bond Required. - Each employee of the Department of Cultural Resources commissioned as a special peace officer under this section shall give a bond with a good surety, payable to the State of North Carolina in a sum not less than one thousand dollars ($1,000), conditioned upon the faithful discharge of his duty as such peace officer. The bond shall be duly approved by and filed in the office of the Commissioner of Insurance, and copies of the same, certified by the Commissioner of Insurance, shall be received in evidence in all actions and proceedings in this State.

(d)   Oaths Required. - Before any employee of the Department of Cultural Resources commissioned as a special peace officer shall exercise any power of arrest under this Article, he shall take the oaths required of public officers before an officer authorized to administer oaths. (1955, c. 543, s. 1; 1973, c. 476, s. 48.)

§ 121-11. Procedures where assistance extended to cities, counties, and other agencies or individuals.

In consideration of the public purpose thereby achieved, the Department of Cultural Resources may assist any county, city, or other political subdivision, corporation or organization, or private individual in the acquisition, maintenance, preservation, restoration, or development of historic or archaeological property by providing a portion of the cost therefor: Provided, that the Department of Cultural Resources may not make any acquisition, maintenance, preservation, restoration, or development of any property, nor any assistance for any property, nor any contribution for these purposes, until:

(1)   The property or properties shall have been approved for these purposes by the Department of Cultural Resources according to criteria adopted by the North Carolina Historical Commission,

(2)   The report and recommendations of the Commission have been received and considered by the Department of Cultural Resources, and

(3)   The Department has found that there is a feasible and practical method of providing funds for the acquisition, restoration, preservation, maintenance, and operation of such property.

In all cases where assistance is extended by the Department of Cultural Resources to nonstate owners of property, whether from State funds or otherwise, it shall be a condition of assistance that

(1)   The property assisted shall, upon its acquisition or restoration, be made accessible to the public at such times and upon such terms as the Department of Cultural Resources shall by rule prescribe;

(2)   That the plans for preservation, restoration, and development be reviewed and approved by the Department of Cultural Resources;

(3)   That the expenditure of such funds be supervised by the Department of Cultural Resources; and

(4)   That such expenditures be accounted to the Department in a manner and at such times as are satisfactory to it.

In further consideration of the public purpose thereby achieved, the Department of Cultural Resources may assist any county, city, or other political subdivision, or corporation nonprofit history museum in the development of interpretive, security or climate control programs or projects. Provided, that the Department of Cultural Resources may not make any assistance or contribution from State funds for a program or project until:

(1)　　The program or project shall have been approved for these purposes by the Department of Cultural Resources according to criteria adopted by the North Carolina Historical Commission;

(2)　　The report and recommendations of the Commission have been received and considered by the Department of Cultural Resources; and

(3)　　The Department has found that there is a feasible and practical method of providing funds for the maintenance and operation of such history museum.

In all cases where assistance is extended by the Department of Cultural Resources to nonstate owners of history museums, whether from State funds or otherwise, it shall be a condition of assistance that:

(1)　　The museum assisted shall be accessible to the public at such times and upon such terms as the Department of Cultural Resources shall by rule prescribe;

(2)　　Plans for the development of museum programs or projects be reviewed and approved by the Department of Cultural Resources;

(3)　　The expenditure of such funds be supervised by the Department of Cultural Resources; and

(4)　　Such expenditures be accounted to the Department in a manner and at such times as are satisfactory to it. (1973, c. 476, s. 48; 1979, c. 861, s. 2; 1985 (Reg. Sess., 1986), c. 1014, s. 171(a).)

§ 121-12. North Carolina Historical Commission.

(a)　　Protection of Properties on National Register. - It shall be the duty of the Historical Commission, meeting at such times and according to such procedures as it shall by rule prescribe, to provide an advisory and coordinative mechanism in and by which State undertakings of every kind that are potentially harmful to the cause of historic preservation within the State may be discussed, and where possible, resolved, giving due consideration to the competing public interests that may be involved. To this end, the head of any State agency having direct or indirect jurisdiction over a proposed State or state-assisted undertaking, or the head of any State department, board, commission, or independent agency having authority to build, construct, operate, license, authorize, assist, or approve any State or state-assisted undertaking, shall, prior to the approval of any State funds for the undertaking, or prior to any approval, license, or authorization, as the case may be, take into account the effect of the undertaking on any district, site, building, structure, or object that is listed in the National Register of Historic Places established pursuant to Public Law 89-665, 16 U.S.C. 470.

Where, in the judgment of the Commission, an undertaking will have an effect upon any listed district, site, building, structure, area, or object, the head of the appropriate State agency shall afford the Commission a reasonable opportunity to comment with regard to such undertaking.

The Historical Commission shall act with reasonable diligence to insure that all State departments, boards, commissions, or agencies potentially affected by the provisions of this section be kept currently informed with respect to the name, location, and other significant particulars of any district, site, building, structure, or object listed or placed upon the National Register of Historic Places. Each affected State department or agency shall furnish, either upon its own initiative or at the request of the Historical Commission such information as may reasonably be required by the Commission for the proper implementation of this section.

(b)   Criteria for State Historic Properties. - The Commission shall prepare and adopt criteria for the evaluation of State historic sites and all other real and personal property which it may consider to be of such historic, architectural, archaeological, or cultural importance as would justify the acquisition and ownership thereof by the State of North Carolina, or for the extension of any assistance or aid thereto by the State, acting by itself or in connection with any county, city, corporation, organization, or individual. The Commission shall cooperate to the fullest practical extent with any local historical organization and with any city or county historic district properties commission. In evaluating whether a building should be a State historic site, the Commission shall request and review plans for the use and maintenance of the building.

(c)   Criteria for State Aid to Historic Properties. - The Commission shall also prepare and adopt criteria for the evaluation of all properties of historic or archaeological importance owned by, under option to, or being considered for

211

acquisition by a county, city, historic properties commission, or other organization or individual for which State aid or assistance is requested from the Department of Cultural Resources. The Commission shall investigate, evaluate, and prepare a written report on all historic or archaeological property for which State aid or appropriations to be administered by the Department of Cultural Resources are proposed. If the property is a building, the Commission shall request and review the plans for the use, maintenance, operation, and purpose of the building and shall comment on the feasibility of the plans in the written report. This report, which shall be filed as a matter of record in the custody of the Department of Cultural Resources, shall set forth the following opinions or recommendations of the Commission:

(1)   Whether the property is historically authentic;

(2)   Whether it is of such educational, historical, or cultural significance as to be essential to the development of a balanced State program of historic and archaeological sites and properties;

(3)   The estimated total cost of the project under consideration and the apportionment of said cost among State and nonstate sources;

(4)   Whether practical plans have been or can be developed for the funding of the nonstate portion of the costs;

(5)   Whether practical plans have been developed for the continued staffing, maintenance and operation of the property without State assistance; and

(6)   Such further comments and recommendations that the Commission may make.

(c1)   Criteria for State Aid to Historical Museums. - The Commission shall also prepare and adopt criteria for the evaluation of all interpretive, security or climate control programs or projects to be installed in nonprofit history museums for which State aid or assistance is requested from the Department of Cultural Resources. The Commission shall investigate, evaluate, and prepare a written report on all interpretive, security, or climate control programs or projects for which State appropriations to be administered by the Department of Cultural Resources are proposed. This report, which shall be filed as a matter of record in the custody of the Department of Cultural Resources, shall set forth the following opinions or recommendations of the Commission:

(1)   The statewide educational significance and the qualitative level of the program or project and whether the program or project is essential to the development of a State program of historical interpretation;

(2)   The local or regional need for such a program or project;

(3)   The estimated total cost of the program or project under consideration and the apportionment of said cost among State and nonstate sources;

(4)   Whether practical plans have been or can be developed for the funding of the nonstate portions of the costs;

(5)   Whether practical plans have been developed for the continued staffing, maintenance, and operating of the museum without State assistance; and

(6)   Such further comments and recommendations that the Commission may make.

(d)   Commission to Furnish Recommendations to Legislative Committees. - The Commission through the Department of Cultural Resources shall furnish as soon as practicable to the chairman of each legislative committee to which is referred any bill seeking an appropriation of State funds to the Department of Cultural Resources for the purpose of acquiring, preserving, restoring, or operating, or otherwise assisting, any property having historic, archaeological, architectural, or other cultural value or significance, and to the chairman of each legislative committee to which is referred any bill seeking an appropriation of State funds to the Department of Cultural Resources for the purpose of assisting a history museum, at least five copies of a report on the findings and recommendations of the Commission relating to such property. (1973, c. 476, s. 48; 1975, c. 19, s. 40; 1979, c. 861, ss. 3-5; 1985 (Reg. Sess., 1986), c. 1014, s. 171(b); 1995, c. 324, s. 12.)

§ 121-12.1. Grants-in-aid.

Under the concepts of reorganization of State government, responsibility for administering appropriations to the Department of Cultural Resources for grants-in-aid to private nonprofit organizations in the areas of history, art, and culture is hereby assigned to the Department of Cultural Resources. It shall be the responsibility of the Department of Cultural Resources to receive, analyze, and recommend to the Governor and the General Assembly the disposition of any request for funding received by it from or for any of these organizations, and to disburse under provisions of law any appropriations made to the Department for them. Appropriations to the Department of Cultural Resources for grants-in-aid to assist in the restoration of historic sites owned by private nonprofit organizations shall in addition be expended only in accordance with G.S. 121-11, 121-12 and 143B-53.1. (1977, c. 802, s. 47; 1985 (Reg. Sess., 1986), c. 955, s. 40; c. 1014, s. 171(c); 2006-203, s. 65.)

§ 121-12.2. Procedures for preparing budget requests and expending appropriations for grants-in-aid.

Requests for funding may be submitted by these organizations to the Department of Cultural Resources. If received by any other department of State government except the General Assembly they shall be forwarded to the Department of Cultural Resources. All such requests shall be subjected to the process described in G.S. 121-12.1 and included in the Department's biennial budget request submitted in compliance with the Executive Budget Act.

The Department of Cultural Resources shall notify on a timely basis and in appropriate detail all those recipients of continuing appropriations as grants-in-aid of the requirements for submission of requests for appropriations for the ensuing fiscal period.

The Secretary of Cultural Resources is empowered and directed, in discharging the responsibilities herein assigned, to make regular and timely reviews, studies and recommendations concerning the operations and needs of these organizations for State funds, and to request from the applicants for grants and the recipients of grants through the Department, operating statements, audit reports and other information deemed appropriate. (1977, c. 802, s. 47; 1985 (Reg. Sess., 1986), c. 1014, s. 171(d).)

§ 121-13. Acquisition of portrait of Governor during term of office.

During the term of office of each Governor of this State and at least six months prior to its expiration, the Secretary of the Department of Cultural Resources is directed to select a skilled artist to paint a portrait of such Governor, and have the same suitably framed. Upon the painting and acquisition of such portrait, the same shall be placed in some appropriate building to be designated by the Department of Cultural Resources and which is located in the City of Raleigh.

The cost of the painting and acquisition of said portrait, including the cost of the frame and other necessary expenses incident thereto, shall be paid from the Contingency and Emergency Fund. (1955, c. 1248; 1973, c. 476, s. 48.)

§§ 121-13.1 through 121-13.2. Repealed by Session Laws 1973, c. 476, s. 48.

Article 2.

Tryon's Palace and Tryon's Palace Commission.

§ 121-14. Acceptance and administration of gifts for restoration of Tryon's Palace; execution of deeds, etc.

The Department of Cultural Resources is hereby authorized and empowered to accept gifts of real or personal property from any source for the restoration of Tryon's Palace at New Bern, North Carolina, and administer the same. All gifts of moneys received by the Department of Cultural Resources shall be deposited in a special account with the Treasurer of North Carolina. The Department of Cultural Resources is hereby given authority to execute such deeds and other instruments as may be necessary. (1945, c. 791, s. 1; 1955, c. 543, s. 8; 1973, c. 476, s. 48.)

§ 121-15. Authority to acquire necessary property for restoration when certain funds available.

The Department of Cultural Resources is hereby authorized and directed to acquire the necessary property in New Bern, North Carolina, for the restoration of Tryon's Palace, when as much as two hundred fifty thousand dollars ($250,000), or securities in said amount as provided in G.S. 121-17, has been

215

provided by private contributions for this purpose: Provided, that the Department of Cultural Resources at such time shall find that there are reasonable grounds to anticipate that from private donations there will thereafter be provided ample funds to restore the Palace. (1945, c. 791, s. 2; 1949, c. 233, s. 1; 1955, c. 543, s. 8; 1973, c. 476, s. 48.)

§ 121-16. Acquiring lands by purchase or condemnation.

The Department of Cultural Resources, within the limits and amounts appropriated by the General Assembly and any funds available from donations or otherwise, when the conditions set forth in G.S. 121-15 of this Article have been met, is hereby granted the power and authority to purchase sufficient lands for the restoration of the Palace, and the Department is hereby authorized to accept title to lands in the name of the State of North Carolina.

The Department of Cultural Resources shall also have the authority to acquire, by condemnation, under the provisions of Chapter 40A of the General Statutes of North Carolina, including the provisions of the Public Works Eminent Domain Law, which is hereby made applicable to such proceedings, any areas of land in New Bern, North Carolina, as it may find necessary for the restoration of the Palace. (1945, c. 791, s. 3; 1949, c. 233, s. 2; 1955, c. 543, s. 8; 1973, c. 476, s. 48; 2001-487, s. 38(g).)

§ 121-17. Funds deposited with trustee.

The Governor as Director of the Budget shall have full authority and discretion to approve the acceptance of donations of cash or securities irrevocably deposited with a trustee in lieu of any requirement that funds provided by outside sources be turned over to the State, and funds or securities placed in trust by private donors for such purpose shall be deemed to be funds turned over to the State for acquisition and restoration of the Palace. (1945, c. 791, s. 4.)

§ 121-18. Closing streets and including area in restoration project; acquiring area originally included in Palace grounds.

Whereas the said Tryon's Palace and grounds originally included all of that area in the City of New Bern known and designated as George Street between Pollock and South Front Streets, and the title thereto is in the State of North Carolina, subject to the easement for use of said street, and the use of such portion of said George Street is essential for a proper restoration of Tryon's Palace, when the governing body of the City of New Bern under its general authority imposed by law shall close George Street between Pollock and South Front Streets, or such portion thereof as may be found by the Commission herein authorized to be essential for the purposes of such restoration, the area within such closed street shall be thereafter used exclusively for the restoration of Tryon's Palace. Provided, that the Department of Cultural Resources is authorized and empowered, in its discretion, to acquire for the use of said Tryon's Palace such part of the area in the City of New Bern originally included in the Palace grounds as may be deemed reasonably necessary for the restoration of said Palace. (1945, c. 791, s. 5; 1949, c. 233, s. 3; 1955, c. 543, s. 8; 1973, c. 476, s. 48.)

§ 121-19. Repealed by Session Laws 1973, c. 476, s. 56.

§ 121-20. Commission to receive and expend funds donated or made available for restoration of Tryon's Palace; Commission to acquire and sell artifacts for Tryon's Palace.

(a)   In addition to exercising the powers and duties imposed upon the Tryon Palace Commission by Chapter 791 of the Session Laws of 1945 and Chapter 233 of the Session Laws of 1949, the Tryon Palace Commission is hereby fully authorized and empowered to receive and expend and disburse, for the restoration of the said Tryon's Palace, all such funds and property which were provided for said purpose by the last will and testament of Maude Moore Latham, deceased, and the said Commission shall likewise have the power and authority to receive and expend all such other funds as may be donated or made available for the purpose of restoring the said Palace or for the purpose of furnishing and equipping same and the grounds on which the same is located at New Bern, North Carolina.

The Tryon Palace Commission is hereby authorized, empowered and directed to designate some person as financial officer and treasurer, to disburse the funds and property devised by Maude Moore Latham to the said Tryon Palace Commission for the aforesaid purpose and all such other funds as may be donated or made available to the said Commission for expenditure for the aforesaid purposes. The said financial officer and treasurer shall be made the custodian of all stocks, bonds and securities and funds hereinbefore referred to and shall be authorized and empowered to sell, convert and transfer any stocks, bonds and securities held for such purpose, subject to and with the advice and approval of a finance committee to be appointed by the Tryon Palace Commission for such purpose. The sale and conversion and transfer of said securities shall be made when necessary to provide funds required for the said restoration and at such time as, in the opinion of the finance officer and treasurer, when approved by the finance committee, will be to the interests and advantage of the Tryon Palace Commission and the purposes for which said funds and securities were provided.

The finance officer and treasurer aforesaid shall be required to give such bond as, in the opinion of the Tryon Palace Commission, is proper for the faithful performance as finance officer and treasurer, and shall render to the Tryon Palace Finance Committee, with copies to the Department of Cultural Resources and the State Treasurer, annual or ad interim detailed reports of moneys and/or securities received, exchanged or converted into cash. Checks issued against such funds shall be countersigned by the chairman of Tryon Palace Commission, or by one duly authorized by the said Commission.

The finance officer and treasurer shall serve without compensation; however, any expenses incurred for the faithful performance of said duties, including the cost of the bond, shall be borne by the Tryon Palace Commission, from the proceeds of the funds thus handled.

The Tryon Palace Commission shall have the power and authority in its discretion to call upon the Treasurer of the State of North Carolina to act as treasurer of the said funds and properties and, if so designated, said treasurer shall exercise all the powers and duties herein imposed upon the financial officer and treasurer hereinbefore referred to.

The Tryon Palace Commission is hereby authorized and empowered to expend the funds hereinbefore referred to and it may disburse said funds through the Department of Cultural Resources in the event it is found more practical to do so, and said Commission shall cooperate with the Department of Cultural Resources of the State of North Carolina in the expenditure of the funds for the restoration of said Tryon's Palace provided by two trust funds created by Maude

Moore Latham in her lifetime, which funds shall be expended in accordance with the terms and provisions of said trusts for the purposes therein set out.

(b)   The Tryon Palace Commission may solicit, accept, and hold artifacts and furnishings, and may acquire them by purchase or gift for the interpretive needs and development of Tryon Palace Historic Sites and Gardens. The Commission may dispose of by trade, sale, or transfer, in accordance with accepted museum practices, any accessioned or unaccessioned artifacts and furnishings in the custody of the Commission, or its appointed officers, that are determined to have no further value for official or administrative purposes or for research, reference, or interpretation. Any proceeds realized through the deaccession and sale of artifacts and furnishings shall be placed in a collections fund administered by the Tryon Palace Commission. Monies received by the Commission, after deduction of the expenses attributable to that sale, shall be used for the acquisition of artifacts and furnishings necessary or desirable for research, reference, and interpretation at Tryon Palace Historic Sites and Gardens. (1953, c. 1100; 1973, c. 1262, s. 86; 1975, c. 387; 1993 (Reg. Sess., 1994), c. 769, s. 12.2.)

§ 121-21. Commission authorized to adopt and copyright certain emblems and lease or license the use of reproductions or replicas.

The Tryon Palace Commission is hereby authorized to adopt an official flag, seal, and other emblems appropriate in connection with the management and operation of the Tryon Palace Restoration, and to copyright the same in the name of the State. The Commission, with the approval of the Governor, is authorized to lease or license the use of reproductions or replicas of such flag, seal, and other emblems upon such terms and conditions as it deems advisable. (1957, c. 1449.)

§ 121-21.1. Tryon Palace Historic Sites and Gardens Fund.

(a)   Fund. - The Tryon Palace Historic Sites and Gardens Fund is hereby created as a special, interest-bearing, and nonreverting fund in the Division of Tryon Palace Historic Sites and Gardens. The Fund shall be treated as a special trust fund and shall be credited with interest by the State Treasurer pursuant to G.S. 147-69.2 and G.S. 147-69.3. The Fund shall be used for repair, renovation, expansion, and maintenance at Tryon Palace Historic Sites and Gardens.

(b)   Disposition of Fees. - All entrance fee receipts shall be credited to the Tryon Palace Historic Sites and Gardens Fund.

(c)   The Tryon Palace Commission shall submit to the Joint Legislative Commission on Governmental Operations, the House and Senate Appropriations Subcommittees on General Government, and the Fiscal Research Division by September 30 of each year a report on the Tryon Palace Historic Sites and Gardens Fund that shall include the source and amounts of all funds credited to the Fund and the purpose and amount of all expenditures from the Fund during the prior fiscal year. (2005-276, s. 19A.1; 2006-180, s. 1.)

Article 3.

Salvage of Abandoned Shipwrecks and Other Underwater Archaeological Sites.

§ 121-22. Title to bottoms of certain waters and shipwrecks, etc., thereon declared to be in State.

Subject to Chapter 82 of the General Statutes, entitled "Wrecks" and to the provisions of Chapter 210, Session Laws of 1963, and to any statute of the United States, the title to all bottoms of navigable waters within one marine league seaward from the Atlantic seashore measured from the extreme low watermark; and the title to all shipwrecks, vessels, cargoes, tackle, and underwater archaeological artifacts which have remained unclaimed for more than 10 years lying on the said bottoms, or on the bottoms of any other navigable waters of the State, is hereby declared to be in the State of North Carolina, and such bottoms, shipwrecks, vessels, cargoes, tackle, and underwater archaeological artifacts shall be subject to the exclusive dominion and control of the State. (1967, c. 533, s. 1.)

§ 121-23. Department is custodian of underwater personal property of the State and may adopt rules concerning the property.

The Department of Cultural Resources is the custodian of shipwrecks, vessels, cargoes, tackle, and underwater archaeological artifacts to which the State has title under G.S. 121-22. The Department of Cultural Resources may adopt rules necessary to preserve, protect, recover, or salvage any or all of these properties. (1967, c. 533, s. 2; 1973, c. 476, s. 48; 1993, c. 249.)

§ 121-24. Department authorized to establish professional staff.

The Department of Cultural Resources is also authorized to establish a professional staff for the purpose of conducting and/or supervising the surveillance, protection, preservation, survey and systematic underwater archaeological recovery of underwater materials as defined in G.S. 121-22 hereof. (1967, c. 533, s. 3; 1973, c. 476, s. 48.)

§ 121-25. License to conduct exploration, recovery or salvage operations.

Any qualified person, firm or corporation desiring to conduct any type of exploration, recovery or salvage operations, in the course of which any part of a derelict vessel or its contents or other archaeological site may be removed, displaced or destroyed, shall first make application to the Department of Cultural Resources and obtain a permit or license to conduct such operations. If the Department of Cultural Resources shall find that the granting of such permit or license is in the best interest of the State, it may grant such applicant a permit or license for such a period of time and under such conditions as the Department may deem to be in the best interest of the State. Such permit or license may include but need not be limited to the following:

(1)   Payment of monetary fee to be set by the Department;

(2)   That a portion or all of the historic material or artifacts be delivered to custody and possession of the Department;

(3)   That a portion of all of such relics or artifacts may be sold or retained by the licensee;

(4)   That a portion or all of such relics or artifacts may be sold or traded by the Department.

221

Permits or licenses may be renewed upon or prior to expiration upon such terms as the applicant and the Department may mutually agree. Holders of permits or licenses shall be responsible for obtaining permission of any federal agencies having jurisdiction, including the United States Coast Guard, the United States Department of the Navy and the United States Army Corps of Engineers prior to conducting any salvaging operations. (1967, c. 533, s. 4; 1973, c. 476, s. 48; 2005-367, s. 2.)

§ 121-25.1. Criminal record checks of applicants for permit or license.

(a)   The following definitions apply to this section:

(1)   Applicant. - A person or entity applying for a permit or license under G.S. 121-25 to conduct any type of exploration, recovery, or salvage operations of any part of a derelict vessel or its contents or other archaeological site.

(2)   Criminal history. - A history of conviction of a state or federal crime, whether a misdemeanor or felony, that bears upon an applicant's fitness to conduct activities related to the surveillance, protection, preservation, and archaeological recovery of property subject to the exclusive dominion and control of the State under G.S. 121-22. The crimes include the criminal offenses set forth in any of the following Articles of Chapter 14 of the General Statutes: Article 5, Counterfeiting and Issuing Monetary Substitutes; Article 5A, Endangering Executive and Legislative Officers and Court Officers; Article 6, Homicide; Article 7A, Rape and Other Sex Offenses; Article 8, Assaults; Article 10, Kidnapping and Abduction; Article 13, Malicious Injury or Damage by Use of Explosive or Incendiary Device or Material; Article 14, Burglary and Other Housebreakings; Article 15, Arson and Other Burnings; Article 16, Larceny; Article 17, Robbery; Article 18, Embezzlement; Article 19, False Pretenses and Cheats; Article 19A, Obtaining Property or Services by False or Fraudulent Use of Credit Device or Other Means; Article 19B, Financial Transaction Card Crime Act; Article 19C, Financial Identity Fraud; Article 20, Frauds; Article 21, Forgery; Article 26, Offenses Against Public Morality and Decency; Article 26A, Adult Establishments; Article 27, Prostitution; Article 28, Perjury; Article 29, Bribery; Article 31, Misconduct in Public Office; Article 35, Offenses Against the Public Peace; Article 36A, Riots, Civil Disorders, and Emergencies; Article 39, Protection of Minors; Article 40, Protection of the Family; Article 59, Public Intoxication; and Article 60, Computer-Related Crime. The crimes also include possession or sale of drugs in violation of the North Carolina Controlled

Substances Act, Article 5 of Chapter 90 of the General Statutes, and alcohol-related offenses such as sale to underage persons in violation of G.S. 18B-302, or driving while impaired in violation of G.S. 20-138.1 through G.S. 20-138.5.

(b)   All applicants shall consent to a criminal history record check. Refusal to consent to a criminal history record check or to the use of fingerprints or other identifying information may constitute grounds for the Department of Cultural Resources to deny a permit or a license to an applicant. The Department of Cultural Resources shall be responsible for providing to the North Carolina Department of Justice the fingerprints of the applicant to be checked, a form signed by the applicant consenting to the criminal record check and the use of fingerprints and other identifying information required by the State or National Repositories of Criminal Histories, and any additional information required by the Department of Justice. If the applicant is not an individual, the applicant shall provide fingerprints for the principals, officers, directors, and controlling persons of the applicant. Each set of fingerprints shall be certified by an authorized law enforcement officer. The Department of Cultural Resources shall keep all information obtained under this section confidential.

(c)   If an applicant's criminal history record check reveals one or more convictions listed under subdivision (a)(2) of this section, the conviction shall not automatically bar the issuance of a permit or a license. When determining whether to issue a permit or license to an applicant, the Department of Cultural Resources shall consider all of the following factors regarding the conviction:

(1)   The level and seriousness of the crime.

(2)   The date of the crime.

(3)   The age of the person at the time of conviction.

(4)   The circumstances surrounding the commission of the crime, if known.

(5)   The nexus between the criminal conduct of the person and the person's responsibilities pursuant to the application.

(6)   The incarceration, probation, parole, rehabilitation, and employment records of the person since the date the crime was committed.

(7)   The subsequent commission by the person of a crime. (2005-367, s. 3; 2012-12, s. 2(ss).)

223

§ 121-26. Funds received by Department under § 121-25.

Any funds which may be paid to or received by the Department of Cultural Resources under the terms of G.S. 121-25 hereof may be allocated for use by the Department of Cultural Resources for continuing its duties under this Article, subject to the approval of the Department of Administration. (1967, c. 533, s. 5; 1973, c. 476, s. 48; 1975, c. 879, s. 46.)

§ 121-27. Law-enforcement agencies empowered to assist Department.

All law-enforcement agencies and officers, State and local, are hereby empowered to assist the Department of Cultural Resources in carrying out its duties under this Article. (1967, c. 533, s. 6; 1973, c. 476, s. 48.)

§ 121-28. Violation of Article a misdemeanor.

Any person violating the provisions of this Article or any rules or regulations established thereunder shall be guilty of a Class 1 misdemeanor. (1967, c. 533, s. 8; 1993, c. 539, s. 917; 1994, Ex. Sess., c. 24, s. 14(c).)

§§ 121-29 through 121-33. Reserved for future codification purposes.

Article 4.

Conservation and Historic Preservation Agreements Act.

§ 121-34. Short title.

The title of this Article shall be known as the "Conservation and Historic Preservation Agreements Act." (1979, c. 747, s. 1; 2004-195, s. 1.3.)

§ 121-35. Definitions.

Subject to any additional definitions contained in this Article, or unless the context otherwise requires:

(1)   A "conservation agreement" means a right, whether or not stated in the form of a restriction, reservation, easement, covenant or condition, in any deed, will or other instrument executed by or on behalf of the owner of land or improvement thereon or in any order of taking, appropriate to retaining land or water areas predominantly in their natural, scenic or open condition or in agricultural, horticultural, farming or forest use, to forbid or limit any or all (i) construction or placing of buildings, roads, signs, billboards or other advertising, utilities or other structures on or above the ground, (ii) dumping or placing of soil or other substance or material as landfill, or dumping or placing of trash, waste or unsightly or offensive materials, (iii) removal or destruction of trees, shrubs or other vegetation, (iv) excavation, dredging or removal of loam, peat, gravel, soil, rock or other mineral substance in such manner as to affect the surface, (v) surface use except for agricultural, farming, forest or outdoor recreational purposes or purposes permitting the land or water area to remain predominantly in its natural condition, (vi) activities detrimental to drainage, flood control, water conservation, erosion control or soil conservation, or (vii) other acts or uses detrimental to such retention of land or water areas.

(2)   "Holder" means any public body of this State, including the State, any of its agencies, any city, county, district or other political subdivision or municipal or public corporation, or any instrumentality of any of the foregoing, any agency, department, or instrumentality of the United States, any nonprofit corporation or trust, or any private corporation or business entity whose purposes include any of those stated in (1) and (3), covering the purposes of preservation and conservation agreements.

(3)   A "preservation agreement" means a right, whether or not stated in the form of a restriction, reservation, easement, covenant, condition or otherwise, in any deed, will or other instrument executed by or on behalf of the owner of the land or any improvement thereon, or in any other [order] of taking, appropriate to preservation of a structure or site historically significant for its architecture, archaeology or historical associations, to forbid or limit any or all (i) alteration, (ii) alterations in exterior or interior features of the structure, (iii) changes in appearance or condition of the site, (iv) uses not historically appropriate, or (v) other acts or uses supportive of or detrimental to appropriate preservation of the structure or site. (1979, c. 747, s. 2; 1995, c. 443, s. 1.)

§ 121-36. Applicability.

225

(a)   This Article shall apply to all conservation and preservation agreements falling within its terms and conditions.

(b)   This Article shall not be construed to make unenforceable any restriction, easement, covenant or condition which does not comply with the requirements of this Article.

(c)   This Article shall not be construed to diminish the powers of any public entity, agency, or instrumentality to acquire by purchase, gift, devise, inheritance, eminent domain or otherwise and to use property of any kind for public purposes. (1979, c. 747, s. 3.)

§ 121-37. Acquisition and approval of conservation and preservation agreements.

Subject to the conditions stated in this Article, any holder may, in any manner, acquire, receive or become a party of a conservation agreement or a preservation agreement. (1979, c. 747, s. 4.)

§ 121-38. Validity of agreements.

(a)   No conservation or preservation agreement shall be unenforceable because of

(1)   Lack of privity of estate or contract, or

(2)   Lack of benefit to particular land or person, or

(3)   The assignability of the benefit to another holder as defined in this Article.

(b)   These agreements are interests in land and may be acquired by any holder in the same manner as it may acquire other interests in land.

(c)   These agreements may be effective perpetually or for shorter stipulated periods of time.

(d)   These agreements may impose present, future, or continuing obligations on either party to the agreement, or their successors, in furtherance of the purposes of the agreement.

(e)   These agreements may contain provisions which require the payment of a fee upon a future conveyance of the property that is subject to the agreement. (1979, c. 747, s. 5; 2008-165, s. 1.)

§ 121-39. Enforceability of agreements.

(a)   Conservation or preservation agreements may be enforced by the holder by injunction and other appropriate equitable relief administered or afforded by the courts of this State. Where appropriate under the agreement, damages, or other monetary relief may also be awarded either to the holder or creator of the agreement or either of their successors for breach of any obligations undertaken by either.

(b)   Such agreements shall entitle representatives of the holder to enter the involved land or improvement in a reasonable manner and at reasonable times to assure compliance. (1979, c. 747, s. 6.)

§ 121-40. Assessment of land or improvements subject to agreement.

For purposes of taxation, land and improvements subject to a conservation or preservation agreement shall be assessed on the basis of the true value of the land and improvement less any reduction in value caused by the agreement. (1979, c. 747, s. 7.)

§ 121-41. Public recording of agreements.

(a)   Except as provided in subsection (c) of this section, conservation agreements shall be recorded in the office of the Register of Deeds of the county or counties in which the subject land or improvement is located, in the same manner as deeds are now recorded.

(b)   Releases or terminations of such agreements shall be recorded in the same waiver. Releases or terminations, or the recording entry, shall appropriately identify by date, parties, and book and pages of recording, the agreement which is the subject of the release or termination.

(c)   A conservation agreement entered into for the purpose of enrolling real property in a voluntary agricultural district pursuant to G.S. 106-737(4) is not required to be recorded unless such conservation agreement is irrevocable as provided pursuant to G.S. 106-743.2. (1979, c. 747, s. 8; 2011-219, s. 2.)

§ 121-42. Citation of Article.

This Article shall be known and may be cited as the "Conservation and Historic Preservation Agreements Act." (1979, c. 747, s. 9; 2004-195, s. 1.4.)

Chapter 122.

Hospitals for the Mentally Disordered.

§§ 122-1 through 122-122: Repealed by Session Laws 1985, c. 589, s. 1.

Chapter 122A.

North Carolina Housing Finance Agency.

§ 122A-1. Short title.

This Chapter shall be known and may be cited as the "North Carolina Housing Finance Agency Act." (1969, c. 1235, s. 1; 1973, c. 1296, s. 1.)

§ 122A-2. Legislative findings and purposes.

The General Assembly hereby finds and declares that as a result of the spread of slum conditions and blight to formerly sound urban and rural neighborhoods and as a result of actions involving highways, public facilities and urban renewal activities there exists in the State of North Carolina a serious shortage of decent, safe and sanitary residential housing available at low prices or rentals to persons and families of lower income. This shortage is severe in certain urban areas of the State, is especially critical in the rural areas, and is inimical to the health, safety, welfare and prosperity of all residents of the State and to the sound growth of North Carolina communities.

The General Assembly hereby finds and declares further that private enterprise and investment have not been able to produce, without assistance, the needed construction of decent, safe and sanitary residential housing at low prices or rentals which persons and families of lower income can afford, or to achieve the urgently needed rehabilitation of much of the present lower income housing. It is imperative that the supply of residential housing for persons and families of lower income affected by the spread of slum conditions and blight and for persons and families of lower income displaced by public actions or natural disaster be increased; and that private enterprise and investment be encouraged to sponsor, build and rehabilitate residential housing for such persons and families, to help prevent the recurrence of slum conditions and blight and assist in their permanent elimination throughout North Carolina.

The General Assembly hereby finds and declares further that the purposes of this Chapter are to provide financing for residential housing construction, new or rehabilitated, for sale or rental to persons and families of lower income.

The General Assembly hereby finds and declares further that in accomplishing this purpose, the North Carolina Housing Finance Agency, a public agency and an instrumentality of the State, is acting in all respects for the benefit of the people of the State in the performance of essential public functions and serves a public purpose in improving and otherwise promoting their health, welfare and prosperity, and that the North Carolina Housing Finance Agency, is empowered to act on behalf of the State of North Carolina and its people in serving this public purpose for the benefit of the general public.

The General Assembly hereby further finds and declares that it shall be the policy of said Agency, whenever feasible, to give first priority in its programs to assisting persons and families of lower income in the purchase and rehabilitation of residential housing, and to undertake its programs in the areas where the greatest housing need exists, and to give priority to projects and individual units which conform to sound principles and practices of comprehensive land use and environmental planning, regional development planning and transportation planning as established by units of local government and regional organizations having jurisdiction over the area within which such projects and units are to be located if such government agencies exist in an area under consideration. However, no area of need shall be penalized because government planning agencies do not exist in such areas.

The General Assembly hereby also further finds and declares that private enterprise and investment have not been able to provide, without assistance, the needed installation of energy saving materials in owner occupied residences of persons and families of lower income. It is imperative for the health, safety and welfare of these persons and the general public that their residences be suitably heated at affordable cost in order to provide decent housing; and that the consumption of nonrenewable sources of energy be reduced. Therefore, the General Assembly finds that one of the purposes of this Chapter is to assist persons and families of lower income to obtain loans for the purpose of heating their homes at affordable cost and at the same time to significantly reduce the amount of consumption of nonrenewable sources of energy. (1969, c. 1235, s. 2; 1973, c. 1296, s. 2; 1977, c. 1083, s. 1.)

§ 122A-3. Definitions.

The following definitions apply in this Chapter:

(1)   Agency. - The North Carolina Housing Finance Agency created by this Chapter.

(2)   Bonds or notes. - The bonds or the bond anticipation notes or construction loan notes authorized to be issued by the Agency under this Chapter.

(3)   Counseling agency. - A nonprofit counseling agency located in North Carolina that is approved by the North Carolina Housing Finance Agency.

(4)   Energy conservation loan. - A loan obtained from a mortgage lender for the purpose of satisfying an existing obligation of a borrower who is the resident owner of a single-family dwelling or of "residential housing." The existing obligation of the owner in an "energy conservation loan" must have been incurred to pay for the purchase of materials or the installation of materials, or both, which results in a significant decrease in the amount of consumption of nonrenewable sources of energy in order to provide or maintain a comfortable level of room temperatures in his residence during the winter. "Energy conservation loan" does not include a loan obtained to refinance an existing

loan agreement unless payment or collection of the original loan was guaranteed by the Agency.

(5)   Federally insured securities. - An evidence of indebtedness secured by a first mortgage lien on residential housing for persons of lower income and insured or guaranteed as to repayment of principal and interest by the United States or any agency or instrumentality thereof.

(6)   Governmental agency. - Any department, division, public agency, political subdivision, or other public instrumentality of the State, the federal government, any other State or public agency, or any two or more thereof.

(7)   Mortgage or mortgage loan. - A mortgage loan for residential housing, including, without limitation, a mortgage loan to finance, either temporarily or permanently, the construction, rehabilitation, improvement, or acquisition and rehabilitation or improvement of residential housing and a mortgage loan insured or guaranteed by the United States or an instrumentality thereof or for which there is a commitment by the United States or an instrumentality thereof to insure such a mortgage. A mortgage obligation may be evidenced by a security document and secured by a lien upon real property, including a deed of trust and land sale agreement. Mortgage also means an obligation evidenced by a security lien on real property upon which an owner-occupied mobile home is located.

(8)   Mortgage lenders. - Any bank or trust company, savings bank, national banking association, savings and loan association, or building and loan association, life insurance company, mortgage banking company, the federal government, and any other financial institution authorized to transact business in the State.

(9)   Mortgagee. - The owner of a beneficial interest in a mortgage loan, the servicer for the owner of a beneficial interest in a mortgage loan, or the trustee for a securitized trust that holds title to a beneficial interest in a mortgage loan.

(10)   Obligations. - Any bonds or bond anticipation notes authorized to be issued by the Agency under the provisions of this Chapter.

(11)   Persons and families of lower income. - Persons and families deemed by the Agency to require such assistance as is made available by this Chapter on account of insufficient personal or family income, taking into consideration, without limitation, (i) the amount of the total income of such persons and families

231

available for housing needs, (ii) the size of the family, (iii) the cost and condition of housing facilities available, (iv) the eligibility of such persons and families for federal housing assistance of any type predicated upon a lower-income basis, and (v) the ability of such persons and families to compete successfully in the normal housing market and to pay the amounts at which private enterprise is providing decent, safe, and sanitary housing and deemed by the Agency therefore to be eligible to occupy residential housing financed wholly or in part, with mortgages, or with other public or private assistance.

(12)   Rehabilitation. - The renovation or improvement of residential housing by the owner of said residential housing.

(13)   Residential housing. - A specific work or improvement undertaken primarily to provide dwelling accommodations for persons and families of lower income, including the rehabilitation of buildings and improvements, and such other nonhousing facilities as may be incidental or appurtenant thereto.

(14)   State. - The State of North Carolina. (1969, c. 1235, s. 3; 1973, c. 1296, ss. 3-6, 8-14, 16, 17; 1975, c. 19, s. 42; 1977, c. 1083, s. 2; 1979, 2nd Sess., c. 1238, s. 1; 1981, c. 344, s. 1; 1983, c. 148, s. 1; 2008-107, s. 21.1(a); 2012-194, s. 24.)

§ 122A-4. North Carolina Housing Finance Agency.

(a)   There is hereby created a body politic and corporate to be known as "North Carolina Housing Finance Agency" which shall be constituted a public agency and an instrumentality of the State for the performance of essential public functions.

(b)   The Agency shall be governed by a board of directors composed of 13 members. The directors of the Agency shall be residents of the State and shall not hold other public office.

(c)   The General Assembly shall appoint eight directors, four upon the recommendation of the Speaker of the House of Representatives (at least one of whom shall have had experience with a mortgage-servicing institution and one of whom shall be experienced as a licensed real estate broker), and four upon the recommendation of the President Pro Tempore of the Senate (at least one of whom shall be experienced with a savings and loan institution and one of whom shall be experienced in home building). Appointments by the General Assembly shall be made in accordance with G.S. 120-121, and vacancies in those appointments shall be filled in accordance with G.S. 120-122. Notwithstanding any other provision of law, the terms of the four noncategorical appointments by the General Assembly shall expire on June 30, 1983. Subsequent noncategorical appointments shall be for terms of two years each. The terms of the initial categorical appointees by the General Assembly upon the recommendation of the Speaker shall expire on June 30, 1983; the terms of subsequent appointees shall be two years. The term of one of the initial categorical appointees by the General Assembly upon the recommendation of the President of the Senate shall expire on June 30, 1983, and the other on June 30, 1985; the terms of subsequent appointees shall be four years.

(d)   The Governor shall appoint four of the directors of the Agency; one of such appointees shall be experienced in community planning, one shall be experienced in subsidized housing management, one shall be experienced as a specialist in public housing policy, and one shall be experienced in the manufactured housing industry. The four appointees of the Governor shall be appointed for staggered four-year terms, two being appointed initially for three years and two for four years, and shall continue in office until their successors are duly appointed and qualified. Any person appointed to fill a vacancy shall serve only for the unexpired term.

(e)   Any member of the board of directors shall be eligible for reappointment. The 12 members of the board shall then elect a thirteenth member to the board by simple majority vote. Each member of the board of directors may be removed by the Governor for misfeasance, malfeasance or neglect of duty after reasonable notice and a public hearing, unless the same are in writing expressly waived. Each member of the board of directors before entering upon his duties shall take an oath of office to administer the duties of his office faithfully and impartially, and a record of such oath shall be filed in the office of the Secretary of State.

(f)   The Governor shall designate from among the members of the Board a chairman and a vice-chairman. The terms of the chairman and vice-chairman shall extend to the earlier of either two years or the date of expiration of their then current terms as members of the Board of Directors of the Agency. The Agency shall exercise all of its prescribed statutory powers independently of any principal State Department except as described in this Chapter. The Executive Director of the Agency shall be appointed by the Board of Directors, subject to approval by the Governor. All staff and employees of the Agency shall be appointed by the Executive Director, subject to approval by the Board of Directors; shall be eligible for participation in the State Employees' Retirement System; and shall be exempt from the provisions of the North Carolina Human Resources Act. All employees other than the Executive Director shall be compensated in accordance with the salary schedules adopted pursuant to the North Carolina Human Resources Act. The salary of the Executive Director shall be fixed by the Board of Directors. The salary of the Executive Director and all staff and employees of the Agency shall not be subject to any limitations imposed pursuant to any salary schedule adopted pursuant to the terms of the North Carolina Human Resources Act. The Board of Directors shall, subject to the approval of the Governor, elect and prescribe the duties of any other officers it finds necessary or advisable, and the Board of Directors shall fix the compensation of these officers. The books and records of the Agency shall be maintained by the Agency and shall be subject to periodic review and audit by the State.

No part of the revenues or assets of the Agency shall inure to the benefit of or be distributable to its members or officers or other private persons. The members of the Agency shall receive no compensation for their services but shall be entitled to receive, from funds of the Agency, for attendance at meetings of the Agency or any committee thereof and for other services for the Agency reimbursement for such actual expenses as may be incurred for travel and subsistence in the performance of official duties and such per diem as is allowed by law for members of other State boards, commissions and committees.

The Executive Director shall administer, manage and direct the affairs and business of the Agency, subject to the policies, control and direction of the members of the Agency Board of Directors. The Secretary of the Agency shall keep a record of the proceedings of the Agency and shall be custodian of all books, documents and papers filed with the Agency, the minute book or journal of the Agency and its official seal. The Secretary may have copies made of all minutes and other records and documents of the Agency and may give certificates under the official seal of the Agency to the effect that such copies are true copies, and all persons dealing with the Agency may rely upon such certificates. Seven members of the Board of Directors of the Agency shall constitute a quorum and the affirmative vote of a majority of the members present at a meeting of the Board of Directors duly called and held shall be necessary for any action taken by the Board of Directors of the Agency, except adjournment; provided, however, that the Board of Directors may appoint an executive committee to act in behalf of said Board during the period between regular meetings of said Board, and said committee shall have full power to act upon the vote of a majority of its members. No vacancy in the membership of the Agency shall impair the rights of a quorum to exercise all the rights and to perform all the duties of the Agency. (1969, c. 1235, s. 4; 1973, c. 476, s. 128; c. 1262, ss. 51, 86; c. 1296, ss. 18-20; 1975, c. 19, s. 43; 1977, c. 673, s. 4; c. 771, s. 4; 1981, c. 895, s. 2; 1981 (Reg. Sess., 1982), c. 1191, s. 32; 1983, c. 148, s. 4; c. 717, ss. 36-37; 1985, c. 479, s. 222; 1987, c. 305, s. 3; 1991 (Reg. Sess., 1992), c. 1039, s. 26; 1995, c. 490, s. 24; 2004-124, s. 31.15(a); 2013-382, s. 9.1(c).)

§ 122A-5. General powers.

The Agency shall have all of the powers necessary or convenient to carry out the provisions of this Chapter, including the power:

(1)   To participate in any federally assisted lease program for housing for persons of lower income under any federal legislation, including, without limitation, section 8 of the National Housing Act; provided, however, that such participation may take place only upon the request and approval of the governing body of the county, city or town in which any such project is to be located;

(2)   To make or participate in the making of mortgage loans to sponsors of residential housing; provided, however, that such loans shall be made only upon the determination by the Agency that mortgage loans are not otherwise available wholly or in part from private lenders upon reasonably equivalent terms and conditions;

(3)   To purchase or participate in the purchase and enter into commitments by itself or together with others for

a.   The purchase of mortgage loans made by mortgage lenders to sponsors of residential housing or to persons of lower income for residential housing where the Agency has given its approval prior to the initial making of the mortgage loan; provided, however, that any such purchase shall be made only upon the determination by the Agency that mortgage loans were, at the time the approval was given, not otherwise available, wholly or in part, from private lenders upon reasonably equivalent terms and conditions, or

235

b.   The purchase of mortgage loans made by mortgage lenders without such prior approval to sponsors of housing for persons and families of any income or to persons of any income for housing upon such terms and conditions requiring the proceeds thereof to be used by such mortgage lenders for the making of new mortgage loans to sponsors of residential housing or to persons of lower income for residential housing as the Agency may prescribe by its rules and regulations; provided, however, that (i) any such purchase of existing mortgage loans shall be made only upon the determination by the Agency that such new mortgage loans are not otherwise available from private lenders upon reasonably equivalent terms and conditions, and (ii) the Agency shall purchase mortgage loans made to sponsors of housing for persons and families not of lower income or to persons not of lower income for housing only upon the determination by the Agency that mortgage loans made to sponsors of residential housing or to persons of lower income for residential housing are not available for purchase by the Agency upon reasonable terms and conditions;

(4)   Repealed by Session Laws 1973, c. 1296, s. 24;

(4a)   To make loans to mortgage lenders on terms and conditions requiring the proceeds thereof to be used by such mortgage lenders to originate new mortgage loans to (i) sponsors of residential housing for persons and families of lower income and persons and families of moderate income and (ii) persons and families of lower income and persons and families of moderate income for residential housing. The loans to mortgage lenders and the loans to be made by such mortgage lenders shall be made on such applicable terms and conditions as are set forth in rules and regulations of the Agency; Provided, however, that loans shall be made by such mortgage lenders only upon the determination by the Agency that such financing is not otherwise available, wholly or in part, from private lenders upon reasonably equivalent terms and conditions;

(5)   To collect and pay reasonable fees and charges in connection with making, purchasing and servicing its loans, notes, bonds, commitments and other evidences of indebtedness;

(6)   To acquire on a temporary basis real property, or an interest therein, in its own name, by purchase, transfer or foreclosure, where such acquisition is necessary or appropriate to protect any loan in which the Agency has an interest and to sell, transfer and convey any such property to a buyer and, in the event such sale, transfer or conveyance cannot be effected with reasonable promptness or at a reasonable price, to rent or lease such property to a tenant pending such sale, transfer or conveyance;

236

(7)   To sell, at public or private sale, all or any part of any mortgage or other instrument or document securing a loan of any type permitted by this Chapter;

(8)   To procure insurance against any loss in connection with its operations in such amounts, and from such insurers, as it may deem necessary or desirable;

(9)   To consent, whenever it deems it necessary or desirable in the fulfillment of its corporate purposes, to the modification of the rate of interest, time of payment of any installment of principal or interest, or any other terms, of any mortgage loan, mortgage loan commitment, contract or agreement of any kind to which the Agency is a party;

(10)   To borrow money as herein provided to carry out and effectuate its corporate purposes and to issue its obligation as evidence of any such borrowing;

(11)   To include in any borrowing such amounts as may be deemed necessary by the Agency to pay financing charges, interest on the obligations for a period not exceeding two years from their date, consultant, advisory and legal fees and such other expenses as are necessary or incident to such borrowing;

(12)   To make and publish rules and regulations respecting its lending programs and such other rules and regulations as are necessary to effectuate its corporate purposes;

(13)   To provide technical and advisory services to sponsors, builders and developers of residential housing and to residents thereof;

(14)   To promote research and development in scientific methods of constructing low-cost residential housing of high durability;

(15)   To service or contract for the servicing of mortgage loans and to make and execute agreements, contracts and other instruments necessary or convenient in the exercise of the powers and functions of the Agency under this Chapter, including contracts with any person, firm, corporation, governmental agency or other entity, and each and any North Carolina governmental agency is hereby authorized to enter into contracts and otherwise cooperate with the Agency to facilitate the purposes of this Chapter;

(16)	To receive, administer and comply with the conditions and requirements respecting any appropriation or any gift, grant or donation of any property or money, including the proceeds of general obligation bonds of the State;

(17)	To sue and be sued in its own name, plead and be impleaded;

(18)	To establish and maintain an office for the transaction of its business in the City of Raleigh and at such place or places as the board of directors deems advisable or necessary in carrying out the purposes of this Chapter;

(19)	To adopt an official seal and alter the same at pleasure;

(20)	To adopt bylaws for the regulation of its affairs and the conduct of its business and to prescribe rules, regulations and policies in connection with the performance of its functions and duties;

(21)	To employ fiscal consultants, engineers, attorneys, real estate counselors, appraisers and such other consultants and employees as may be required in the judgment of the Agency and to fix and pay their compensation from funds available to the Agency therefor;

(22)	To purchase or to participate in the purchase and enter into commitments by itself or together with others for the purchase of federally insured securities; provided, however, that the Agency shall first determine that the proceeds of such securities will be utilized for the purpose of making new mortgage loans to sponsors of residential housing or to persons of lower income for residential housing, all as specified in regulations to be adopted by the Agency;

(23)	To provide, or contract for the providing of, management and counseling services whenever, in the judgment of the Agency, no other satisfactory low-income housing counseling service is available for occupants of rental projects for persons of lower income or for prospective homeowners of lower income; provided, however, that no such program shall be undertaken until the Agency shall have made a study of its feasibility and shall have determined that the undertaking of such program will not adversely affect other programs of the Agency;

(24)	To advise the Governor regarding the coordination of public and private low- and moderate-income housing programs;

(25)   To participate in and administer federal housing programs, including housing rehabilitation, construction of new housing, assistance to the homeless, and home ownership assistance;

(26)   To acquire, hold, rent, encumber, transfer, convey, and otherwise deal with real property and utilities in the same manner as a private person or corporation, subject only to the approval of the Governor and Council of State. The Board of Directors may pledge or encumber income and assets of the Agency to secure financing for real property; and

(27)   To select and retain, subject to the approval of the Local Government Commission, the financial consultants, underwriters, and bond attorneys to be associated with the issuance of any bonds and to pay for services rendered by underwriters, financial consultants, or bond attorneys out of the proceeds of any such issue with regard to which the services were performed.

(28)   Repealed by Session Laws 2010-31, s. 23.1(b).

§ 122A-5.1. Rules and regulations governing Agency activity.

(a)   The Agency shall from time to time adopt, modify or repeal rules and regulations governing the purchase of federally insured securities by the Agency and the purchase and sale of mortgage loans and the application of the proceeds thereof, including rules and regulations as to any or all of the following:

(1)   Procedures for the submission of requests or the invitation of proposals for the purchase and sale of mortgage loans or for the purchase of federally insured securities;

(2)   Limitations or restrictions as to the number of family units, location or other qualifications or characteristics of residences to be financed by mortgage loans and requirements as to the income limits of persons and families of lower income occupying such residences;

(3)   Restrictions as to the interest rates on mortgage loans or the return which may be realized by mortgage lenders on any mortgage loans or on the sale of federally insured securities to the Agency;

(4)   Requirements as to commitments by mortgage lenders with respect to the use of the proceeds of sale of any federally insured securities;

(5)   Schedules of any fees and charges necessary to provide for expenses and reserves of the Agency; and

(6)   Any other matters related to the duties and the exercise of the powers of the Agency to purchase and sell mortgage loans, or to purchase federally insured securities.

Such rules and regulations shall be designed to effectuate the general purposes of this Chapter and the following specific objectives: (i) the construction of decent, safe and sanitary residential housing at low prices or rentals which persons and families of lower income can afford; (ii) the rehabilitation of present lower-income housing; (iii) increasing the supply of residential housing for persons and families of lower income affected by the spread of slum conditions and blight and for persons and families of lower income displaced by public action or natural disaster; (iv) the encouraging of private enterprise and investment to sponsor, build and rehabilitate residential housing for such persons and families to prevent the recurrence of slum conditions and blight and assist in their permanent elimination throughout the State; and (v) the restriction of the financial return and benefit to that necessary to protect against the realization by mortgage lenders of an excessive financial return or benefit as determined by prevailing market conditions.

(b)   The interest rate or rates and other terms of federally insured securities or mortgage loans purchased from the proceeds of any issue of bonds of the Agency shall be at least sufficient to assure the payment of said bonds and the interest thereon as the same become due from the amounts received by the Agency in repayment of such federally insured securities or such loans and interest thereon.

(c)   The Agency shall require as a condition of the purchase of federally insured securities from a mortgage lender and the purchase or the making of a commitment to purchase mortgage loans from a mortgage lender where the Agency has not given its approval prior to the initial making of the mortgage loan that such mortgage lender shall on or prior to the one-hundred-eightieth day (or such earlier day as may be prescribed by rules and regulations of the Agency) following the receipt of the sale proceeds have entered into written commitments to make, and shall thereafter proceed as promptly as practicable to make from such sale proceeds, new mortgage loans with respect to

240

residential housing in the State having a stated maturity of not less than 20 years from the date thereof in an aggregate principal amount equal to the amount of such sale proceeds. The Agency shall not purchase nor make commitment to purchase mortgage loans, federally insured securities or other obligations from a mortgage lender from which it has previously purchased federally insured securities or mortgage loans initially made without such prior approval unless said mortgage lender has either made or entered into written commitments to make such new mortgage loans. (1973, c. 1296, s. 44; 1975, c. 616, s. 3.)

§ 122A-5.2. Mortgage insurance authority.

(a)   The Agency may upon application of a proposed mortgagee insure and make advance commitments to insure payments required by a loan for residential housing for persons of lower income upon such terms and conditions as the Agency may prescribe. Mortgage loans insured by the Agency under this Chapter may provide financing for related ancillary facilities to the extent permitted by applicable Agency regulations. Mortgage loans insured by the Agency under this Chapter shall be secured by a first mortgage.

The aggregate principal amount of all mortgages so insured by the Agency under this Chapter and outstanding at any one time shall not exceed 10 times the average annual balance for the preceding calendar year of funds on deposit in the housing mortgage insurance fund, the creation of which is hereby authorized. The aggregate amount of principal obligations of all mortgages so insured shall not be deemed to constitute a debt, liability or obligation of the State or of any political subdivision thereof or a pledge of the faith and credit of the State or of any such political subdivision, but shall be payable solely from moneys on deposit to the credit of the housing mortgage insurance fund. Any contract of insurance executed by the Agency under this section shall be conclusive evidence of eligibility for such mortgage insurance and the validity of any contract of insurance so executed or of an advance commitment to issue such shall be incontestable in the hands of a mortgagee from the date of execution of such contract or commitment, except for fraud or misrepresentation on the part of such mortgagee and, as to commitments to insure, noncompliance with the terms of the advance commitment or Agency regulations in force at the time of issuance of the advance commitment.

(b)   For mortgage payments to be eligible for insurance under the provisions of this Chapter, the underlying mortgage loan shall:

(1)   Be one which is made and held by a mortgagee approved by the Agency as responsible and able to service the mortgage properly;

(2)   Not exceed (i) ninety percent (90%) of the estimated cost of the proposed housing if owned or to be owned by a profit-making sponsor or (ii) one hundred percent (100%) of the estimated cost of such proposed housing if owned or to be owned by a nonprofit housing sponsor or, if owned by a person or family of lower income, in the case of a single family dwelling or condominium;

(3)   Have a maturity satisfactory to the Agency but in no case longer than eighty percent (80%) of the Corporation's [Agency's] estimate of the remaining useful life of said housing or 40 years from the date of the issuance of insurance, whichever is earlier;

(4)   Contain amortization provisions satisfactory to the Agency requiring periodic payments by the mortgagor not in excess of his ability to pay as determined by the Agency;

(5)   Be in such form and contain such terms and provisions with respect to maturity, property insurance, repairs, alterations, payment of taxes and assessments, default reserves, delinquency charges, default remedies, anticipation of maturity, additional and secondary liens, equitable and legal redemption rights, prepayment privileges and other matters as the Agency may prescribe.

(c)   All applications for mortgage insurance shall be forwarded, together with an application fee prescribed by the Agency, to the executive director of the Agency. The Agency shall cause an investigation of the proposed housing to be made, review the application and the report of the investigation, and approve or deny the application. No application shall be approved unless the Agency finds that it is consistent with the purposes of this Chapter and further finds that the financing plan for the proposed housing is sound. The Agency shall notify the applicant and the proposed lender of its decision. Any such approval shall be conditioned upon payment to the Agency, within such reasonable time and after notification of approval as may be specified by the Agency, of the commitment fee prescribed by the Agency.

(d)   The Agency shall fix mortgage insurance premiums for the insurance of mortgage payments under the provision of this Chapter. Such premiums shall be computed as a percentage of the principal of the mortgage outstanding at the beginning of each mortgage year, but shall not be more than one half of one percent (1/2 of 1%) per year of such principal amount. The amount of premium need not be uniform for all insured loans. Such premiums shall be payable by mortgagors or mortgagees in such manner as prescribed by the Agency.

(e)   In the event of default by the mortgagor, the mortgagee shall notify the Agency both of the default and the mortgagee's proposed course of action. When it appears feasible, the Agency may for a temporary period upon default or threatened default by the mortgagor authorize mortgage payments to be made by the Agency to the mortgagee which payments shall be repaid under such conditions as the Agency may prescribe. The Agency may also agree to revised terms of financing when such appear prudent. The mortgagee shall be entitled to receive the benefits of the insurance provided herein upon:

(1)   Any sale of the mortgaged property by court order in foreclosure or a sale with the consent of the Agency by the mortgagor or a subsequent owner of the property or by the mortgagee after foreclosure or acquisition by deed in lieu of foreclosure, provided all claims of the mortgagee against the mortgagor or others arising from the mortgage, foreclosure, or any deficiency judgment shall be assigned to the Agency without recourse except such claims as may have been released with the consent of the Agency; or

(2)   The expiration of six months after the mortgagee has taken title to the mortgaged property under judgment of strict foreclosure, foreclosure by sale or other judicial sale, or under a deed in lieu of foreclosure if during such period the mortgagee has made a bona fide attempt to sell the property, and thereafter conveys the property to the Agency with an assignment, without recourse, to the Agency of all claims of the mortgagee against the mortgagor or others arising out of the mortgage foreclosure, or deficiency judgment; or

(3)   The acceptance by the Agency of title to the property or an assignment of the mortgage, without recourse to the Agency, in the event the Agency determines it imprudent to proceed under (1) or (2) above.

Upon the occurrence of either (1), (2) or (3) hereof, the obligation of the mortgagee to pay premium charges for insurance shall cease, and the Agency shall, within 30 days thereafter, pay to the mortgagee ninety-eight percent (98%) of the sum of (i) the then unpaid principal balance of the insured indebtedness,

(ii) the unpaid interest to the date of conveyance or assignment to the Agency, as the case may be, (iii) the amount of all payments made by the mortgagee for which it has not been reimbursed for taxes, insurance, assessments and mortgage insurance premiums, and (iv) such other necessary fees, costs or expenses of the mortgagee as may be approved by the Agency.

(f)   Upon request of the mortgagee, the Agency may at any time, under such terms and conditions as it may prescribe, consent to the release of the mortgagor from his liability or consent to the release of parts of the property from the lien of the mortgage, or approve a substitute mortgagor or sale of the property or part thereof.

(g)   No claim for the benefit of the insurance provided in this Chapter shall be accepted by the Agency except within one year after any sale or acquisition of title of the mortgaged premises described in subdivisions (1) or (2) of subsection (e) of this section.

(h)   There shall be paid into the housing mortgage insurance fund (i) all premiums received by the Agency for the granting of such mortgage insurance, (ii) any moneys or other assets received by the Agency as a result of default or delinquency on mortgage loans insured by the Agency, including any proceeds from the sale or lease of real property, (iii) any moneys appropriated and made available by the State for the purpose of such fund. (1973, c. 1296, s. 45.)

§ 122A-5.3. Energy conservation loan authority.

(a)   The Agency may guarantee the payment or collection of energy conservation loans pursuant to and in accordance with the provisions of this Chapter when the Agency has given its approval prior to the initial making of the loan; provided that any such guarantee shall be made only upon determination by the Agency that energy conservation loans were at the time of approval not otherwise available from private lenders upon reasonably equivalent terms and conditions; and provided further, no single guarantee of payment or collection shall exceed the sum of twelve hundred dollars ($1200) and no person or family of lower income shall be entitled to more than one loan guarantee.

(b)   At no time may the Agency have outstanding loan guarantees in which the liability of the Agency exceeds 15 times any amounts remaining unspent from the specific funds appropriated by the General Assembly for the energy conservation loan guarantee program plus any specific grants or donations for this purpose; but the Agency is authorized to expend any unspent amounts from these sources to satisfy its liabilities under the loan guarantee program; provided no other assets of the Agency shall be obligated or expended in satisfaction of its energy conservation loan guarantee liability.

(c)   The Agency shall from time to time adopt, modify, or repeal rules and regulations governing the guaranteeing of energy conservation loans including rules and regulations as to any or all of the following:

(1)   Procedures for the submission and approval of requests to guarantee energy conservation loans including advance commitments by the Agency to guarantee loans;

(2)   Limitations and restrictions on the number of family units, location or other qualifications or characteristics of residences in regard to which energy conservation work is performed to qualify for a loan guarantee;

(3)   Restrictions as to interest rates on energy conservation loans or the return which may be realized by mortgage lenders on energy conservation loans guaranteed by the Agency;

(4)   Schedules of any fees and charges necessary to provide for the administrative expenses of the Agency allocable to the administration of the energy conservation loan guarantee program;

(5)   Procedures regarding the servicing of energy conservation loan guarantees including procedures for honoring defaults and procedures to be implemented to enforce the obligations of the borrowers to repay guaranteed energy conservation loans;

(6)   Any other matters related to the duties and the exercise of the power of the Agency with respect to the energy conservation loan guarantee program deemed necessary to effectuate the purposes of this act. (1977, c. 1083, s. 3.)

§ 122A-5.4. Housing for persons and families of moderate income.

(a)   The General Assembly hereby finds and determines that there is a serious shortage of decent, safe and sanitary housing which persons and families of moderate income in the State can afford; that it is in the best interests of the State to encourage home ownership by persons and families of moderate income; that the assistance provided by this section will enable persons and families of moderate income to acquire existing decent, safe and sanitary housing without undue financial hardship and will encourage private enterprise to sponsor, build and rehabilitate additional housing for such persons and families; and that the Agency in providing such assistance is promoting the health, welfare and prosperity of all citizens of the State and is serving a public purpose for the benefit of the general public.

(b)   The terms "persons and families of lower income" and "persons of lower income" wherever they appear in this Chapter, except where they appear in G.S. 122A-2 and G.S. 122A-3, shall be deemed to include "persons and families of moderate income" as defined in clause (c) of this section.

(c)   "Persons and families of moderate income" means persons and families deemed by the Agency to require the assistance made available by this Chapter on account of insufficient personal or family income taking into consideration, without limitation, (i) the amount of the total income of such persons and families available for housing needs, (ii) the size of the family, (iii) the cost and condition of housing facilities available and (iv) the eligibility of such persons and families for federal housing assistance of any type predicated upon a moderate or low and moderate income basis. (1979, c. 810; 2008-107, s. 21.1(b).)

§ 122A-5.5. Rehabilitation Loan Authority.

(a)   In order to effectuate the authority of the Agency to participate in commitments to purchase and to purchase mortgage loans for the rehabilitation of existing residential housing the Agency is hereby empowered to adopt, modify or repeal rules and regulations governing the making or participation in the making of mortgage loans and the purchase or participation in commitments for the purchase of mortgage loans for the rehabilitation of existing residential housing.

(b)   The rules and regulations of the Agency adopted pursuant to this section shall provide at a minimum that:

(1)   Rehabilitation mortgage loans shall be for the purpose of owner-financed improvements to or renovation of residential housing;

246

(2)   Requirements for eligibility for rehabilitation mortgage loans shall be consistent with all applicable federal laws and regulations governing bonds for rehabilitation mortgage loans in order to insure that such bonds are exempt from taxation. (1981, c. 344, s. 2.)

§ 122A-5.6. Terms and conditions of loans to and by mortgage lenders.

(a)   The Agency shall from time to time adopt, modify, amend or repeal rules and regulations governing the making of loans to mortgage lenders and the application of the proceeds thereof. These rules and regulations shall be designed to effectuate the general purposes of this Chapter and the following specific objectives: (i) the construction and rehabilitation of decent, safe and sanitary residential housing available to persons and families of lower income and persons and families of moderate income at prices or rentals that they can afford; (ii) the encouragement of private enterprise and investment to sponsor, build and rehabilitate residential housing for persons and families of lower income and persons and families of moderate income; and (iii) the restriction of the financial return and benefit to the mortgage lenders from such loans to an amount that is necessary to induce their participation and that is not excessive as determined by prevailing market conditions.

(b)   Notwithstanding any other provision of this section, the interest rate or rates and other terms of the loans to mortgage lenders made from the proceeds of any issue of bonds of the Agency shall provide that the amounts received by the Agency in repayment of the loans and interest thereon shall be at least sufficient to assure the payment of the principal of and the interest on the bonds as they become due.

(c)   The Agency shall enter into a written agreement with each mortgage lender that shall require as a condition of each loan to such mortgage lender that the mortgage lender shall originate new mortgage loans within a reasonable period of time as determined by the Agency's rules and regulations and that such new mortgage loans shall have such stated maturities as determined by the Agency's rules and regulations.

(d)   The loans to mortgage lenders shall be general obligations of the respective mortgage lenders owing them. The Agency shall require that such loans shall be additionally secured as to payment of both principal and interest

247

by a pledge and lien upon collateral security. The collateral security itself shall be in such amount as the Agency determines will assure the payment of the principal of and the interest on the bonds as they become due. Collateral security shall be deemed to be sufficient if the principal of and the interest on the collateral security, when due, will be sufficient to pay the principal of and the interest on the bonds. The collateral security shall consist of any of the following items: (i) direct obligations of, or obligations guaranteed by, the State or the United States of America; (ii) bonds, debentures, notes or other evidences of indebtedness, satisfactory to the Agency, issued by any of the following federal agencies: Bank for Cooperatives, Federal Intermediate Credit Bank, Federal Home Loan Bank System, Export-Import Bank of Washington, Federal Land Banks, Fannie Mae or the Government National Mortgage Association; (iii) direct obligations of or obligations guaranteed by the State; (iv) mortgages insured or guaranteed by the United States of America or an instrumentality of it as to payment of principal and interest; (v) any other mortgages secured by real estate on which there is located a residential structure, the collateral value of which shall be determined by the regulations issued from time to time by the Agency; (vi) obligations of Federal Home Loan Banks; (vii) certificates of deposit of banks or trust companies, including the trustee, organized under the laws of the United States or any state, which have a combined capital and surplus of at least fifteen million dollars ($15,000,000); (viii) Bankers Acceptances; and (ix) commercial paper that has been classified for rating purposes by Dun & Bradstreet, Inc., as Prime-1 or by Standard & Poor's Corp. as A-1.

(e)   The Agency may require as a condition of any loan to a mortgage lender such representations and warranties that it determines to be necessary to secure such loans and to carry out the purposes of this section. (1983, c. 148, s. 3; 2001-487, s. 14(i).)

§ 122A-5.7. Homeownership Assistance Fund authorized; authority.

The North Carolina Housing Finance Agency is authorized to establish a Homeownership Assistance Fund (hereinafter referred to as "the Fund") to assist families of low and moderate income in the purchase of affordable residential housing. To achieve this purpose, the Agency may use the Fund to provide additional security for eligible loans, to subsidize down payments, principal payments and interest payments, and to provide any type of mortgage assistance the Agency deems necessary. The Fund shall operate as a revolving fund. The Agency shall adopt rules for the operation and use of the Fund. These funds shall be used for people who otherwise would be unable to receive subsidized loans from the Housing Finance Agency. (1983, c. 923, s. 203.)

§ 122A-5.8. Distressed multi-family residential rental housing provisions.

(a)   The General Assembly hereby finds and determines that a serious shortage of decent, safe and sanitary multi-family residential rental housing which persons and families of low and moderate income in the State can afford continues to exist; that it is in the best interests of the State to continue to promote and maintain the viability of such housing and to encourage private enterprise to sponsor, build and rehabilitate additional multi-family residential rental housing for such low and moderate income persons and families; that certain multi-family residential rental housing projects financed by the Agency are currently experiencing financial difficulties due to low occupancy levels; that measures to facilitate higher occupancy levels by extending occupancy on a temporary basis to those with incomes in excess of required low and moderate levels will help to maintain certain multi-family residential rental housing for persons and families of low and moderate income to prevent foreclosure and the use of such facilities without regard to income limitations; and that the Agency in providing such temporary assistance is promoting the health, welfare and property of all citizens of the State and is serving a public purpose for the benefit of the general public.

(b)   "Distressed rental housing project" means any multi-family residential rental housing project heretofore or hereafter financed by the Agency that, as determined by resolution of the Board of Directors of the Agency, has an occupancy level below that required for sustaining operation and as a result thereof needs to increase its occupancy levels in order to avoid foreclosure and the subsequent use of such facilities without regard to the Agency's income limitations. In determining the foregoing, the Board of Directors of the Agency shall take into consideration (1) occupancy rates of the project, (2) market conditions affecting the project, (3) costs of operation of the project, (4) debt service for the project, (5) management of the project and such other factors as the Board of Directors may deem relevant.

(c)   The Board of Directors of the Agency may determine, by resolution, to permit not in excess of ten percent (10%) of the rental units in any distressed rental housing project to be rented to persons or families without regard to

249

income until the project's occupancy levels, in the judgment of the Agency, will sustain operations at a level sufficient to prevent delinquency or default.

(d)   The Board of Directors may also determine, by resolution, to permit additional rental units at any such distressed rental housing project, to be rented to persons or families without regard to income, subject to the restriction contained in subsection (c) of this section, provided that: (1) the units therein that have been available for rental without regard to income have been available for a period of time not less than three months, (2) the Agency has determined that permitting additional units, in excess of ten percent (10%), to be rented without regard to income is necessary in order for such distressed rental housing project to avoid foreclosure, and (3) the total number of housing units at any distressed rental housing project rented without regard to income shall not exceed fifteen percent (15%) of the total number of units therein.

(e)   Once a distressed rental housing project attains sustaining occupancy at a level satisfactory to the Agency, the Agency will thereafter require the owners of such distressed rental housing project to rent only to persons and families of low and moderate income and will require that any units that were leased without regard to income limitations pursuant to the provisions of this section will next be leased, when such units become vacant, only to persons and families whose incomes fall within the then current Agency income limitations. (1987, c. 305, s. 1; 1989, c. 454, ss. 1-3; 1989, c. 454, s. 3.)

§ 122A-5.9. Formation of subsidiary corporations to own and operate housing projects.

(a)   The Agency may acquire, by purchase or otherwise, construct, acquire, develop, own, repair, maintain, improve, rehabilitate, renovate, furnish, equip, operate, and manage residential rental housing projects to rent to persons and families of lower and moderate income.

(b)   The Agency may form a nonprofit corporation or corporations under the laws of this State which may acquire, construct, develop, repair, improve, rehabilitate, renovate, furnish, equip, operate and manage residential rental housing projects for persons and families of lower and moderate income. All of the stock of a nonprofit corporation formed by the Agency shall be owned by the Agency and its Board of Directors shall be elected or appointed by the Agency.

(c)   No statutory provisions with respect to the acquisition, operation or disposition of property by other public bodies shall be applicable to the Agency or to any nonprofit corporation formed pursuant to this section. (1987, c. 305, s. 2.)

§ 122A-5.10. Housing Coordination and Policy Council; creation; duties.

(a)   There is created the Housing Coordination and Policy Council in the Office of the Governor. The Housing Coordination and Policy Council shall have the following functions and duties:

(1)   To advise the Governor regarding the coordination of various public and private low-and moderate-income housing programs;

(2)   To advise the Governor in the preparation of an overall, comprehensive State housing plan with specific recommendations to address identified areas of need, which report shall be presented to the General Assembly;

(3)   To advise the Governor with respect to the best use of housing resources; and

(4)   To advise the Governor regarding any other matter relating to housing the Governor may refer to it.

(b)   Nothing herein shall abrogate the existing statutory responsibility of any other agency to develop housing plans and policies relating to specific housing programs. (1993, c. 321, s. 305(d).)

§ 122A-5.11. Council membership; compensation; procedures.

(a)   The Housing Coordination and Policy Council shall consist of 15 representatives, as follows:

(1)   One member of the N.C. Housing Partnership who is experienced with housing programs for low-income persons, as designated by the chair.

(2)   One member of the Community Development Council who is experienced with federal, State, and local housing programs, as designated by the chair.

(3)   One member of the N.C. Housing Finance Agency Board of Directors who is experienced with real estate finance and development, as designated by the chair.

(4)   One member of the Weatherization Policy Advisory Council who is experienced with community weatherization programs, as designated by the chair.

(5)   One member of the State protection and advocacy agency designated under the Developmental Disabilities Assistance and Bill of Rights Act 2000, P.L. 106-402, who is familiar with the housing needs of the disabled.

(6)   The executive director of the Commission of Indian Affairs, or a designee familiar with Indian housing programs.

(7)   The Assistant Secretary of Community Development and Housing, or a designee familiar with housing programs related to community development and housing functions.

(8)   The director of the Division of Aging, or a designee familiar with the housing programs of the Division.

(9)   The executive director of the N.C. Housing Finance Agency, or a designee familiar with the housing programs of the Agency.

(10)   The director of the Division of Mental Health, or a designee familiar with housing for those with mental disabilities.

(11)   The executive director of the N.C. Human Relations Commission, or a designee familiar with federal and State fair housing laws.

(12)   The head of the AIDS Care Branch, or a designee familiar with the housing programs of the Division of Adult Health Promotion.

(13)   The director of the Office of Economic Opportunity, or a designee familiar with programs for the homeless.

252

(14)   Two members of nonprofit organizations who are experienced with housing advocacy for low-income persons and State and federal housing programs.

(b)   All members except those serving ex officio shall be appointed by the Governor. The Governor shall designate one member of the Council to serve as Chair.

(c)   The initial members of the Council other than those serving ex officio shall be appointed to serve for terms of four years and until their successors are appointed and qualified. Any appointment to fill a vacancy created by resignation, dismissal, death, or disability of a member shall be for the balance of the term.

(d)   Members of the Council may receive per diem and necessary travel and subsistence expenses in accordance with the provisions of G.S. 138-5.

(e)   A majority of the Council shall constitute a quorum for the transaction of business.

(f)   All clerical and other services required by the Council shall be supplied by the Housing Finance Agency. (1993, c. 321, s. 305(d); 1995, c. 263, s. 1; 2007-323, s. 19.1(d).)

§ 122A-5.12. Council meetings; report.

(a)   The Housing Coordination and Policy Council shall meet at least quarterly and may hold special meetings at any time and place within the State at the call of the Chair or upon written request of a majority of the members.

(b)   The Council shall assist in the preparation and filing of an annual written report which contains a review of work completed, a review of ongoing activities, and housing policy recommendations. This report shall be filed with the General Assembly and the Governor by May 1. (1993, c. 321, s. 305(d).)

§ 122A-5.13. Adult Care Home, Group Home, and Nursing Home Fire Protection Fund authorized; authority.

(a)   The North Carolina Housing Finance Agency shall establish an Adult Care Home, Group Home, and Nursing Home Fire Protection Fund (hereinafter "Fire Protection Fund") to assist owners of adult care homes, group homes for developmentally disabled adults, and nursing homes with the purchase and installation of fire protection systems and emergency generators in existing and new adult care homes, group homes for developmentally disabled adults, and nursing homes. The Fire Protection Fund shall be a revolving fund.

(b)   The Agency, in consultation with the Department of Health and Human Services, shall adopt rules for the management and use of the Fire Protection Fund. These rules at a minimum shall provide for the following:

(1)   Financial incentives for owners of facilities who utilize Fire Protection Fund monies to install sprinkler systems instead of smoke detection equipment.

(2)   Maximum loan amounts of one dollar and seventy-five cents ($1.75) per square foot for advanced smoke detectors and digital communication equipment, three dollars and seventy-five cents ($3.75) per square foot for residential sprinkler systems, and six dollars ($6.00) per square foot for institutional sprinkler systems.

(3)   Interest rates from three percent (3%) to six percent (6%) for a period not to exceed 20 years for sprinkler systems and 10 years for smoke detection systems.

(4)   Documentary verification that owners of facilities obtain fire protection systems and emergency generators at a reasonable cost.

(5)   Acceleration of a loan when statutory fire protection requirements are not met by the facility for which the loan was made.

(6)   Loan approval priority criteria that considers the frailty level of residents at a facility.

(7)   Loan origination and servicing fees.

(c)   Proceeds from the Fire Protection Fund, not to exceed ten thousand dollars ($10,000) annually, may be used to provide staff support to the North Carolina Housing Finance Agency for loan processing under this section and to the Department of Health and Human Services for review and approval of fire protection plans and inspection of fire protection systems. (1996, 2nd Ex. Sess.,

c. 18, s. 24.26B(a); 1997-443, s. 11A.118(a); 1999-237, s. 11.17; 2000-67, s. 11.10.)

§ 122A-5.14. Home Protection Program and Fund.

(a)   The North Carolina Housing Finance Agency shall establish and administer the Home Protection Program ("Program") to assist North Carolina workers who have lost jobs as a result of changing economic conditions in North Carolina when the workers are in need of assistance to avoid losing their homes to foreclosure. The Agency shall do all of the following:

(1)   Develop and administer the Home Protection Program Fund ("Fund") to ensure that workers in North Carolina have assistance to avoid losing their homes to foreclosure.

(2)   Make loans secured by liens on residential real property located in North Carolina to property owners who are eligible for those loans.

(3)   Develop and administer procedures by which property owners at risk of being foreclosed upon may qualify for assistance.

(4)   Designate, approve, and fund nonprofit counseling agencies in North Carolina to be available to assist the Agency in implementing the provisions of this section, provide services such as direct mortgagee negotiations on behalf of unemployed workers, and process loan applications for the Agency.

(5)   Develop and fund enhanced methods by which workers may be notified of foreclosure mitigation services, may easily contact local nonprofit counseling agencies, and may apply for loans from the Agency.

(b)   Home Protection Period. - Notwithstanding Chapters 23, 24, and 45 of the General Statutes or any other provision of law, upon the proper filing of an application for loan assistance by a mortgagor under this section, a mortgagee shall not do the following for a period of 120 days following the date of the mortgagor's properly filed application:

(1)   Accelerate the maturity of any mortgage obligation covered under this section.

(2)   Commence or continue any legal action, including mortgage foreclosure pursuant to Chapter 45 of the General Statutes, to recover the mortgage obligation.

(3)   Take possession of any security of the mortgagor for the mortgage obligation.

(4)   Procure or receive a deed in lieu of foreclosure.

(5)   Enter judgment by confession pursuant to a note accompanying a mortgage.

(6)   Proceed to enforce the mortgage obligation pursuant to applicable rules of civil procedure.

The provisions of this section shall not apply if the mortgagee receives notice from the Agency that the mortgagor's application has been denied.

If a mortgagee acts as proscribed in subdivisions (1) through (6) of this subsection, a mortgagor shall be entitled to injunctive relief without the necessity of providing a bond. This relief shall be in addition to any defenses available under G.S. 45-21.16(d) and any other remedies at law or equity.

Upon the Agency's receipt of a properly filed mortgagor's application for loan assistance, the Agency shall mail notice of the application to the mortgagor's mortgagee within 10 business days of the Agency's receipt of the application. The Agency shall also mail notice of the acceptance or denial of the mortgagor's application to the mortgagee within five days of the Agency's determination. Notice shall be deemed sufficient if sent to the last known address of the mortgagee.

(c)   Rule Making. - Solely with respect to the adoption of procedures for the program by which property owners at risk of being foreclosed upon may qualify for assistance, the Agency is exempt from the requirements of Article 2A of Chapter 150B of the General Statutes. Prior to adoption or amendment of procedures, the Agency shall:

(1)   Publish the proposed procedures in the North Carolina Register at least 30 days prior to the adoption of the final procedures.

(2)   Accept oral and written comments on the proposed procedures.

(3)   Hold at least one public hearing on the proposed procedures.

(d)   Annual Report. - By April 1 of each year, the Agency shall report to the House Appropriations Subcommittee on General Government and Senate Appropriations Subcommittee on General Government and Information Technology on the effectiveness of the Program in accomplishing its purposes and provide any other information the Agency determines is pertinent or that the General Assembly requests. (2008-107, s. 21.1(c).)

§ 122A-6. Credit of State not pledged.

Obligations issued under the provisions of this Chapter shall not be deemed to constitute a debt, liability or obligation of the State or of any political subdivision thereof or a pledge of the faith and credit of the State or of any such political subdivision, but shall be payable solely from the revenues or assets of the Agency. Each obligation issued under this Chapter shall contain on the face thereof a statement to the effect that the Agency shall not be obligated to pay the same nor the interest thereon except from the revenues or assets pledged therefor and that neither the faith and credit nor the taxing power of the State or of any political subdivision thereof is pledged to the payment of the principal of or the interest on such obligation.

Expenses incurred by the Agency in carrying out the provisions of this Chapter may be made payable from funds provided pursuant to this Chapter and no liability shall be incurred by the Agency hereunder beyond the extent to which moneys shall have been so provided. Provided the provisions of this section do not apply to the liability of the Agency with respect to energy conservation loan guarantees. (1969, c. 1235, s. 6; 1973, c. 1296, s. 46; 1977, c. 1083, s. 4.)

§ 122A-6.1. Credit of State not pledged to satisfy liabilities under energy conservation loan guarantees.

Energy conservation loan guarantees issued under the provisions of this Chapter shall not be deemed to constitute a debt, liability, obligation of the State or of any political subdivision thereof, or a pledge of the faith and credit of the State or of any political subdivision thereof, but shall be payable solely from any unspent specific appropriations by the General Assembly for the energy conservation loan guarantee program and any donations and grants for this specific purpose. Each guarantee issued by the Agency shall contain on its face a statement to the effect that the Agency shall not be obligated to pay the same nor the interest thereon except from the unspent specific appropriations by the General Assembly for the energy conservation loan guarantee program and any specific donations and grants for this purpose, and that neither the faith and credit nor the taxing power of the State or of any political subdivision thereof is pledged to the payment of the principal of or the interest on such guarantees.

Provided any recoveries from the borrower or others which ultimately reduce the amounts paid out by the Agency in satisfaction of its liabilities under the energy conservation loan guarantee program shall be deemed unspent appropriations, donations or grants. (1977, c. 1083, s. 5.)

§ 122A-7. Repealed by Session Laws 1973, c. 1296, s. 47.

§ 122A-8. Bonds and notes.

The Agency is hereby authorized to provide for the issuance, at one time or from time to time, of bonds and notes of the Agency to carry out and effectuate its corporate purposes. The Agency also is hereby authorized to provide for the issuance, at one time or from time to time of (i) bond anticipation notes in anticipation of the issuance of such bonds and (ii) construction loan notes to finance the making or purchase of mortgage loans to sponsors of residential housing for the construction, rehabilitation or improvement of residential housing. The total amount of bonds, bond anticipation notes, and construction loan notes outstanding at any one time shall not exceed three billion dollars ($3,000,000,000) excluding therefrom any bond anticipation notes for the payment of which bonds have been issued. The principal of and the interest on such bonds or notes shall be payable solely from the funds herein provided for such payment. Any such notes may be made payable from the proceeds of bonds or renewal notes or, in the event bond or renewal note proceeds are not available, such notes may be paid from any available revenues or assets of the Agency. The bonds or notes of each issue shall be dated and may be made redeemable before maturity at the option of the Agency at such price or prices and under such terms and conditions as may be determined by the Agency. Any such bonds or notes shall bear interest at such rate or rates as may be

258

determined by the Local Government Commission of North Carolina with the approval of the Agency. Notes shall mature at such time or times not exceeding 10 years from their date or dates and bonds shall mature at such time or times not exceeding 43 years from their date or dates, as may be determined by the Agency. The Agency shall determine the form and manner of execution of the bonds or notes, including any interest coupons to be attached thereto, and shall fix the denomination or denominations and the place or places of payment of principal and interest, which may be any bank or trust company within or without the State. In case any officer whose signature or a facsimile of whose signature shall appear on any bonds or notes or coupons attached thereto shall cease to be such officer before the delivery thereof, such signature or such facsimile shall nevertheless be valid and sufficient for all purposes the same as if he had remained in office until such delivery. The Agency may also provide for the authentication of the bonds or notes by a trustee or fiscal agent. The bonds or notes may be issued in coupon or in registered form, or both, as the Agency may determine, and provision may be made for the registration of any coupon bonds or notes as to principal alone and also as to both principal and interest, and for the reconversion into coupon bonds or notes of any bonds or notes registered as to both principal and interest, and for the interchange of registered and coupon bonds or notes. Upon the filing with the Local Government Commission of North Carolina of a resolution of the Agency requesting that its bonds and notes be sold, such bonds or notes may be sold in such manner, either at public or private sale, and for such price as the Commission shall determine to be for the best interest of the Agency and best effectuate the purposes of this Chapter, as long as the sale is approved by the Agency.

The proceeds of any bonds or notes shall be used solely for the purposes for which issued and shall be disbursed in such manner and under such restrictions, if any, as the Agency may provide in the resolution authorizing the issuance of such bonds or notes or in the trust agreement hereinafter mentioned securing the same.

Prior to the preparation of definitive bonds, the Agency may, under like restrictions, issue interim receipts or temporary bonds, with or without coupons, exchangeable for definitive bonds when such bonds shall have been executed and are available for delivery. The Agency may also provide for the replacement of any bonds or notes which shall become mutilated or shall be destroyed or lost.

Bonds or notes may be issued under the provisions of this Chapter without obtaining, except as otherwise expressly provided in this Chapter, the consent of any department, division, commission, board, body, bureau or agency of the State, and without any other proceedings or the happening of any conditions or things other than those proceedings, conditions or things which are specifically required by this Chapter and the provisions of the resolution authorizing the issuance of such bonds or notes or the trust agreement securing the same. (1969, c. 1235, s. 8; 1973, c. 1296, s. 48; 1979, c. 844; 1979, 2nd Sess., c. 1238, s. 2; 1981, c. 343; 1983 (Reg. Sess., 1984), c. 1062, s. 2; 1985, c. 769, s. 2; 1997-13, s. 1; 2001-185, s. 1.)

§ 122A-8.1: Repealed by Session Laws 2008-194, s. 1(b), effective August 8, 2008.

§ 122A-9. Trust agreement or resolution.

In the discretion of the Agency any obligations issued under the provisions of this Chapter may be secured by a trust agreement by and between the Agency and a corporate trustee, which may be any trust company or bank having the powers of a trust company within or without the State. Such trust agreement or the resolution providing for the issuance of such obligations may pledge or assign all or any part of the revenues or assets of the Agency, including, without limitation, mortgage loans, mortgage loan commitments, contracts, agreements and other security or investment obligations, the fees or charges made or received by the Agency, the moneys received in payment of loans and interest thereon and any other moneys received or to be received by the Agency. Such trust agreement or resolution may contain such provisions for protecting and enforcing the rights and remedies of the holders of any such obligations as may be reasonable and proper and not in violation of law, including covenants setting forth the duties of the Agency in relation to the purposes to which obligation proceeds may be applied, the disposition or pledging of the revenues or assets of the Agency, the terms and conditions for the issuance of additional obligations, and the custody, safeguarding and application of all moneys. It shall be lawful for any bank or trust company incorporated under the laws of the State which may act as depositary of the proceeds of obligations, revenues or other money hereunder to furnish such indemnifying bonds or to pledge such securities as may be required by the Agency. Any such trust agreement or resolution may set forth the rights and remedies of the holders of any obligations and of the trustee, and may restrict the individual right of action by any such holders. In addition to the foregoing, any such trust agreement or resolution may contain such other provisions as the Agency may deem reasonable and proper for the security of the holders of any obligations. All expenses incurred in carrying out the provisions of such trust agreement or resolution may be paid from the revenues or assets pledged or assigned to the payment of the principal of and the interest on obligations or from any other funds available to the Agency. (1969, c. 1235, s. 9; 1973, c. 1296, s. 49.)

§ 122A-10. Validity of any pledge.

The pledge of any assets or revenues of the Agency to the payment of the principal of or the interest on any obligations of the Agency shall be valid and binding from the time when the pledge is made and any such assets or revenues shall immediately be subject to the lien of such pledge without any physical delivery thereof or further act, and the lien of any such pledge shall be valid and binding as against all parties having claims of any kind in tort, contract or otherwise against the Agency, irrespective of whether such parties have notice thereof. Nothing herein shall be construed to prohibit the Agency from selling any assets subject to any such pledge except to the extent that any such sale may be restricted by the trust agreement or resolution providing for the issuance of such obligations. (1969, c. 1235, s. 10; 1973, c. 1296, s. 50.)

§ 122A-11. Trust funds.

Notwithstanding any other provisions of law to the contrary, all moneys received pursuant to the authority of this Chapter shall be deemed to be trust funds to be held and applied solely as provided in this Chapter. The resolution authorizing any obligations or the trust agreement securing the same may provide that any of such moneys may be temporarily invested pending the disbursement thereof and shall provide that any officer with whom, or any bank or trust company with which, such moneys shall be deposited shall act as trustee of such moneys and shall hold and apply the same for the purposes hereof, subject to such regulations as this Chapter and such resolution or trust agreement may provide.

Any moneys received pursuant to the authority of this Chapter and any other moneys available to the Agency for investment may be invested:

(1)   As provided in G.S. 159-30, except that for purposes of G.S. 159-30(b) the Agency may deposit moneys at interest in banks or trust companies outside as well as in this State, as long as any moneys at deposit outside this State are collateralized to the same extent and manner as if at deposit in this State;

(2)   In evidences of ownership of, or fractional undivided interests in, future interest and principal payments on either direct obligations of the United States government or obligations the principal of and the interest on which are guaranteed by the United States government, which obligations are held by a bank or trust company organized and existing under the laws of the United States of America or any state in the capacity of custodian;

(3)   In obligations which are collateralized by mortgage pass-through securities guaranteed by the Government National Mortgage Association, the Federal Home Loan Mortgage Corporation, or Fannie Mae;

(4)   In a trust certificate or similar instrument evidencing an equity investment in a trust or other similar arrangement which is formed for the purpose of issuing obligations which are collateralized by mortgage pass-through or participation certificates guaranteed by the Government National Mortgage Association, the Federal Home Loan Mortgage Corporation or Fannie Mae; and

(5)   In repurchase agreements with respect to (i) direct obligations of the United States government, (ii) obligations the principal of and the interest on which are guaranteed by the United States government, or (iii) obligations described in G.S. 159-30(c)(2), (3), (6), or (7), if all of the following conditions are met:

a.   The repurchase agreement is entered into with an institution whose ability to pay its unsecured long-term obligations (including, if the institution is an insurance company, its claims paying ability) is rated in one of the two highest ratings categories by a nationally recognized securities rating agency. If the term of the repurchase agreement is for a period of one year or less, however, the repurchase agreement may be entered into with an institution that does not have such a long-term rating if its ability to pay its unsecured short-term obligations is rated in one of the two highest ratings categories by a nationally recognized securities rating agency. If the institution with which the agreement is to be entered does not meet the ratings requirement of this subparagraph, the repurchase agreement may nevertheless be entered into with the institution if the obligations of the institution under the repurchase agreement are fully guaranteed by another institution that does meet the ratings requirement of this subparagraph.

b.   The repurchase agreement provides that it shall be terminated, without penalty, if the institution with which the repurchase agreement is entered or by whom the institution's obligations are guaranteed fails to maintain (i) in the event that the repurchase agreement was entered into in reliance upon the rating of the institution's long-term obligations, a rating of its long-term obligations in one of the three highest ratings categories by at least one nationally recognized securities rating agency, or (ii) in the event that the repurchase agreement was entered into in reliance upon the rating of the institution's short-term obligations, a rating of its short-term obligations in one of the two highest ratings categories by at least one nationally recognized securities rating agency. The repurchase agreement does not have to be terminated, however, if a new guarantor meeting the rating requirement set forth in subparagraph a. as the requirement necessary for the Agency to enter the repurchase agreement agrees to fully guarantee the obligations of the institution under the repurchase agreement.

c.   The obligations that are subject to the repurchase agreement are delivered (in physical or in book entry form) to the Agency, or any financial institution serving either as trustee for obligations issued by the Agency or as fiscal agent for the Agency or the State Treasurer or are supported by a safekeeping receipt issued by a depository satisfactory to the Agency. The repurchase agreement must provide that the value of the underlying obligations shall be maintained at a current market value, calculated at least daily, of not less than one hundred percent (100%) of the repurchase price. The financial institution serving either as trustee or as fiscal agent for the Agency holding the obligations subject to the repurchase agreement hereunder or the depository issuing the safekeeping receipt shall not be the provider of the repurchase agreement.

d.   A valid and perfected first security interest in the obligations which are the subject of the repurchase agreement has been granted to the Agency or its assignee or book entry procedures, conforming, to the extent practicable, with federal regulations and satisfactory to the agency have been established for the benefit of the Agency or its assignee.

e.   The securities are free and clear of any adverse third-party claims.

f.   The repurchase agreement is in a form satisfactory to the Agency.
(1969, c. 1235, s. 11; 1973, c. 1296, s. 51; 1985, c. 479, s. 149(b); 1985 (Reg.
Sess., 1986), c. 1014, s. 185; 1997-13, s. 2; 2001-181, s. 1.)

§ 122A-12. Remedies.

Any holder of obligations issued under the provisions of this Chapter or any
coupons appertaining thereto, and the trustee under any trust agreement or
resolution authorizing the issuance of such obligations, except to the extent the
rights herein given may be restricted by such trust agreement or resolution,
may, either at law or in equity, by suit, action, mandamus or other proceeding,
protect and enforce any and all rights under the laws of the State or granted
hereunder or under such trust agreement or resolution, or under any other
contract executed by the Agency pursuant to this Chapter, and may enforce and
compel the performance of all duties required by this Chapter or by such trust
agreement or resolution to be performed by the Agency or by any officer
thereof. (1969, c. 1235, s. 12; 1973, c. 1296, s. 52.)

§ 122A-13. Negotiable instruments.

Notwithstanding any of the foregoing provisions of this Chapter or any recitals in
any obligations issued under the provisions of this Chapter, all such obligations
and interest coupons appertaining thereto shall be and are hereby made
negotiable instruments under the laws of this State, subject only to any
applicable provisions for registration. (1969, c. 1235, s. 13.)

§ 122A-14. Obligations eligible for investment.

Obligations issued under the provisions of this Chapter are hereby made
securities in which all public officers and public bodies of the State and its
political subdivisions, all insurance companies, trust companies, banking
associations, investment companies, executors, administrators, trustees and
other fiduciaries may properly and legally invest funds, including capital in their
control or belonging to them. Such obligations are hereby made securities which
may properly and legally be deposited with and received by any State or

municipal officer or any agency or political subdivision of the State for any purpose for which the deposit of bonds, notes or obligations of the State is now or may hereafter be authorized by law. (1969, c. 1235, s. 14.)

§ 122A-15. Refunding obligations.

The Agency is hereby authorized to provide for the issuance of refunding obligations for the purpose of refunding any obligations then outstanding which shall have been issued under the provisions of this Chapter, including the payment of any redemption premium thereon and any interest accrued or to accrue to the date of redemption of such obligations and, if deemed advisable by the Agency, for any corporate purpose of the Agency. The issuance of such obligations, the maturities and other details thereof, the rights of the holders thereof, and the rights, duties and obligations of the Agency in respect of the same shall be governed by the provisions of this Chapter which relate to the issuance of obligations, insofar as such provisions may be appropriate therefor.

Refunding obligations may be sold or exchanged for outstanding obligations issued under this Chapter and, if sold, the proceeds thereof may be applied, in addition to any other authorized purposes, to the purchase, redemption or payment of such outstanding obligations. Pending the application of the proceeds of any such refunding obligations, with any other available funds, to the payment of the principal, accrued interest and any redemption premium on the obligations being refunded, and, if so provided or permitted in the resolution authorizing the issuance of such refunding obligations or in the trust agreement securing the same, to the payment of any interest on such refunding obligations and any expenses in connection with such refunding, such proceeds may be invested in direct obligations of, or obligations the principal of and the interest on which are unconditionally guaranteed by, the United States of America which shall mature or which shall be subject to redemption by the holders thereof, at the option of such holders, not later than the respective dates when the proceeds, together with the interest accruing thereon, will be required for the purposes intended. (1965, c. 1235, s. 15; 1973, c. 1296, s. 55.)

§ 122A-16. Oversight by committees of General Assembly; annual reports.

The Finance Committee of the House of Representatives and the Finance Committee of the Senate shall exercise continuing oversight of the Agency in order to assure that the Agency is effectively fulfilling its statutory purpose; provided, however, that nothing in this Chapter shall be construed as required by the Agency to receive legislative approval for the exercise of any of the powers granted by this Chapter. The Agency shall, promptly following the close of each fiscal year, submit an annual report of its activities for the preceding year to the Governor, the Office of State Budget and Management, State Auditor, the aforementioned committees of the General Assembly and the Local Government Commission. Each such report shall set forth a complete operating and financial statement of the Agency during such year. The Agency shall cause an audit of its books and accounts to be made at least once in each year by an independent certified public accountant and the cost thereof may be paid from any available moneys of the Agency. The Agency shall on January 1 and July 1 of each year submit a written report of its activities to the Joint Legislative Commission on Governmental Operations. The Agency shall also at the end of each fiscal year submit a written report of its budget expenditures by line item to the Joint Legislative Commission on Governmental Operations. (1969, c. 1235, s. 16; 1973, c. 1296, s. 56; 1977, c. 673, s. 3; c. 771, s. 4; 1981, c. 895, s. 4; 1981 (Reg. Sess., 1982), c. 1191, s. 34; 1983 (Reg. Sess., 1984), c. 1034, s. 134; 2000-140, s. 93.1(a); 2001-424, s. 12.2(b); 2006-203, s. 67.)

§ 122A-17. Officers not liable.

No member or other officer of the Agency shall be subject to any personal liability or accountability by reason of his execution of any obligations or the issuance thereof. (1969, c. 1235, s. 17; 1973, c. 1296, s. 57.)

§ 122A-18. Authorization to accept appropriated moneys.

The Agency is authorized to accept such moneys as may be appropriated from time to time by the General Assembly for effectuating its corporate purposes including, without limitation, the payment of the initial expenses of administration and operation and the establishment of a reserve or contingency fund to be available for the payment of the principal of and the interest on any bonds or notes of the Agency. (1969, c. 1235, s. 18; 1973, c. 1296, s. 58.)

§ 122A-19. Tax exemption.

The exercise of the powers granted by this Chapter will be in all respects for the benefit of the people of the State, for their well-being and prosperity and for the improvement of their social and economic conditions, and the Agency shall not be required to pay any tax or assessment on any property owned by the Agency under the provisions of this Chapter or upon the income therefrom.

Any obligations issued by the Agency under the provisions of this Chapter shall at all times be free from taxation by the State or any local unit or political subdivision or other instrumentality of the State, excepting inheritance or gift taxes, income taxes on the gain from the transfer of the obligations, and franchise taxes. The interest on the obligations is not subject to taxation as income. (1969, c. 1235, s. 19; 1973, c. 1296, s. 59; 1995, c. 46, s. 10.)

§ 122A-20. Conflict of interest.

If any member, officer or employee of the Agency shall be interested either directly or indirectly, or shall be an officer or employee of or have an ownership interest in any firm or corporation interested directly or indirectly in any contract with the Agency, including any loan to any sponsor, builder or developer, such interest shall be disclosed to the Agency and shall be set forth in the minutes of the Agency, and the member, officer or employee having such interest therein shall not participate on behalf of the Agency in the authorization of any such contract. (1969, c. 1235, s. 20; 1973, c. 1296, s. 60.)

§ 122A-21. Additional method.

The foregoing sections of this Chapter shall be deemed to provide an additional and alternative method for the doing of the things authorized thereby and shall be regarded as supplemental and additional to powers conferred by other laws, and shall not be regarded as in derogation of any powers now existing; provided, however, that the issuance of bonds or notes under the provisions of this Chapter need not comply with the requirements of any other law applicable to the issuance of bonds or notes. (1969, c. 1235, s. 21.)

§ 122A-22. Chapter liberally construed.

This Chapter, being necessary for the prosperity of the State and its inhabitants, shall be liberally construed to effect the purposes thereof. (1969, c. 1235, s. 22.)

§ 122A-23. Inconsistent laws inapplicable.

Insofar as the provisions of this Chapter are inconsistent with the provisions of any general or special laws, or parts thereof, the provisions of this Chapter shall be controlling. (1969, c. 1235, s. 24.)

Chapter 122B.

North Carolina Agricultural Facilities Finance Act.

§§ 122B-1 through 122B-29. Repealed by Session Laws 1985 (Reg. Sess., 1986), c. 1011, s. 2.1(a), effective July 15, 1986.

Chapter 122C.

Mental Health, Developmental Disabilities, and Substance Abuse Act of 1985.

Article 1.

General Provisions.

§ 122C-1. Short title.

This Chapter may be cited as the Mental Health, Developmental Disabilities, and Substance Abuse Act of 1985. (1985, c. 589, s. 2; 1989, c. 625, ss. 1, 2.)

§ 122C-2. Policy.

The policy of the State is to assist individuals with needs for mental health, developmental disabilities, and substance abuse services in ways consistent with the dignity, rights, and responsibilities of all North Carolina citizens. Within available resources it is the obligation of State and local government to provide mental health, developmental disabilities, and substance abuse services through a delivery system designed to meet the needs of clients in the least restrictive, therapeutically most appropriate setting available and to maximize their quality of life. It is further the obligation of State and local government to provide community-based services when such services are appropriate, unopposed by the affected individuals, and can be reasonably accommodated within available resources and taking into account the needs of other persons for mental health, developmental disabilities, and substance abuse services.

State and local governments shall develop and maintain a unified system of services centered in area authorities or county programs. The public service system will strive to provide a continuum of services for clients while considering the availability of services in the private sector. Within available resources, State and local government shall ensure that the following core services are available:

(1)   Screening, assessment, and referral.

(2)   Emergency services.

(3)   Service coordination.

(4)   Consultation, prevention, and education.

Within available resources, the State shall provide funding to support services to targeted populations, except that the State and counties shall provide matching funds for entitlement program services as required by law.

As used in this Chapter, the phrase "within available resources" means State funds appropriated and non-State funds and other resources appropriated, allocated or otherwise made available for mental health, developmental disabilities, and substance abuse services.

The furnishing of services to implement the policy of this section requires the cooperation and financial assistance of counties, the State, and the federal government. (1977, c. 568, s. 1; 1979, c. 358, s. 1; 1983, c. 383, s. 1; 1985, c. 589, s. 2; c. 771; 1989, c. 625, s. 2; 2001-437, s. 1.1.)

§ 122C-3. Definitions.

The following definitions apply in this Chapter:

(1)   "Area authority" means the area mental health, developmental disabilities, and substance abuse authority.

(2)   "Area board" means the area mental health, developmental disabilities, and substance abuse board.

(2a)   "Area director" means the administrative head of the area authority program appointed pursuant to G.S. 122C-121.

(2b)   "Board of county commissioners" includes the participating boards of county commissioners for multicounty area authorities and multicounty programs.

(3)   "Camp Butner reservation" means the original Camp Butner reservation as may be designated by the Secretary as having been acquired by the State and includes not only areas which are owned and occupied by the State but also those which may have been leased or otherwise disposed of by the State, and shall also include those areas within the municipal boundaries of the Town of Butner and that portion of the extraterritorial jurisdiction of the Town of Butner consisting of lands not owned by the State of North Carolina.

(4)   "City" has the same meaning as in G.S. 153A-1(1).

(5)   "Catchment area" means the geographic part of the State served by a specific area authority or county program.

(6)   "Client" means an individual who is admitted to and receiving service from, or who in the past had been admitted to and received services from, a facility.

(7)   "Client advocate" means a person whose role is to monitor the protection of client rights or to act as an individual advocate on behalf of a particular client in a facility.

(8)   "Commission" means the Commission for Mental Health, Developmental Disabilities, and Substance Abuse Services, established under Part 4 of Article 3 of Chapter 143B of the General Statutes.

(9)   "Confidential information" means any information, whether recorded or not, relating to an individual served by a facility that was received in connection with the performance of any function of the facility. "Confidential information" does not include statistical information from reports and records or information regarding treatment or services which is shared for training, treatment, habilitation, or monitoring purposes that does not identify clients either directly or by reference to publicly known or available information.

(9a)   "Core services" are services that are necessary for the basic foundation of any service delivery system. Core services are of two types: front-end service capacity such as screening, assessment, and emergency triage, and indirect services such as prevention, education, and consultation at a community level.

(10)   "County of residence" of a client means the county of his domicile at the time of his admission or commitment to a facility. A county of residence is not changed because an individual is temporarily out of his county in a facility or otherwise.

(10a)   "County program" means a mental health, developmental disabilities, and substance abuse services program established, operated, and governed by a county pursuant to G.S. 122C-115.1.

(11)   "Dangerous to himself or others" means:

a.   "Dangerous to himself" means that within the relevant past:

1.   The individual has acted in such a way as to show:

I.   That he would be unable, without care, supervision, and the continued assistance of others not otherwise available, to exercise self-control, judgment, and discretion in the conduct of his daily responsibilities and social relations, or to satisfy his need for nourishment, personal or medical care, shelter, or self-protection and safety; and

II.   That there is a reasonable probability of his suffering serious physical debilitation within the near future unless adequate treatment is given pursuant to this Chapter. A showing of behavior that is grossly irrational, of actions that the individual is unable to control, of behavior that is grossly inappropriate to the situation, or of other evidence of severely impaired insight and judgment shall create a prima facie inference that the individual is unable to care for himself; or

271

2.   The individual has attempted suicide or threatened suicide and that there is a reasonable probability of suicide unless adequate treatment is given pursuant to this Chapter; or

3.   The individual has mutilated himself or attempted to mutilate himself and that there is a reasonable probability of serious self-mutilation unless adequate treatment is given pursuant to this Chapter.

Previous episodes of dangerousness to self, when applicable, may be considered when determining reasonable probability of physical debilitation, suicide, or self-mutilation.

b.   "Dangerous to others" means that within the relevant past, the individual has inflicted or attempted to inflict or threatened to inflict serious bodily harm on another, or has acted in such a way as to create a substantial risk of serious bodily harm to another, or has engaged in extreme destruction of property; and that there is a reasonable probability that this conduct will be repeated. Previous episodes of dangerousness to others, when applicable, may be considered when determining reasonable probability of future dangerous conduct. Clear, cogent, and convincing evidence that an individual has committed a homicide in the relevant past is prima facie evidence of dangerousness to others.

(11a)   "Dayight service" means a service provided on a regular basis, in a structured environment that is offered to the same individual for a period of three or more hours within a 24-hour period.

(12)   "Department" means the North Carolina Department of Health and Human Services.

(12a)   "Developmental disability" means a severe, chronic disability of a person which:

a.   Is attributable to a mental or physical impairment or combination of mental and physical impairments;

b.   Is manifested before the person attains age 22, unless the disability is caused by a traumatic head injury and is manifested after age 22;

c.   Is likely to continue indefinitely;

272

d.   Results in substantial functional limitations in three or more of the following areas of major life activity: self-care, receptive and expressive language, capacity for independent living, learning, mobility, self-direction and economic self-sufficiency; and

e.   Reflects the person's need for a combination and sequence of special interdisciplinary, or generic care, treatment, or other services which are of a lifelong or extended duration and are individually planned and coordinated; or

f.   When applied to children from birth through four years of age, may be evidenced as a developmental delay.

(13)   "Division" means the Division of Mental Health, Developmental Disabilities, and Substance Abuse Services of the Department.

(13a)   Repealed by Session Laws 2000-67, s. 11.21(c), effective July 1, 2000.

(13a1) Recodified as subdivision (13c).

(13b)   Recodified as subdivision (13d).

(13c)   "Eligible infants and toddlers" means children with or at risk for developmental delays or atypical development until:

a.   They have reached their third birthday;

b.   Their parents have requested to have them receive services in the preschool program for children with disabilities established under Article 9 of Chapter 115C of the General Statutes; and

c.   They have been placed in the program by the local educational agency.

In no event shall a child be considered an eligible toddler after the beginning of the school year immediately following the child's third birthday, unless the Secretary and the State Board enter into an agreement under G.S. 115C-106.4(c) [G.S. 115C-107.1(c)].

The early intervention services that may be provided for these children and their families include early identification and screening, multidisciplinary evaluations, case management services, family training, counseling and home visits, psychological services, speech pathology and audiology, and

273

occupational and physical therapy. All evaluations performed as part of early intervention services shall be appropriate to the individual child's age and development.

(13d) "Eligible psychologist" means a licensed psychologist who has at least two years' clinical experience. After January 1, 1995, "eligible psychologist" means a licensed psychologist who holds permanent licensure and certification as a health services provider psychologist issued by the North Carolina Psychology Board.

(14)   "Facility" means any person at one location whose primary purpose is to provide services for the care, treatment, habilitation, or rehabilitation of the mentally ill, the developmentally disabled, or substance abusers, and includes:

a.   An "area facility", which is a facility that is operated by or under contract with the area authority or county program. For the purposes of this subparagraph, a contract is a contract, memorandum of understanding, or other written agreement whereby the facility agrees to provide services to one or more clients of the area authority or county program. Area facilities may also be licensable facilities in accordance with Article 2 of this Chapter. A State facility is not an area facility;

b.   A "licensable facility", which is a facility that provides services to individuals who are mentally ill, developmentally disabled, or substance abusers for one or more minors or for two or more adults. These services shall be day services offered to the same individual for a period of three hours or more during a 24-hour period, or residential services provided for 24 consecutive hours or more. Facilities for individuals who are substance abusers include chemical dependency facilities;

c.   A "private facility", which is a facility that is either a licensable facility or a special unit of a general hospital or a part of either in which the specific service provided is not covered under the terms of a contract with an area authority;

d.   The psychiatric service of the University of North Carolina Hospitals at Chapel Hill;

e.   A "residential facility", which is a 24-hour facility that is not a hospital, including a group home;

f.   A "State facility", which is a facility that is operated by the Secretary;

274

g.   A "24-hour facility", which is a facility that provides a structured living environment and services for a period of 24 consecutive hours or more and includes hospitals that are facilities under this Chapter; and

h.   A Veterans Administration facility or part thereof that provides services for the care, treatment, habilitation, or rehabilitation of the mentally ill, the developmentally disabled, or substance abusers.

(15)   "Guardian" means a person appointed as a guardian of the person or general guardian by the court under Chapters 7A or 35A or former Chapters 33 or 35 of the General Statutes.

(16)   "Habilitation" means training, care, and specialized therapies undertaken to assist a client in maintaining his current level of functioning or in achieving progress in developmental skills areas.

(17)   "Incompetent adult" means an adult individual adjudicated incompetent.

(18)   "Intoxicated" means the condition of an individual whose mental or physical functioning is presently substantially impaired as a result of the use of alcohol or other substance.

(19)   "Law-enforcement officer" means sheriff, deputy sheriff, police officer, State highway patrolman, or an officer employed by a city or county under G.S. 122C-302.

(20)   "Legally responsible person" means: (i) when applied to an adult, who has been adjudicated incompetent, a guardian; (ii) when applied to a minor, a parent, guardian, a person standing in loco parentis, or a legal custodian other than a parent who has been granted specific authority by law or in a custody order to consent for medical care, including psychiatric treatment; or (iii) when applied to an adult who is incapable as defined in G.S. 122C-72(c) and who has not been adjudicated incompetent, a health care agent named pursuant to a valid health care power of attorney.

(20a)   "Local funds" means fees from services, including client payments, Medicare and the local and federal share of Medicaid receipts, fees from agencies under contract, gifts and donations, and county and municipal funds, and any other funds not administered by the Division.

(20b) "Local management entity" or "LME" means an area authority, county program, or consolidated human services agency. It is a collective term that refers to functional responsibilities rather than governance structure.

(20c) "Local management entity/managed care organization" or "LME/MCO" means a local management entity that is under contract with the Department to operate the combined Medicaid Waiver program authorized under Section 1915(b) and Section 1915(c) of the Social Security Act.

(21) "Mental illness" means: (i) when applied to an adult, an illness which so lessens the capacity of the individual to use self-control, judgment, and discretion in the conduct of his affairs and social relations as to make it necessary or advisable for him to be under treatment, care, supervision, guidance, or control; and (ii) when applied to a minor, a mental condition, other than mental retardation alone, that so impairs the youth's capacity to exercise age adequate self-control or judgment in the conduct of his activities and social relationships so that he is in need of treatment.

(22) "Mental retardation" means significantly subaverage general intellectual functioning existing concurrently with deficits in adaptive behavior and manifested before age 22.

(23) "Mentally retarded with accompanying behavior disorder" means an individual who is mentally retarded and who has a pattern of maladaptive behavior that is recognizable no later than adolescence and is characterized by gross outbursts of rage or physical aggression against other individuals or property.

(23a) "Minimally adequate services" means a level of service required for compliance with all applicable State and federal laws, rules, regulations, and policies and with generally accepted professional standards and principles.

(24) "Next of kin" means the individual designated in writing by the client or his legally responsible person upon the client's acceptance at a facility; provided that if no such designation has been made, "next of kin" means the client's spouse or nearest blood relation in accordance with G.S. 104A-1.

(25) "Operating costs" means expenditures made by an area authority in the delivery of services for mental health, developmental disabilities, and substance abuse as provided in this Chapter and includes the employment of legal counsel on a temporary basis to represent the interests of the area authority.

(26)   Repealed by Session Laws 1987, c. 345, s. 1.

(26a)   "Other recipient" means an individual who is not admitted to a facility but who receives a service other than care, treatment, or rehabilitation services. The services that the "other recipient" may receive include consultative, preventative, educational, and assessment services.

(27)   "Outpatient treatment" as used in Part 7 of Article 5 means treatment in an outpatient setting and may include medication, individual or group therapy, day or partial day programming activities, services and training including educational and vocational activities, supervision of living arrangements, and any other services prescribed either to alleviate the individual's illness or disability, to maintain semi-independent functioning, or to prevent further deterioration that may reasonably be predicted to result in the need for inpatient commitment to a 24-hour facility.

(28)   "Person" means any individual, firm, partnership, corporation, company, association, joint stock association, agency, or area authority.

(29)   "Physician" means an individual licensed to practice medicine in North Carolina under Chapter 90 of the General Statutes or a licensed medical doctor employed by the Veterans Administration.

(29a)   "Program director" means the director of a county program established pursuant to G.S. 122C-115.1.

(30)   "Provider of support services" means a person that provides to a facility support services such as data processing, dosage preparation, laboratory analyses, or legal, medical, accounting, or other professional services, including human services.

(30a)   "Psychologist" means an individual licensed to practice psychology under Chapter 90. The term "eligible psychologist" is defined in subdivision (13a).

(30b)   "Public services" means publicly funded mental health, developmental disabilities, and substance abuse services, whether provided by public or private providers.

(31)   "Qualified professional" means any individual with appropriate training or experience as specified by the General Statutes or by rule of the Commission in

277

the fields of mental health or developmental disabilities or substance abuse treatment or habilitation, including physicians, psychologists, psychological associates, educators, social workers, registered nurses, certified fee-based practicing pastoral counselors, and certified counselors.

(32)   "Responsible professional" means an individual within a facility who is designated by the facility director to be responsible for the care, treatment, habilitation, or rehabilitation of a specific client and who is eligible to provide care, treatment, habilitation, or rehabilitation relative to the client's disability.

(33)   "Secretary" means the Secretary of the Department of Health and Human Services.

(33a)   "Severe and persistent mental illness" means a mental disorder suffered by persons of 18 years of age or older that leads these persons to exhibit emotional or behavioral functioning that is so impaired as to interfere substantially with their capacity to remain in the community without supportive treatment or services of a long term or indefinite duration. This disorder is a severe and persistent mental disability, resulting in a long-term limitation of functional capacities for the primary activities of daily living, such as interpersonal relations, homemaking, self-care, employment, and recreation.

(34)   Repealed by Session Laws 2001-437, s. 1.2(c), effective July 1, 2002.

(35)   Repealed by Session Laws 2001-437, s. 1.2(c), effective July 1, 2002.

(35a)   Renumbered as subdivision (35e).

(35b)   "Specialty services" means services that are provided to consumers from low-incidence populations.

(35c)   "State" or "Local" Consumer Advocate means the individual carrying out the duties of the State or Local Consumer Advocacy Program Office in accordance with Article 1A of this Chapter.

(35d)   "State Plan" means the State Plan for Mental Health, Developmental Disabilities, and Substance Abuse Services.

(35e)   "State resources" means State and federal funds and other receipts administered by the Division.

(36)   "Substance abuse" means the pathological use or abuse of alcohol or other drugs in a way or to a degree that produces an impairment in personal, social, or occupational functioning. "Substance abuse" may include a pattern of tolerance and withdrawal.

(37)   "Substance abuser" means an individual who engages in substance abuse.

(38)   "Targeted population" means those individuals who are given service priority under the State Plan.

(39)   "Uniform portal process" means a standardized process and procedures used to ensure consumer access to, and exit from, public services in accordance with the State Plan. (1899, c. 1, s. 28; Rev., s. 4574; C.S., s. 6189; 1945, c. 952, s. 18; 1947, c. 537, s. 12; 1949, c. 71, s. 3; 1955, c. 887, s. 1; 1957, c. 1232, s. 13; 1959, c. 1028, s. 4; 1963, c. 1166, ss. 2, 10; c. 1184, s. 1; 1965, c. 933; 1973, c. 475, s. 2; c. 476, s. 133; c. 726, s. 1; c. 1408, ss. 1, 3; 1977, c. 400, ss. 2, 12; c. 568, s. 1; c. 679, s. 7; 1977, 2nd Sess., c. 1134, s. 2; 1979, c. 164, ss. 3, 4; c. 171, s. 2; c. 358, ss. 2, 26; c. 915, s. 1; c. 751, s. 28; 1981, c. 51, ss. 2-4; c. 539, s. 1; 1983, c. 280; c. 383, s. 2; c. 638, s. 2; c. 718, s. 1; c. 864, s. 4; 1983 (Reg. Sess., 1984), c. 1110, s. 4; 1985, c. 589, s. 2; c. 695, s. 1; c. 777, s. 2; 1985 (Reg. Sess., 1986), c. 863, s. 7; 1987, c. 345, s. 1; c. 830, ss. 47(a), (b); 1989, c. 141, s. 8; c. 223; c. 486, s. 2; c. 625, s. 2; 1989 (Reg. Sess., 1990), c. 823, s. 11; c. 1003, s. 2; c. 1024, s. 26(a); 1993, c. 321, s. 220(a)-(c); c. 375, s. 6; c. 396, ss. 1, 2; 1995, c. 249, s. 1; c. 406, s. 5; 1997-443, s. 11A.118(a); 1997-456, s. 27; 1998-198, s. 3; 1998-202, s. 4(r); 1999-186, s. 1; 2000-67, s. 11.21(c); 2001-437, ss. 1.2(b), 1.2(c); 2001-437, s. 1.2(a); 2003-313, s. 1; 2006-69, s. 3(n); 2006-142, ss. 4(a), 7; 2007-269, s. 3.1; 2007-502, s. 15(a); 2008-107, s. 10.15(dd); 2013-85, s. 1.)

§ 122C-4. Use of phrase "client or his legally responsible person."

Except as otherwise provided by law, whenever in this Chapter the phrase "client or his legally responsible person" is used, and the client is a minor or an incompetent adult, the duty or right involved shall be exercised not by the client, but by the legally responsible person. (1985, c. 589, s. 2.)

§ 122C-5. Report on restraint and seclusion.

The Secretary shall report annually on October 1 to the Joint Legislative Oversight Committee on Health and Human Services on the following for the immediately preceding fiscal year:

(1)   The level of compliance of each facility with applicable State and federal laws, rules, and regulations governing the use of restraints and seclusion. The information shall indicate areas of highest and lowest levels of compliance.

(2)   The total number of facilities that reported deaths under G.S. 122C-31, the number of deaths reported by each facility, the number of deaths investigated pursuant to G.S. 122C-31, and the number found by the investigation to be related to the use of restraint or seclusion. (2000-129, s. 3(b); 2003-58, s. 1; 2011-291, s. 2.40.)

§ 122C-6. Smoking prohibited; penalty.

(a)   Smoking is prohibited inside facilities licensed under this Chapter. As used in this section, "smoking" means the use or possession of any lighted cigar, cigarette, pipe, or other lighted smoking product. As used in this section, "inside" means a fully enclosed area.

(b)   The person who owns, manages, operates, or otherwise controls a facility subject to this section shall:

(1)   Conspicuously post signs clearly stating that smoking is prohibited inside the facility. The signs may include the international "No Smoking" symbol, which consists of a pictorial representation of a burning cigarette enclosed in a red circle with a red bar across it.

(2)   Direct any person who is smoking inside the facility to extinguish the lighted smoking product.

(3)   Provide written notice to individuals upon admittance that smoking is prohibited inside the facility and obtain the signature of the individual or the individual's representative acknowledging receipt of the notice.

(c)   The Department may impose an administrative penalty not to exceed two hundred dollars ($200.00) for each violation on any person who owns, manages, operates, or otherwise controls a facility licensed under this Chapter and fails to comply with subsection (b) of this section. A violation of this section constitutes a civil offense only and is not a crime.

(d)   This section does not apply to State psychiatric hospitals. (2007-459, s. 3.)

§ 122C-7. Reserved for future codification purposes.

§ 122C-8. Reserved for future codification purposes.

§ 122C-9. Reserved for future codification purposes.

Article 1A.

MH/DD/SA Consumer Advocacy Program.

(This article has a contingent effective date)

§ 122C-10. (This article has a contingent effective date - see note) MH/DD/SA Consumer Advocacy Program.

The General Assembly finds that many consumers of mental health, developmental disabilities, and substance abuse services are uncertain about their rights and responsibilities and how to access the public service system to obtain appropriate care and treatment. The General Assembly recognizes the importance of ensuring that consumers have information about the availability of services and access to resources to obtain timely quality care. There is established the MH/DD/SA Consumer Advocacy Program. The purpose of this

Program is to provide consumers, their families, and providers with the information and advocacy needed to locate appropriate services, resolve complaints, or address common concerns and promote community involvement. It is further the intent of the General Assembly that the Department, within available resources and pursuant to its duties under this Chapter, ensure that the performance of the mental health care system in this State is closely monitored, reviews are conducted, findings and recommendations and reports are made, and that local and systemic problems are identified and corrected when necessary to promote the rights and interests of all consumers of mental health, developmental disabilities, and substance abuse services. (2001-437, s. 2; 2002-126, s. 10.30; 2003-284, s. 10.10; 2005-276, s. 10.27.)

§ 122C-11. (This article has a contingent effective date - see notes) MH/DD/SA Consumer Advocacy Program/definitions.

Unless the context clearly requires otherwise, as used in this Article:

(1)   "MH/DD/SA" means mental health, developmental disabilities, and substance abuse.

(2)   "State Consumer Advocate" means the individual charged with the duties and functions of the State MH/DD/SA Consumer Advocacy Program established under this Article.

(3)   "State Consumer Advocacy Program" means the State MH/DD/SA Consumer Advocacy Program.

(4)   "Local Consumer Advocate" means an individual employed and certified by the State Consumer Advocate to perform the duties and functions of the MH/DD/SA Local Consumer Advocacy Program in accordance with this Article.

(5)   "Local Consumer Advocacy Program" means a local MH/DD/SA Local Consumer Advocacy Program.

(6)   "Consumer" means an individual who is a client or a potential client of public services from a State or area facility. (2001-437, s. 2; 2002-126, s. 10.30; 2003-284, s. 10.10; 2005-276, s. 10.27.)

§ 122C-12. (This article has a contingent effective date - see note) State MH/DD/SA Consumer Advocacy Program.

The Secretary shall establish a State MH/DD/SA Consumer Advocacy Program office in the Office of the Secretary of Health and Human Services. The Secretary shall appoint a State Consumer Advocate. In selecting the State Consumer Advocate, the Secretary shall consider candidates recommended by citizens' organizations representing the interest of individuals with needs for mental health, developmental disabilities, and substance abuse services. The State Consumer Advocate may hire individuals to assist in executing the State Consumer Advocacy Program and to act on the State Consumer Advocate's behalf. The State Consumer Advocate shall have expertise and experience in MH/DD/SA, including expertise and experience in advocacy. The Attorney General shall provide legal staff and advice to the State Consumer Advocate. (2001-437, s. 2; 2002-126, s. 10.30; 2003-284, s. 10.10; 2005-276, s. 10.27.)

§ 122C-13. (This article has a contingent effective date - see note) State Consumer Advocate duties.

The State Consumer Advocate shall:

(1)   Establish Local Quality Care Consumer Advocacy Programs described in G.S. 122C-14 and appoint the Local Consumer Advocates.

(2)   Establish certification criteria and minimum training requirements for Local Consumer Advocates.

(3)   Certify Local Consumer Advocates. The certification requirements shall include completion of the minimum training requirements established by the State Consumer Advocate.

(4)   Provide training and technical Advocacy to Local Consumer Advocates.

(5)   Establish procedures for processing and resolving complaints both at the State and local levels.

(6)   Establish procedures for coordinating complaints with local human rights committees and the State protection and advocacy agency.

(7)   Establish procedures for appropriate access by the State and Local Consumer Advocates to State, area authority, and county program facilities and records to ensure MH/DD/SA. The procedures shall include, but not be limited to, interviews of owners, consumers, and employees of State, area authority, and county program facilities, and on-site monitoring of conditions and services. The procedures shall ensure the confidentiality of these records and that the identity of any complainant or consumer will not be disclosed except as otherwise provided by law.

(8)   Provide information to the public about available MH/DD/SA services, complaint procedures, and dispute resolution processes.

(9)   Analyze and monitor the development and implementation of federal, State, and local laws, regulations, and policies relating to consumers and recommend changes as considered necessary to the Secretary.

(10)   Analyze and monitor data relating to complaints or concerns about access and issues to identify significant local or systemic problems, as well as opportunities for improvement, and advise and assist the Secretary in developing policies, plans, and programs for ensuring that the quality of services provided to consumers is of a uniformly high standard.

(11)   Submit a report annually to the Secretary, the Joint Legislative Oversight Committee on Health and Human Services, and the Joint Legislative Health Care Oversight Committee containing data and findings regarding the types of problems experienced and complaints reported by or on behalf of providers, consumers, and employees of providers, as well as recommendations to resolve identified issues and to improve the administration of MH/DD/SA facilities and the delivery of MH/DD/SA services throughout the State. (2001-437, s. 2; 2002-126, s. 10.30; 2003-284, s. 10.10; 2005-276, s. 10.27; 2011-291, s. 2.41.)

§ 122C-14. (This article has a contingent effective date - see note) Local Consumer Advocate; duties.

(a)   The State Consumer Advocate shall establish a Local MH/DD/SA Consumer Advocacy Program in locations in the State to be designated by the Secretary. In determining where to locate the Local Consumer Advocacy Programs, the Secretary shall ensure reasonable consumer accessibility to the Local Consumer Advocates. Local Consumer Advocates shall administer the

Local Consumer Advocacy Programs. The State Consumer Advocate shall appoint a Local Consumer Advocate for each of the Local Consumer Advocacy Programs. The State Consumer Advocate shall supervise the Local Consumer Advocates.

(b)   Pursuant to policies and procedures established by the State Consumer Advocate, the Local Consumer Advocate shall:

(1)   Assist consumers and their families with information, referral, and advocacy in obtaining appropriate services.

(2)   Assist consumers and their families in understanding their rights and remedies available to them from the public service system.

(3)   Serve as a liaison between consumers and their families and facility personnel and administration.

(4)   Promote the development of consumer and citizen involvement in addressing issues relating to MH/DD/SA.

(5)   Visit the State, area authority, or county program facilities to review and evaluate the quality of care provided to consumers and submit findings to the State Consumer Advocate.

(6)   Work with providers and consumers and their families or advocates to resolve issues of common concern.

(7)   Participate in regular Local Consumer Advocate training established by the State Consumer Advocate.

(8)   Report regularly to area authorities and county programs, county and area authority boards, and boards of county commissioners about the Local Consumer Advocate's activities, including the findings made pursuant to subdivision (5) of this subsection.

(9)   Provide training and technical assistance to counties, area authority boards, and providers concerning responding to consumers, evaluating quality of care, and determining availability of services and access to resources.

(10)   Coordinate activities with local human rights committees based on procedures developed by the State Consumer Advocate.

(11)   Provide information to the public on MH/DD/SA issues.

(12)   Perform any other related duties as directed by the State Consumer Advocate. (2001-437, s. 2; 2002-126, s. 10.30; 2003-284, s. 10.10; 2005-276, s. 10.27.)

§ 122C-15. (This Article has a contingent effective date - see note) State/Local Consumer Advocate; authority to enter; communication with residents, clients, patients; review of records.

(a)   For purposes of this section, G.S. 122C-16 and G.S. 122C-17, "Consumer Advocate" means either the State Consumer Advocate or any Local Consumer Advocate.

(b)   In performing the Consumer Advocate's duties, a Consumer Advocate shall have access at all times to any State or area facility and shall have reasonable access to any consumer or to an employee of a State or area facility. Entry and access to any consumer or to an employee shall be conducted in a manner that will not significantly disrupt the provision of services. If a facility requires visitor registration, then the Consumer Advocate shall register.

(c)   In performing the Consumer Advocate's duties, a Consumer Advocate may communicate privately and confidentially with a consumer. A consumer shall not be compelled to communicate with a Consumer Advocate. When initiating communication, a Consumer Advocate shall inform the consumer of the Consumer Advocate's purpose and that a consumer may refuse to communicate with the Consumer Advocate. A Consumer Advocate also may communicate privately and confidentially with State and area facility employees in performing the Consumer Advocate's duties.

(d)   Notwithstanding G.S. 8-53, G.S. 8-53.3, or any other law relating to confidentiality of communications involving a consumer, in the course of performing the Consumer Advocate's duties, the Consumer Advocate may access any information, whether recorded or not, concerning the admission, discharge, medication, treatment, medical condition, or history of any consumer to the extent permitted by federal law and regulations. Notwithstanding any State law pertaining to the privacy of personnel records, in the course of the Consumer Advocate's duties, the Consumer Advocate shall have access to personnel records of employees of State, area authority, or county program facilities. (2001-437, s. 2; 2002-126, s. 10.30; 2003-284, s. 10.10; 2005-276, s. 10.27.)

§ 122C-16. (This Article has a contingent effective date - see note) State/Local Consumer Advocate; resolution of complaints.

(a)   Following receipt of a complaint, a Consumer Advocate shall attempt to resolve the complaint using, whenever possible, informal mediation, conciliation, and persuasion.

(b)   If a complaint concerns a particular consumer, the consumer may participate in determining what course of action the Consumer Advocate should take on the consumer's behalf. If the consumer has an opinion concerning a course of action, the Consumer Advocate shall consider the consumer's opinion.

(c)   Following receipt of a complaint, a Consumer Advocate shall contact the service provider to allow the service provider the opportunity to respond, provide additional information, or initiate action to resolve the complaint.

(d)   Complaints or conditions adversely affecting consumers that cannot be resolved in the manner described in subsection (a) of this section shall be referred by the Consumer Advocate to the appropriate licensing agency under Article 2 of this Chapter. (2001-437, s. 2; 2002-126, s. 10.30; 2003-284, s. 10.10; 2005-276, s. 10.27.)

§ 122C-17. (This Article has a contingent effective date - see note) State/Local Consumer Advocate; confidentiality.

(a)   Except as required by law, a Consumer Advocate shall not disclose the following:

(1)   Any confidential or privileged information obtained pursuant to G.S. 122C-15 unless the affected individual authorizes disclosure in writing; or

(2)   The name of anyone who has furnished information to a Consumer Advocate unless the individual authorizes disclosure in writing.

(b)   Violation of this section is a Class 3 misdemeanor, punishable only by a fine not to exceed five hundred dollars ($500.00).

(c)   All confidential or privileged information obtained under this section and the names of persons providing information to a Consumer Advocate are exempt from disclosure pursuant to Chapter 132 of the General Statutes. Access to substance abuse records and redisclosure of protected information shall be in compliance with federal confidentiality laws protecting medical records. (2001-437, s. 2; 2002-126, s. 10.30; 2003-284, s. 10.10; 2005-276, s. 10.27.)

§ 122C-18. (This Article has a contingent effective date - see note) State/Local Consumer Advocate; retaliation prohibited.

No one shall discriminate or retaliate against any person, provider, or facility because the person, provider, or facility in good faith complained or provided information to a Consumer Advocate. (2001-437, s. 2; 2002-126, s. 10.30; 2003-284, s. 10.10; 2005-276, s. 10.27.)

§ 122C-19. (This Article has a contingent effective date - see note) State/Local Consumer Advocate; immunity from liability.

(a)   The State and Local Consumer Advocate shall be immune from liability for the good faith performance of official Consumer Advocate duties.

(b)   A State or area facility, its employees, and any other individual interviewed by a Consumer Advocate are immune from liability for damages resulting from disclosure of any information or documents to a Consumer Advocate pursuant to this Article. (2001-437, s. 2; 2002-126, s. 10.30; 2003-284, s. 10.10; 2005-276, s. 10.27.)

§ 122C-20. (This Article has a contingent effective date - see note) State/Local Consumer Advocate; penalty for willful interference.

Willful interference by an individual other than the consumer or the consumer's representative with the State or a Local Consumer Advocate in the performance of the Consumer Advocate's official duties is a Class 1 misdemeanor. (2001-437, s. 2; 2002-126, s. 10.30; 2003-284, s. 10.10; 2005-276, s. 10.27.)

§ 122C-20.1: Reserved for future codification purposes.

§ 122C-20.2: Reserved for future codification purposes.

§ 122C-20.3: Reserved for future codification purposes.

§ 122C-20.4: Reserved for future codification purposes.

Article 1B.

Transitions to Community Living.

Part 1. North Carolina Supportive Housing Program.

§ 122C-20.5. Definitions.

The following definitions apply in this Article:

(1)   Individual with serious and persistent mental illness or SPMI. - A person who is 18 years of age or older who meets one of the following criteria:

a.   Has a mental illness or disorder that is so severe and chronic that it prevents or erodes development of functional capacities in primary aspects of daily life such as personal hygiene and self-care, decision making, interpersonal relationships, social transactions, learning, and recreational activities.

b.   Is receiving Supplemental Security Income or Social Security Disability Income due to mental illness.

(2)   Individual with serious mental illness or SMI. - An individual who is 18 years of age or older with a mental illness or disorder that is described in the Diagnostic and Statistical Manual of Mental Disorders, Fourth Edition, that impairs or impedes functioning in one or more major areas of living and is unlikely to improve without treatment, services, supports, or all three. The term

does not include a primary diagnosis of Alzheimer's disease or dementia. (2013-397, s. 6(a).)

§ 122C-20.6. Department to establish statewide supportive housing program for individuals transitioning into community living; purpose.

The Department of Health and Human Services, in consultation with the North Carolina Housing Finance Agency, shall establish and administer a tenant-based rental assistance program known as the North Carolina Supportive Housing Program. The purpose of the program is to transition individuals diagnosed with serious mental illness or serious and persistent mental illness from institutional settings to more integrated community-based settings appropriate to meet their needs. Under the program, the Department, in consultation with the North Carolina Housing Finance Agency and LME/MCOs, shall arrange for program participants to be transitioned to housing slots available through the program with all the rights and obligations created by a landlord-tenant relationship. (2013-397, s. 6(a).)

§ 122C-20.7. Administration of housing subsidies for supportive housing.

The Department may enter into a contract with a private vendor to serve as the housing subsidy administrator for the North Carolina Supportive Housing Program with responsibility for distributing rental vouchers and community living vouchers to program participants based on a formula developed by the Department. (2013-397, s. 6(a).)

§ 122C-20.8. Eligibility requirements for NC Supportive Housing Program.

The Division of Aging and Adult Services shall adopt rules to establish eligibility requirements for the program. The eligibility requirements shall, at a minimum, include income eligibility requirements and requirements to give priority for program participation and transition services to individuals diagnosed with serious mental illness or serious and persistent mental illness who are currently residing in institutional settings. The Division may adopt temporary rules necessary to implement this Article. (2013-397, s. 6(a).)

§ 122C-20.9. In-reach activities for supportive housing.

The Department shall have ongoing responsibility for developing and distributing a list of potentially eligible program participants for each LME/MCO by catchment area. Upon receipt of this information, each LME/MCO shall have ongoing responsibility for prioritizing the list of individuals to whom it will provide in-reach activities in order to (i) arrange an in-person meeting with potentially eligible participants to determine their eligibility and level of interest and (ii) report back to the Department on the LME/MCO's recommended list of program participants on a daily basis. Upon receipt of an LME/MCO's recommended list of program participants, the Department shall make a final determination of eligibility. (2013-397, s. 6(a).)

§ 122C-20.10. Allocation of supportive housing slots to LME/MCOs.

The Department shall annually determine the number of housing slots to be allocated to each LME/MCO as follows:

(1)   Each year, the Department shall distribute at least fifty percent (50%) of the housing slots available through this program equally among all LME/MCOs.

(2)   The Department shall award additional housing slots to LME/MCOs based on local need, as determined by the information provided by LME/MCOs to the Department in accordance with G.S. 122C-20.9. (2013-397, s. 6(a).)

§ 122C-20.11. Transition of program participants into housing slots.

The LME/MCO shall develop a written transition plan for each individual determined to be eligible and interested in participating in the North Carolina Supportive Housing Program. The transition plan for the approved housing slot shall identify at least all of the following:

(1)   Available housing units that meet the individual's needs.

(2)   Any transition services that will be necessary for the individual, including, but not limited to, a one-time transition stability payment, not to

291

exceed two thousand dollars ($2,000) per individual, for up-front move-in costs approved by the Department or the housing subsidy administrator.

(3)   Solutions to potential barriers to the individual's successful transition to community-based supported housing.

(4)   Any other information the Department deems necessary for the individual program participant's successful transition into community-based supported housing. (2013-397, s. 6(a).)

§ 122C-20.12. Transition services.

LME/MCOs shall provide individualized transition services to program participants within their respective catchment areas for the 90-day period following the individual's transition into a housing slot provided through the program. (2013-397, s. 6(a).)

§ 122C-20.13. Tenancy support services.

The Department or the housing subsidy administrator shall provide ongoing tenancy support services to program participants. (2013-397, s. 6(a).)

§ 122C-20.14. Approval of landlords and housing units.

The Department shall develop an application process for owners of housing units seeking to participate in the program as landlords. The application process shall, at a minimum, include an inspection of the owners' selected housing units and a requirement that owners receive educational information from the Department about the North Carolina Supportive Housing Program prior to being approved as landlords. (2013-397, s. 6(a).)

§ 122C-20.15. Annual reporting on NC Supportive Housing Program.

Annually on October 1, the Department shall report to the Joint Legislative Oversight Committee on Health and Human Services of the General Assembly on the number of individuals within each LME/MCO catchment area who transitioned into housing slots available through the North Carolina Supportive Housing Program during the preceding calendar year. The report shall include a breakdown of all funds expended by each LME/MCO for transitioning these individuals into the housing slots. (2013-397, s. 6(a).)

§ 122C-20.16. NC Supportive Housing Program not an entitlement.

The Department shall not be required to provide housing slots to individuals beyond the number that can be supported by funds appropriated by the General Assembly for this purpose. The supportive housing program established under this Part, whether administered by the Department or a private entity, is not an entitlement, and nothing in this Part shall create any property right. (2013-397, s. 6(a).)

Article 2.

Licensure of Facilities for the Mentally Ill, the Developmentally Disabled, and Substance Abusers.

§ 122C-21. Purpose.

The purpose of this Article is to provide for licensure of facilities for the mentally ill, developmentally disabled, and substance abusers by the development, establishment, and enforcement of basic rules governing:

(1)   The provision of services to individuals who receive services from licensable facilities as defined by this Chapter, and

(2)   The construction, maintenance, and operation of these licensable facilities that in the light of existing knowledge will ensure safe and adequate treatment of these individuals. The Department shall ensure that licensable facilities are inspected every two years to determine compliance with physical

plant and life-safety requirements. (1983, c. 718, s. 1; 1985, c. 589, s. 2; 1989, c. 625, s. 4; 2005-276, s. 10.40A(c).)

§ 122C-22. Exclusions from licensure; deemed status.

(a)   All of the following are excluded from the provisions of this Article and are not required to obtain licensure under this Article:

(1)   Physicians and psychologists engaged in private office practice.

(2)   General hospitals licensed under Article 5 of Chapter 131E of the General Statutes, that operate special units for the mentally ill, developmentally disabled, or substance abusers.

(3)   State and federally operated facilities.

(4)   Adult care homes licensed under Chapter 131D of the General Statutes.

(5)   Developmental child care centers licensed under Article 7 of Chapter 110 of the General Statutes.

(6)   Persons subject to licensure under rules of the Social Services Commission.

(7)   Persons subject to rules and regulations of the Division of Vocational Rehabilitation Services.

(8)   Facilities that provide occasional respite care for not more than two individuals at a time; provided that the primary purpose of the facility is other than as defined in G.S. 122C-3(14).

(9)   Twenty-four-hour nonprofit facilities established for the purposes of shelter care and recovery from alcohol or other drug addiction through a 12-step, self-help, peer role modeling, and self-governance approach.

(10)   Inpatient chemical dependency or substance abuse facilities that provide services exclusively to inmates of the Division of Adult Correction of the Department of Public Safety, as described in G.S. 148-19.1.

(11)   A charitable, nonprofit, faith-based, adult residential treatment facility that does not receive any federal or State funding and is a religious organization exempt from federal income tax under section 501(a) of the Internal Revenue Code.

(12)   A home in which up to three adults, two or more having a disability, co-own or co-rent a home in which the persons with disabilities are receiving three or more hours of day services in the home or up to 24 hours of residential services in the home. The individuals who have disabilities cannot be required to move if the individuals change services, change service providers, or discontinue services.

(b)   The Commission may adopt rules establishing a procedure whereby a licensable facility certified by a nationally recognized agency, such as the Joint Commission on Accreditation of Hospitals, may be deemed licensed under this Article by the Secretary. Any facility licensed under the provisions of this subsection shall continue to be subject to inspection by the Secretary. (1983, c. 718, s. 1; 1983 (Reg. Sess., 1984), c. 1110, s. 5; 1985, c. 589, s. 2; c. 695, s. 13; 1987, c. 345, s. 2; 1989, c. 625, s. 5; 1995, c. 535, s. 7; 1997-506, s. 43; 2000-67, s. 11.25A; 2001-424, s. 25.19(b); 2004-199, s. 32; 2011-145, s. 19.1(h); 2011-202, s. 1; 2012-15, s. 1; 2013-410, s. 11.)

Vision Books Order Form

Fax Orders: 1-980-299-5965

Phone Orders: 1-704-898-0770

E-mail Orders: www.visionbooks.org

Mail Orders: Vision Books, LLC
                       P.O. Box 42406
                       Charlotte, NC 28215

Shipp To:
Name_____
Address_____
City_____State_____Zip_____
Phone_____Fax_____
Email_____@_____

Bill To: We can bill a third party on your behalf.
Name_____
Address_____
City_____State_____Zip_____
Phone___(_____)_____Fax_____
Email_____@_____

Pamphlet Number ($15.00 Each)	Qty	Total Cost
_____	_____	_____
_____	_____	_____
_____	_____	_____
_____	_____	_____
_____	_____	_____
_____	_____	_____
_____	_____	_____
Full Volume Set 1-92	92 Pamphlets	1,380.00

Free Shipping Shipping & Handling on Full Volume Orders
Add $1.00 Shipping & Handling per pamphlet $_____

Total Cost $_____

Thank you for your support. Management!

DID YOU ENJOY THIS BOOK?

Vision Books, LLC would like to hear from you! If you or someone you know has been fasely imprisoned, we would like to hear your story. If the 'North Carolina Criminal Law and Procedure' has had an effect in your life or if you have suggestions, we would like to hear from you. Send your letters to:

Vision Books, LLC
Attn: Staff Writers
P.O. Box 42406
Charlotte, NC 28215
Email: staff@visionbooks.org

Order Additional Copies:

Fax Orders: 1-980-299-5965

Phone Orders: 1-704-898-0770

E-mail Orders: www.visionbooks.org

Mail Orders: Vision Books, LLC
                        P.O. Box 42406
                        Charlotte, NC 28215

www.ingramcontent.com/pod-product-compliance
Lightning Source LLC
Chambersburg PA
CBHW051630170526
45167CB00001B/136